D1121522

WARRIOR
The World's First Ironclad
Then and Now

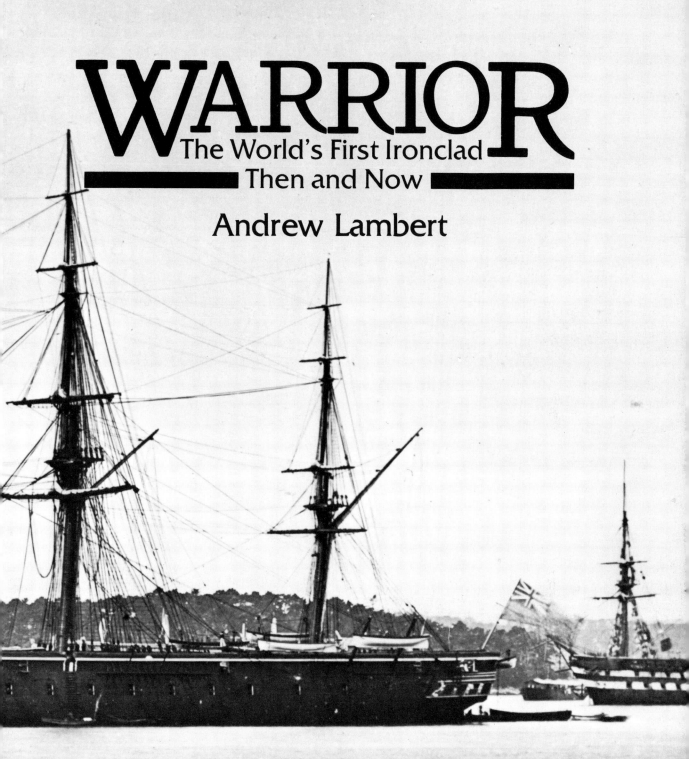

WARRIOR
The World's First Ironclad
Then and Now

Andrew Lambert

NAVAL INSTITUTE PRESS

This book is dedicated to the memory of all those involved in the conception, design and construction of HMS *Warrior*; and to their successors, the team that saved the ship 120 years later.

Frontispiece.
The first, and one of the best known, photographs of *Warrior*. She is seen here at Devonport possibly in mid 1863. The ship astern is the wooden two decker *Edgar*, flagship of the Channel Fleet. *IWM*

© 1987 Dr Andrew Lambert
First published in 1987 by Conway Maritime Press Ltd
24 Bride Lane, Fleet Street, London EC4Y 8DR

All rights reserved

Published and distributed in the United States of America and Canada by the Naval Institute Press, Annapolis, Maryland 21402

Library of Congress Catalog Card No. 86–63792

ISBN 0-87021-986-3

This edition is authorized for sale only in the United States and its territories and possessions, and Canada

Contents

FOREWORD   6
INTRODUCTION   7
ACKNOWLEDGEMENTS,
GLOSSARY & ABBREVIATIONS   8
CHAPTER ONE: ORIGINS   9
CHAPTER TWO: IN SERVICE   27
CHAPTER THREE: RECONSTRUCTION   45
CHAPTER FOUR: HULL AND ARMOUR   63
CHAPTER FIVE: GUNS   81
CHAPTER SIX: MACHINERY   103
CHAPTER SEVEN: RIG   123
CHAPTER EIGHT: DETAIL   145
CHAPTER NINE: CONCLUSIONS   171

APPENDIX I: THE WORKFORCE
                    AND ASSOCIATED
                    FIRMS   175
APPENDIX II: EXPENDITURE ON
                    WARRIOR   177
APPENDIX III: SPECIFICATION   182
INDEX   190
BIBLIOGRAPHY   192

Foreword

This book is the record of a great achievement. It also shows how one thing leads to another – how the need to do the work exactly right has caused much long-forgotten information about Victorian ships and engineering to be rediscovered; and how individuals with indispensable knowledge or skill have appeared out of the blue to help – and have stayed on to become friends.

It has taken nineteen years, since first we saw her blackened plates in Milford Haven, to secure *Warrior* and then to restore her. Like most novel and original projects, it has been carried through by quite a small band of people, without any one of whom it could not have been done at all. Their vision, determination and staying power has brought this great ship back from the dead, one of the most influential warships ever built and the sole surviving nineteenth century capital ship in the world, forerunner and survivor of all those castles of steel that once ruled the waves.

It has been a desperate enterprise – more of a burning deck than a bandwagon – but all who have worked on or for *Warrior* can justly pride themselves that they have done something really difficult and have made a wonderful present to the British people.

Our aim is to show her without modern alterations or additions of any sort, without notices or concessions to comfort which would break the spell, but exactly like a modern warship on a Navy Day, functional and purposeful in every detail. In this way we hope that she will now have a long and useful future, not just as one more tourist attraction, but as an example of good work well planned and done, and as a reminder to all who see her of the virtues of courage and service.

John Smith

Introduction

HMS *Warrior* was designed and built as a direct response to the French ship *Gloire*, the first sea-going ironclad warship. *Gloire* symbolised two important aspects of international politics in the mid nineteenth century. The Navy of Emperor Napoleon III was challenging Britain for supremacy at sea. Whilst Louis Napoleon Bonaparte, nephew of the great Napoleon, was not personally hostile to Britain, his Imperial regime depended upon popular support at home, and important elements of French opinion were implacably opposed to Britain. The Imperial Navy was a symbol of French power, and it was intended to defy the Royal Navy. It is even possible that Louis Napoleon considered that a powerful French fleet would make the British government anxious to retain his friendship, and thus prepared to support his programme of radical political change in Europe. This hope was without foundation: the end result was entirely counterproductive. The similar policy of Kaiser Wilhelm II and Admiral Tirpitz between 1898 and 1912 failed for the same reasons.

Popular opinion in Britain considered the French to be pathologically hostile, determined to avenge Waterloo and probably Trafalgar as well, consequently the naval policy of the day was intended to counter the challenge implicit in French construction. There was no thought of being influenced by the Emperor.

Britain and France had been allies during the Russian War (1854–1856) but at the Peace of Paris the French affected a reconciliation with Russia. During the period 1854–8 the French steam battlefleet had momentarily achieved a numerical equality with the British. This fact, in combination with the laying down of *Gloire* in March 1858, sparked off the invasion scare of 1858–9.

The French had not laid down a battleship since 1855. With *Gloire* they demonstrated a complete faith in the ironclad. In the 1820s the French introduced the shell firing gun, in the late 1840s they began the first steam powered battleship, *Le Napoleon*; the ironclad was a further development of the same policy of supporting new technology. The British response was always the same – Outbuild. Having lost every naval race the French merely changed the rules and started again, with even less chance of success.

In this sense *Warrior* was the complete answer both to *Gloire* and the policy that she symbolised. *Warrior* was in every important respect a more advanced ship than *Gloire*, indeed she was so advanced that she could not have been built in France. However the British did not share the confidence of the French in the ironclad, and so they conceived and built *Warrior* solely to counter *Gloire*. The ship demonstrated the clear resolve of Britain to retain her technological superiority and naval mastery, whatever the cost.

Viewed in isolation as ships of the late 1850s *Gloire* and *Warrior* stand on opposite sides of the most significant dividing line in the history of the fighting ship. *Gloire* was a refinement of the wooden warship of the preceeding centuries. Her steam engine, rifled guns and armour were new, but the ship was still constrained by the limits of wood as a shipbuilding material. *Warrior* was the first iron-hulled, armoured sea-going warship. She freed designers from the limits of wood, allowing them to make the best use of the new elements already employed in *Gloire*. *Warrior* pointed to the future, *Gloire* was the end of the line. In this respect France had lost the new naval race even before it had properly begun.

Acknowledgements

I must take the opportunity to thank all those without whom the completion of this book would not have been possible. Few authors can owe a greater debt to so many people and if I have omitted anyone, I can only beg their indulgence.

The staff of the Warrior Preservation Trust, both at Hartlepool and in London, were unfailingly helpful, both in dealing with often simple questions and in giving the benefit of their experience. The staff of the Draught Room, Reading Room and Historic Photograph Department at the National Maritime Museum were again most helpful; similarly the Photograph Department at the Imperial War Museum provided valuable assistance. Among others not directly associated with the project D K Brown RCNC and John Campbell gave me the benefit of their extensive knowledge and Len Robinson-Smith of Paul Popper Ltd used his skill to reprint the photographs of the *Narcissus* from the faded 1860s originals. I owe a further debt of gratitude to Zohra, for her unfailing support and enthusiasm. Without the help of these people this book would not have been written. Even so the errors, omissions and failings of the end result are my responsibility.

Andrew Lambert
Norfolk 1986

GLOSSARY

Battleship Any large warship in which the combat features of offensive and defensive strength are given greater weight than speed and endurance the features emphasised in a cruiser.

Corvette Originally a small warship with a single open gundeck. In the ironclad era the term was used to describe any ship thought too small for the title of frigate.

Displacement The modern method of determining the size of a ship, came into widespread use in Britain at the end of the 1850s, but was not used by the Navy for another decade.

Floating battery A French-designed armoured vessel of limited sea-going ability, intended for the bombardment of coastal forts.

Frigate The cruiser of the sailing age, a single covered gundeck, 32 to 60 guns. Properly used for scouting and commerce protection, but in this era the frigate was too closely configured to a small battleship to avoid service in the line of battle.

Indicated horse power Determined by a mechanical indicator fitted to the engine; a rather more reliable expression of performance than nhp.

Ironclad Any sea-going ship with armour.

Nominal horse power A rating of large steam engines computed from the dimensions of the cylinders. Not an accurate assessment of an engine's potential after 1845.

Paddle frigate The first steam warships, large single-decked ships with paddle wheel propulsion. No more than 20 guns fitted, but normally of a large calibre.

Sail of the Line The battleship of the sailing age, two or three covered gundecks, 70 to 120 guns.

Screw frigate The classic sailing frigate with screw propulsion. In the 1850s the type became enlarged to an unfortunate degree and lost contact with the functions of the Nelson era.

Shot and Shell These terms are often confused. *Shot* in the 1850s were solid, cast iron or steel projectiles, spherical for the smooth bore guns, conical for the rifled weapons. Hollow shot were, in effect, empty shells. *Shells* were hollow projectiles filled with gunpowder and ignited by a percussion or primitive time fuze. Red-hot-shot and molten iron shells were specially designed for incendiary effect.

Tonnage The old method of determining the size of a ship, approximately one-third too small in terms of actual displacement.

Wooden steam battleship Any ship of the line built for, or fitted with screw steam propulsion, two or three covered gundecks, 60 to 131 guns.

ABBREVIATIONS USED IN THE TEXT

CPL	Conway Picture Library
IWM	Imperial War Museum
M de la M	Musée de la Marine, Paris
MSC	Manpower Services Commission
MT	Maritime Trust
nhp	Nominal Horse Power
NMM	National Maritime Museum
Paris	*Souvenirs de Marine*
RNM	Royal Naval Museum
SPT	Ship's Preservations Trust
WPT	Warrior Preservation Trust

CHAPTER ONE
Origins

In 1815 the most powerful ships afloat were 120-gun three-decker sailing line of battleships some 20ft longer than the *Victory*. Their extra length and more practical construction reflected the reforms of Sir Robert Seppings, Surveyor of the Navy 1813–1832, the first great technological innovator of the nineteenth century naval revolution.

In the 1820s the French artillery expert Henri Paixhans developed a system of firing explosive shells from cannon that made wooden ships appear little more than large inflammable targets. However, the obvious response, to create a defence to keep the shells out, was not considered as a practical proposition until the Russian War. By that time the other ideas that went into *Warrior* had been brought to fruition.

The advance of steam engines at sea, symbolised by Brunel's *Great Western* and *Great Britain*, was paralleled in the world's navies, but only in small vessels. So long as the paddle wheel was the only method of propelling ships no battleship would be given a steam engine, for the wheels obscured the broadside of the ship, the focus of her offensive power. Only at the mid-point of the century did the screw propeller and im-

Nelson's famous flagship, veteran of many battles, HMS *Victory*. She spent almost one hundred years as the floating flagship of the Naval Commander-in-Chief at Portsmouth. *POPPERFOTO*

Brunel's epochal iron screw steamship the SS *Great Britain*, now preserved in the drydock in Bristol where she was built. She marked the greatest step forward yet seen in the rise of iron shipbuilding, completing for sea in 1845. She is seen here as rebuilt in 1857 for the Australian service. *POPPERFOTO*

The largest and most powerful of the paddle frigates, the *Terrible* of 1845. Larger than the 74-gun ships that fought at Trafalgar, she still only mounted 19 guns, admittedly of a heavier calibre. *Terrible* gave long and distinguished service, in the Black Sea during the Russian War, and as the 'rudder' of the Bermuda dock in 1869. She was finally sold in 1879. *CPL*

proved engines lead to a steam-powered battleship. Dupuy de Lôme's *Le Napoleon* and Isaac Watt's *Agamemnon*, both 90-gun two-deckers, began a brief Anglo-French Naval race during the 1850s. Over 100 two- and three-decked wooden battleships were built or converted into steam battleships in Britain and France before the type vanished almost as suddenly as it had appeared.

The unsuitability of wood for large steam-powered ships quickly became apparent, but it was the menace of improved artillery that finally ended the long reign of the wooden fighting ship.

The idea of building iron warships was first adopted in the mid-1840s. Just as these iron frigates were nearing completion gunnery experiments revealed that

The first successful steam powered battleship, Dupuy de Lôme's 960nhp 90-gun two-decker *Le Napoleon*, completed for service in early 1852. Unlike earlier attempts to introduce steam into the line of battle, this ship was primarily a steamer, sail was the auxilliary. Her principal role was to secure communications between Toulon and Algiers, hence the sacrifice of endurance for speed. Her original machinery was unreliable, especially when used at full power, when the vibration was unbearable. Note the two funnels. One of the *Algeciras* class, improved half sisters, can be seen astern. *M DE LA M*

The British reply to *Le Napoleon*, Isaac Watts' 91-gun 600nhp
Agamemnon. In most respects she was a superior ship, especially in regard
to her machinery. She was fitted with a smaller version of the Penn
Trunk engines later used in *Warrior*. *Agamemnon* is seen here at
Greenwich in 1856 loading the first, unsuccessful, Transatlantic telegraph
cable. *NMM*

rather than taking the initiative with any more novel
designs. The British response to *Le Napoleon* was the
obvious result.

Iron was once again employed in building warships
when armour plate was perfected, and this meant that
additional buoyancy was required to carry the weight.
After the Russian Black Sea Fleet had annihilated the
Turkish squadron at Sinope Bay in November 1853
Napoleon III decided that warships could not face up
to shell fire. He therefore proposed a scheme of armour
to protect them. His original idea, for an iron box full of
6lb shot, was impractical; once the box had been
broken by the first shot the 6lb balls rolled away.
However, the British Chief Naval Engineer, Thomas
Lloyd, suggested 4in thick wrought iron plate. This
proved quite adequate to keep out the most powerful
shot. France, and later Britain, built floating batteries
covered with 4in plates. These slow, ugly and unsea-
worthy vessels were only intended to bombard the
numerous Russian forts. They were not regular sea-
going warships. Three of the French batteries,
Dévastation, *Lave* and *Tonnant* went into action on 17
October 1855 assisting the Allied fleets to demolish the
fort at Kinburn. British, French and Russian authorities were all suitably impressed. Only the French had
the intellectual courage to realise the full implications
of what had happened. They ordered no more wooden
battleships, although it must be pointed out that they
lacked the necessary dockyard space.

their ½in shell plating made very good shrapnel, once
fractured by shot. The ships already built were converted into troopships and the loss of the *Birkenhead*
only served to confirm a prejudice against iron in 1852.
Too much had been attempted without a thorough
trial, a lesson taken to heart by the Admiralty. This resulted in a policy of reacting to foreign developments

Gibraltar, 101 guns, sister of *Duncan*. While the French were happy to
repeat *Napoleon*, the British expanded the *Agamemnon*. This ship, the end
of the design process, was 25ft longer and fitted with more powerful
machinery. The *Bulwark* class 90-gun ships later converted into ironclads
used the same hull form and dimensions. The *Gibraltar* is seen at
Devonport in 1867, just prior to final paying off. *IWM*

The French carried out a series of armour trials and on 1 January 1857 Stanislas Dupuy de Lôme was appointed *Directeur du Material* (Chief Constructor). De Lôme, already famous for *Le Napoleon*, was a determined advocate of iron ships and armour plate. He designed *Gloire* to carry a complete 4½in belt from stem to stern on a hull only slightly longer than *Le Napoleon*. She was built of wood because France lacked the iron shipbuilding resources and experience of Britain. One ship of the 1858 programme, *Couronne*, was built of iron to an alternative design by M Audenet. Although laid down before *Warrior*, she was not completed until after the British ship, which therefore can claim to be the first iron-hull ironclad warship.

Whatever the merits of *Gloire* the decision to lay down a total of six ironclads in March 1858 produced profound alarm in all circles in Britain. This galvanised the hitherto reluctant Admiralty and forced it to respond.

ADMIRAL SIR BALDWIN WALKER AND THE IRONCLAD

If any one man can take a major share of the credit for the success of *Warrior* it must be the Surveyor of the Navy, Admiral Sir Baldwin Walker. As Surveyor, (1848–1861) Walker was responsible to the Board of Admiralty for the ships built for the Navy. After problems with the previous Surveyor Walker had been appointed to liaise between the Admiralty and the constructors to ensure that the Navy received the best

Simoom, one of the 1845 iron frigates, seen here in her later role as a troopship. Note the large number of boats, which reflect her new task. In this configuration she played a valuable part in the Crimean campaign notably in carrying fresh meat and vegetables from Sinope to Balaklava. As a part of her conversion the original 700nhp engines were removed and replaced by 250 nhp machinery originally intended for the conversion of a small wooden frigate. *Simoom*'s engines were later used in the 131-gun steam battleship *Duke of Wellington*. The placement of the funnel abaft the mainmast was a feature of many screw steamers up to the battleship *Agamemnon*. The experience gained with ships so fitted, where the mainmast and mainyard were badly damaged by smoke and heat, ensured that by the time *Warrior* was built the funnels were placed between the main and foremasts. The all black colour scheme reflects *Simoom*'s subordinate role, and not the new aesthetics of the ironclad era. *CPL*

A model of one of the British floating batteries. Based on a French design, these simple armoured boxes used armour to solve the age-old problem of how ships could meet forts on equal terms. In October 1855 three French batteries played a major part in the capture of the Russian fort at Kinburn. This encouraged Dupuy de Lôme and Napoleon III to consider the potential of a sea-going ironclad. However it must be recalled that in Britain Sir Baldwin Walker was also giving his attention to this, for him, unwelcome possibility. *SCIENCE MUSEUM*

ships. His reputation as a seaman and an administrator was unrivalled.

While the final decision always rested with the politicians, Walker's professional advice carried enormous weight with almost all the First Lords of the Admiralty of the period. The respect given to his opinions was in direct proportion to the competence of those First Lords.

During the next ten years he created the steam battlefleet and marshalled the resources of the nation to meet the needs of war with Russia and a simultaneous naval challenge from Britain's erstwhile ally, France. By 1856 his career had reached its zenith; he was honoured by Queen and Country and admired and trusted by the nation, the Navy and the politicians. Walker dominated British construction policy.

He was a conservative and methodical man; in an age of dramatic innovation he remained firmly wedded to the doctrine of evolution rather than revolution in naval technology. Under his control the Surveyor's Department produced a succession of classes of wooden warship, each an improvement on the last. Walker was hardly the man to take a leap in the dark with a revolutionary new concept, yet that was exactly what he did with *Warrior*.

Under the relaxed direction of the First Lord, Sir Charles Wood (1855–8), the Admiralty investigated armour in the years following the Russian War. While Wood felt that Kinburn had not been a thorough test for armour as the guns there were too small, the concept of a floating battery was accepted unquestion-

ingly. The new trials were specifically intended to prepare the way for a sea-going ironclad. Unlike the French, who wanted to overturn the existing order of seapower at a stroke, the Admiralty was quite happy to consider the implications of armour at leisure. The trials progressed to the extent that in February 1858 Walker proposed building an experimental ironclad corvette; significantly this was before *Gloire* had been laid down. The dimensions and specification of this vessel repay study (see p22). This early wooden-hulled project was inferior to *Gloire* in only two respects: 4in as against 4½in armour, and a speed of only 10kts. In reality the former was of little consequence. Armour trials at Woolwich in late 1856 and throughout 1857 had established that 4in plates would resist 68pdr solid shot at 600yd, even if repeated hits demolished the target. The 8in 68pdr gun, weighing 95cwt was the most powerful naval gun then available. Walker's estimated speed for the projected ship was very low in comparison with other ships of that size and engine power. The wooden hull reflected his conservatism and a desire to build a ship for worldwide service. Iron hulls were prone to rapid fouling that reduced speed and made them reliant on drydocks for regular cleaning.

In many ways the first project was similar to *Gloire*. Her dimensions and machinery reflected experience with the wooden two-deckers. She would have been a stretched version of the 100-gun *Duncan* (see p22) with only one gun deck. As befits an experimental ship the design had only one novel feature, the armour – everything else was tried and tested. In that way the essential

Brunel's last ship, the colossal *Great Eastern*, was a testimony to the potential of iron. She remained the largest ship afloat throughout her long and unhappy career. Brunel's vision of trans-oceanic steaming, London to Bombay, inspired Scott-Russell to call for ironclads of similar size. Seen here beached in the Mersey awaiting demolition in 1888. *POPPERFOTO*

Sir Baldwin Walker's original essay at a first class single-decked fighting ship, the *Mersey* of 1859. With her sister, *Orlando*, she demonstrated the outer limits of wooden shipbuilding. Built to counter the American *Merrimac*s they were condemned to futility by the failure of the American ships and their own enormous cost of maintenance. They were sold in 1875 and 1871 respectively. *IWM*

purpose – to test armour on a sea-going ship – would not be compromised by the failure of any other aspect of the design. There was however no requirement for such a vessel, even as an experiment, and she was not ordered. The reasons were simple: Britain had no desire to encourage the French to start another naval race, expecially at a time when the Admiralty Estimates were being heavily cut back. Furthermore, Walker, unlike de Lôme, did not see the ironclad as the inevitable future of the fighting ship. His policy was to wait on French developments, keeping up to date with the latest technology. This would enable him to make a proper response when the French adopted a new type. Until then the best interests of Britain were served by

The four masted *Achilles* was effectively a modified *Warrior* taking into account the criticism levelled, by Reed in particular, at the *Warrior*'s unarmoured ends. She had a 13ft deep complete waterline belt and a 212ft long battery, closed off by 4½in armoured bulkheads, as in *Warrior*. The steering gear was fully protected. As seen here in 1864 with her original rig she spread 44,000 sq ft of canvas, the largest amount ever in a British warship. By 1866 she had been altered to a three-masted rig along the lines of *Warrior*. She was a fast ship under steam or sail and a superb gun platform. As a result her reputation stood far higher than that of *Warrior*, and she remained in front rank service with the Channel Fleet until 1885, by which time *Warrior* had been fifteen years in the reserve. *IWM*

The bow of *Minotaur*, seen here at Portsmouth after 1875 refit: the heavy bow scroll, a substitute for the old figurehead, is clearly shown. Note how the bow is cut back, where the group of seamen are standing, to permit ahead fire from the upper deck guns. The bowsprit is fitted so as to pivot upwards, when the ship cleared for action, the outward curve of the bow indicates the ram stem. *CPL*

The stern of *Northumberland*. A comparison with that of *Warrior* demonstrates the new style adopted to facilitate carrying armour round the stern, covering the rudderhead. This form was first adopted by the French, for *Napoleon* and then *Gloire*. Only the light stern walk and the name scroll are left of the baroque splendour of the preceding centuries. Note the spherical life preservers under the starboard end of the stern walk. *CPL*

the wooden navy. During this period Walker began to be influenced by John Scott-Russell, the controversial constructor of the *Great Eastern*. This relationship would bear fruit in the overall concept of *Warrior*, although not, as Scott-Russell later claimed, in her detailed design.

THE INVASION SCARE

When the first reports of *Gloire*'s laying down reached London in May 1858 the rumoured power of the French ship and the supposed numerical equality of the two battlefleets created a panic. Under pressure from the Queen and the Prince Consort, Lord Derby, the Tory Prime Minister, established a Parliamentary Committee of Enquiry. Although they were given a very wide field of investigation, the members of the Committee were directed to pay special attention to the opinions of Walker. The Report of the 'Derby' Committee reflected Walker's views, as did the naval policy of the First Lord of the Admiralty, Sir John Pakington.

Walker still did not feel that ironclads would inevitably replace wooden battleships. However, he did feel it essential to match the six French vessels as soon as possible, for the safety of the country. In a submission to the Board of Admiralty of 22 June, repeated before the 'Derby' Committee six days later, he laid down the rationale of British Construction policy as he understood it.

> Although I have frequently stated it is not in the interest of Great Britain, possessing as she does so large a navy, to adopt any important change in the construction of ships of war which might have the effect of rendering necessary the introduction of a new class of very costly vessels until such a course is forced upon her by the adoption by Foreign Powers of formidable ships of a novel character requiring similar ships to cope with them, yet it then becomes a matter not only of expediency but of absolute necessity. This time has arrived. France has now commenced to build frigates of great speed with their sides protected by thick metal plates, and this renders it imperative for this country to do the same without a moment's delay.

The original letter to the Board included a proposal that six ironclads be ordered at once: two, with wooden hulls, at the Naval Dockyards of Chatham and Pembroke; the other four, with iron hulls, at private yards. These vessels would have been modified versions of the first proposal; primarily enlarged and fitted with more powerful machinery to match the design speed of *Gloire*, as yet unlaunched and unproven. The wooden-hulled ships would cost £197,560, those with iron hulls being £4000 cheaper. At this stage of the wooden battleship naval race timber suitable for large warships was scarce, and correspondingly expensive.

Although the Board of Admiralty expressed deep concern at the six new French ships it preferred to

The last and largest of the wooden three deckers to enter service, the *Victoria*. She is lying at Malta during her years as flagship of the Mediterranean Fleet, 1864–7. Note the two lowered funnels, one either side of the mainmast. *NMM*

follow Walker's other recommendation, to convert wooden sailing ships into steamers, and deferred a decision on ironclads until the following year. Even then they anticipated ordering only two, with the possibility of more. One major reason for this was the anticipated success of the new Armstrong gun, a rifled breechloader that promised to supersede the old muzzle-loading smooth bores. Walker felt that it might have the power to render armour irrelevant. The Committee's willingness to follow Walker's opinions, where they offered economy, reflected the influence of the Treasury, and in particular of the Chancellor, Disraeli. Disraeli had a violent dislike of Walker, dating back to the brief Tory Ministry of 1852–3, when his professional integrity had defeated a crude Tory attempt to use the Dockyards for political advantage. As a result he, almost alone, hated the Surveyor. He told the Prime Minister:

> I am assured on the highest authority that nothing could be worse than the condition of the Admiralty as far as the naval members were concerned. All the men that Pakington has chosen ... are the most inefficient that could be selected. The Admiralty is governed by Sir B. Walker who has neither talents, nor science – & as far as I believe – nor honour – but the last is suspicion, the first are facts. He has frightened the country and has lowered its tone & his only remedy is building colossal ships which have neither speed nor power & which are immensely expensive from their enormous crews...

Disraeli favoured large frigates rather than battleships, on economic grounds. Derby also doubted Walker's honour, although he upheld his judgement on naval matters. Yet the uncertainty of the two Tory leaders was reflected in their preference for makeshift solutions and their failure to order more than a single ironclad. They both distrusted Pakington, their own selection for the Admiralty, and behind his back claimed that he was

urging large estimates to curry favour with the Navy. Derby still recognised the need to match the French; Disraeli, had he been Prime Minister, would have dismissed Walker and there would have been no *Warrior*. His point about Walker dominating the Admiralty is perhaps the most interesting part of the letter. It helps to emphasise the prestige that the Surveyor had earned during his term in office.

On the vital question of the purpose of ironclads, Walker lagged behind the French. He still favoured wooden conversions, placed his hopes in the Armstrong gun and did not think that ironclads would replace wooden battleships. In a submission to the Board of 27 July, repeated to the Derby Committee on 13 November, he argued:

> They must be regarded as an addition to our force, as a balance to those of France, and not as calculated to supersede any existing class of ship; indeed no prudent man would, at present, consider it safe to risk upon the performance of ships of this novel character, the Naval Supremacy of Great Britain.

Such sentiments were hardly likely to endear him to politicians, offering only an addition to naval expenditure. It required a more powerful political intellect than

either Derby or Disraeli possessed to suggest moving in advance of naval opinion and securing strength with economy by replacing wooden battleships with iron-clads.

The Report of the Derby Committee was published on 4 April 1859, but long before then the first British ironclad, *Warrior*, had been ordered.

ARMOUR TRIALS

During October 1858 a further series of gun *versus* armour trials produced more data on the design and performance of armour plate. HMS *Excellent*, the Naval Gunnery School moored in Portsmouth Harbour, used the old wooden battleship *Alfred* as a mounting for iron plates. After resisting 68pdrs, the plates were eventually penetrated by a single wrought iron shot from an experimental Whitworth rifled muzzle-loader. While this pointed out the potential of artillery it was rendered irrelevant as the gun had burst in firing the shot. Another six years would pass before any gun in service could penetrate 4½in armour with regularity, and even longer before shells could follow the shot. The *Alfred* trials also established that one 68lb shot had approximately the same effect on armour as five 32lb shot striking close together.

Later in October the Russian War floating batteries *Erebus* and *Meteor* were subjected to a series of trials. The wooden-hulled *Meteor* proved to be far stronger than the iron-hulled *Erebus*. This demonstrated satisfactorily the value of a heavy wooden backing for the plates, something that French engineers had anticipated when they inspected the iron-hulled batteries in 1855 (see Chapter 4 for a modern explanation of these trials).

When the Political Secretary to the Board of Admiralty, Henry Thomas Lowry Corry, persuaded his colleagues to call for an ironclad design, on 27 November, they specified a wooden ship with 4½in armour. However, influenced by Corry, Scott-Russell, Walker and members of his staff moved away from wooden-hulled ironclads in June. By calling for four iron-hulled ships to be built alongside their two wooden sisters he had admitted their suitability. Only

The nearest British equivalent to *Gloire* were the converted *Bulwark* class two-deckers. *Royal Oak*, seen here barque rigged as originally built, was the first to enter service, in 1863. In British service this class, eventually totalling seven ships, were second rank units suitable for the Mediterranean and more distant stations. *Warrior* and her iron-hulled contemporaries were kept at home, near the French threat, and the necessary graving dock. Note the canvas ventilators. *CPL*

blind prejudice could prevent the final success of iron and of this Walker had none. Wood was a better backing for armour, but it could not be trusted in long ships and lacked the strength and load-carrying capability of iron, as demonstrated by Brunel's colossal *Great Eastern*. An iron hull could be built with the length and fine extremities that contemporary ideas on hydrodynamics required for high speed. Walker explained his rationale for iron hulls to the Board in a letter of 28 September 1860:

> speed is of the utmost importance in all ships of war, and absolutely essential in sea-going ships cased with iron, both for their own safety and for attack, it becomes necessary to build them of extraordinary length, and in order to obtain the necessary strength they must be constructed of iron.

The tactical value of speed was inestimable for an ironclad – a term which was still firmly linked with the frigate in Walker's mind. Speed would allow the ship to avoid the concentrated close-range fire of wooden battleships and would also allow her to force an unwilling enemy to fight, solving the single greatest tactical problem of the sailing era: how to bring a flying enemy to decisive action. However, speed was not a vital element in fleet actions, where all were governed by the speed of the slowest. *Warrior* was not conceived as a battleship. Walker's thoughts were greatly influenced by Captain Hewlett of *Excellent*, the officer in charge of the most recent armour trials. He pressed for the ironclad to have the speed to choose the range at which it fought. This would enable it to use armour and heavy guns to the best advantage, keeping outside the effective range of the enemy's weapons while destroying him. This tactical concept had very little to do with battleships; it was the rationale for a powerful frigate. It demonstrates that *Warrior* was not conceived as a battleship, and was in this respect, as in many others, very different from *Gloire*. Had *Warrior* been designed as a line of battleship she would have carried a larger number of guns, an armament suitable for close-range fire. Walker was still convinced that future naval actions would be decided at point blank range. Only his large frigates were armed for long-range fire with a small number of heavy guns.

After due consideration of the Board's request Walker sent in the outline of the ship he considered most suitable. His letter stands as a remarkable exposition of the ideas that inspired *Warrior*.

Department of the Surveyor of the Navy.
Confidential.

Frigate of 36 Guns cased with Wrought Iron Plates – Designs obtain

Admiralty S W
27th January 1859

With reference to the question of Building Ships to be cased with Iron to render them Shot-proof, I beg to state that having given this important subject my best consideration, and it appearing that the most judicial course would be *not only to call on the Master Shipwrights* in the Dockyards, but *also* to request some of the *most eminent private shipbuilders* who have had considerable experience in Iron Shipbuilding, to furnish designs. I beg to submit that the Parties named in the margin be informed that their Lordships having under their consideration the subject of shot proof vessels would be glad to receive designs and suggestions for vessels of this description, and that the proposed particulars be sent for their information, observing that if they are disposed to furnish a Design not in accordance with these conditions, but which in their opinion would be better calculated to answer the intended purpose, their Lordships would be glad to receive it also.

The Design to be for a Frigate of 36 guns cased with $4\frac{1}{2}$ inch Wrought Iron Plates from the Upper Deck to 5 feet below the Load Water Line.

The Vessel to be capable of carrying the weights as per accompanying statement in addition to Machinery, Boilers, and Water, and Coals for full steaming for at least seven days, with a height of Midship Port of at least 9 feet above the water:- also to possess sufficient stability to enable her Guns to be used effectively both when Coals and Stores are expended, and when fully laden.

As *Iron* appears to be the *most suitable* material for a ship of this kind both as regards strength and durability, the Design should be for an Iron Ship, but if it is considered by any of the Parties called on that a more satisfactory arrangement could be made with wood than iron, a Plan and the particulars of a wooden ship may be forwarded for consideration; observing that in a wood ship *the Armour Plates* must necessarily extend from the stem to the stern, whereas *in an iron ship* it might be considered advisable to *limit their extent to about 200 feet* of the middle point of the vessel, separating the part cased from the parts not cased by strong athwartship Bulkheads, covered also with $4\frac{1}{2}$ inch Plates to extend down to about 5 feet below the Plates on the sides.

If this arrangement be adopted the ends of the ship not cased should have as great a number of watertight compartments as can be conveniently constructed, to afford strength for running down, and security against damage by Collisions or shot.

A full description of the proposed arrangements for this purpose should be given, as well as of the proposed mode of securing the Armour Plates, which in the case of an Iron ship should have a bed or backing of Timbers and planks of hard wood placed between them and the ordinary Plating of the ship, equal in substance and strength to the Timbering and Planking of the Topsides of a Ship of the Line, and the edges of the Armour Plates should be planed and closely fitted.

The Main Deck to be of 4 inch Dantzic Oak with

Beams sufficient in number and strength to bear the heavy guns and other weights.

The Upper Deck to be of Iron ⅝ of an inch thick, and to be covered with Dantzic Fir 3 inches in thickness.

The Ship to be Masted and Rigged as an 80-Gun ship and to have sufficient steam power to give a speed of at least 13½ knots under steam alone when fully equipped and with all stores on board.

The Horse Power of the Engines to be stated, and the space required for them and the boilers to be shewn on the drawings.

I further submit that the Private Shipbuilders be informed that as it is important their Lordships should know the probable cost of such a vessel before coming to any decisions, that it is desireable that an estimate of the cost of building her, and of the time required, be furnished with the Design, and that the information requested should be forwarded on the 1st March next.

B W Walker   Surveyor

Mr Chatfield Deptford Yard
Mr Rice Woolwich Yard
Mr Laing Chatham Yard
Mr Henwood Sheerness Yard
Mr Abthell Portsmouth Yard
Mr Peake Devonport Yard
Mr Cradock Pembroke Yard

*The Thames Shipbuilding
   Company* Blackwall
Mr Mare Millwall
Mr Scott-Russell Millwall
Messrs Samuda Blackwall
Westwood & Baillie Millwall
Mr Laird Birkenhead
Mr Palmer Jarrow on Tyne
Mr Napier Glasgow

Warrior during her first commission. She is trimmed heavily by the stern in contrast to the reports that she was bow heavy. *CPL*

Achilles in the late 1860s, when she had adopted a three-masted rig. Note that her funnels and steam pipes are of the same length, unlike *Warrior*. Although a half-sister sharing the same hull form, *Achilles* lacks the archaic knee bow and frigate stern of *Warrior*. *CPL*

Weights to be received on board the proposed 36-gun screw frigate

	Tons
Water for 6 weeks for 550 men – including casks	124
Provisions and spirits for 4 months for 550 men	105
Officer's stores and slops	14
Wood, sand and holystones	16
Officers, men and effects	75
Masts and yards, including spare spars, booms etc	119
Rigging, blocks and sails	70
Cables and anchors	121
Boatswain's and Warrant Officers' Stores:	92
main deck 34 100cwt 68pdr 10ft 0in	
Guns & Carriages:	215
Upper Deck 2 Pivors 68pdr 10ft 10in	
Small Arms and Ammunition	8
Powder: 550 cases	42
Shot and shell – 100 rounds, all taken as sold shot	109
Grape and canister shot	14
Galley and condensors	10
Engineers' stores	15
Spare screw, etc	12
	1161

Engines and Boilers complete, with spare gear etc
Coals for 7 days at 10lb nhp per hour
Weight of hull
Weight of armour plates
Total Displacement required

fore & aft	3ft 6in
Main deck ports deep	3ft 10in
distance between ports	12ft 0in
lower sill	1ft 6in
from deck	

In this letter Walker demonstrated the various elements that went into the eventual design of *Warrior*. Calling on eight private ship-builders for designs was unprecedented. During the Wars of the French Revolution and Empire, 1792–1815, private yards had built some ships of the line, but their use was abandoned after the war. None had ever been invited to submit designs for such an important class of ship. However, the Royal Dockyards, where all the major warships of the era were built, had neither the experience nor the facilities to build large iron ships. The iron frigates of 1845 had been contracted out, and any new iron ship would have to follow their example. The provision in Walker's letter for wooden-hulled ships was a placebo to allow the Master Shipwrights to compete. The private builders suggested in the margin of the letter were all famous for their work with iron ships, especially Scott-Russell, Mare and Napier. Walker realised that some, or all of them, would have to be called on to build any iron-hulled ships. It was only common sense to get them involved in the process at at

early stage, supplementing the limited iron experience at the Admiralty.

The parameters drawn up by Walker ensured that the designs sent in were for a long ship. With 34 guns to be mounted on the main deck, each occupying 15ft of space for convenient working, and a speed of at least 13½kts they would have to be longer than the *Mersey* class frigates, at that time the longest warships afloat. This made iron the preferred material for two clear reasons: first, to provide greater hull strength, something that was found to be lacking in *Mersey*, and secondly to avoid the need to armour the bow and stern. Walker, along with his contemporaries, feared that carrying the weight of armour up to the extremities would cause plunging in a head sea, making for a poor seaboat. The central 200ft long armoured citadel would protect the gun crews, while the watertight subdivision fore and after preserved flotation in the event of damage. Wooden hulls, being inflammable and unsuited to subdivision had, of necessity, to be armoured overall. Only after experience with ships armoured overall was the fallacy of poor sea-keeping exposed.

The detailed breakdown of weights was included to allow for a calculation of stability. This was essential if the ship was to be a stable fighting platform both fully loaded and empty. Walker's empirical approach was also reflected in his description of the wooden backing to be provided for the armour, equal to the topsides of a line of battle ship. Every aspect of the specification, and later of the detailed design, reflected the experience of a decade spent perfecting the wooden steam ship.

The various replies to Walker's circular were studied and ultimately rejected. All were defective in important areas, notably undercalculation of weights, stability or power requirements. Watts had the moral courage to prefer his own design, but the best of the commercial efforts, by Mare and Napier, were preferred when tenders for *Warrior* and *Black Prince* were offered.

The *Warrior* design was submitted to the Board in January 1859, and finally approved on 29 April. The decision to order was taken on 6 May, after great misgivings about the size and cost of the ship. The support of Corry and Pakington was vital at this stage. Without them Walker could never have built *Warrior*, especially in view of Disraeli's hostility. Watts' final design was an expansion of the original 26-gun corvette. Both earlier projects would have resembled *Warrior* in profile, albeit on a reduced scale. The first project would also have had only one funnel, on account of her 800nhp engines.

DETAILED DESIGN

The inspiration for *Warrior* came from many diverse sources. This was reflected in the detailed design. Walker provided the 'staff requirements' that governed the functional aspects of the ship. Scott-Russell, a talented iron shipbuilder, and rather better self-publicist, helped with conceptual matters and some minor aspects of construction technique. He persuaded

Table showing the responses to Walker's Letter

Designer	Length (ft)	Beam (ft)	Displ (tons)	Speed (knots)	Wt of armour (displ)	Wt of hull (displ)	ihp
Laird	400	60	9779	13½	.11	.51	3250
Thames Co.	430	60	11,180		.10	.58	4000
Mare	380	57	7341		.13	.46	3000
Scott Russell	385	58	7256		.18	.38	3000
Napier	365	56	8000	13½			4120
Westwood and Baillie	360	55	7600	13½	.16	.36	4000
Samuda	382	55					
			8084	13½	.16	.15	2500
Palmer	340	58	7690	13½			4500
Aberthell (Portsmouth)	336	57	7668				2500
Henwood (Sheerness)	372	52	6507		.18	.4	2500
† Peake	355	56	7000		.14	.46	3000
† Chatfield	343.6	59.6	7791		.14		
Lang (Chatham)	400	55	8511	15	.14	.53	2500
† Craddock	360	57.6	7724		.2	.42	2500
Admiralty (Office)	380	58	8625	14	.18	.52	5000

† To be built of wood.

Walker to build a long ship with fine lines, especially the hollow bow, which displayed some similarities to his 'Wave Line' theory. Even after the success of HMS *Bellerophon* had vindicated Edward Reed's ideas on shorter ships, Scott-Russell still called for very long ships, with bunkers large enough for oceanic steaming. The idea was Brunel's, and formed the basis of the *Great Eastern* design. Scott-Russell's later shift to favour small rams was the action of a man desperate for the limelight.

Scott-Russell's claim to a half share in the credit for designing *Warrior* was, like many of his statements, exaggerated. However, it did have an element of truth. In 1855 the floating battery *Aetna* was burnt out at his yard. He then proposed to the Admiralty that the armour be used in a sea-going ironclad frigate. The Admiralty understandably did not want to attempt anything so revolutionary. The materials were ordered to be reused in the replacement *Aetna*. When tenders were invited from private yards to build *Warrior* Scott-Russell's conceits received a direct rebuff. Walker explained to the Admiralty:

> Mr Scott-Russell asserts his rights to have preference over other parties who have tendered for the building of the Iron Cased Frigates on the grounds that he was the original inventor and proposer of them.
>
> The Surveyor reports that he has no such right and that his prices are higher than those of others.

Isaac Watts never gave Scott-Russell any credit for *Warrior*. Instead he admitted in 1861 before a Parliamentary Committee that the ship being 'of a novel character', the design involved frequent communication between himself, Walker and the Chief Engineer, the same Thomas Lloyd who had originally proposed 4in wrought iron plates as armour. This triumvirate were entirely respons-ible for *Warrior*. Scott-Russell, through Walker exerted a degree of influence, but in the last resort Watts designed *Warrior*, with engineering advice from Lloyd, to meet the conception of the Surveyor.

Watts was not entirely at home as a designer of iron ships, yet his mastery of design was such that within 18 months of the launch of *Warrior* he produced *Achilles*, a perfected *Warrior* and one of the finest ironclads ever built. It was an indication of Watts' ability that *Achilles* was a distinct improvement over *Warrior* in almost every respect, even though she was a half-sister with the same hull.

In conclusion it must be argued that Scott-Russell's contribution to the design of *Warrior* came in the form of conceptual elements, like the unarmoured ends and internal subdivision, along with details of the latest merchant ship practice. He did not assist Watts to design the ship. Watts was an autocrat and highly unlikely to tolerate the presence of an egregious and conceited merchant shipbuilder in his office, even under orders. The real basis of Scott-Russell's claim lies in his own subsequent statements; they must be reduced in scale.

Watts final design for *Warrior* was competent, if rather conservative. It reflected his experience with the large wooden steamers, notably in adopting very heavy frames. Walker designed the middle of the ship, leaving Watts to provide a hull that could carry the guns and armour, while allowing the large engines to reach at least 13½kt. Experience with the wooden steam battle-ship had demonstrated that only long and very fine hulls could reach such speeds. *Warrior* had a length-to-beam ratio of 6½ to 1, and was therefore slightly finer than the preceding class of very long frigates, the 330ft *Mersey*. As if to emphasise the conservatism of the design, Watts left *Warrior* with the profile of *Mersey*.

This provided two of the least satisfactory elements in the design: the knee bow and the frigate stern. These features made *Warrior* and *Black Prince* the most elegant of the ironclads, but were entirely anachronistic. The knee bow was especially futile: on a wooden ship it served to support the bowsprit; but on an iron hull it had no purpose – it only added 40 tons of useless weight to the marginally buoyant bow section. A glance at *Achilles* will show the less elegant, but more functional, form of her extremities that resulted from simply leaving off the knee bow and carrying the form of the side right round the stern in the French fashion first seen with *Le Napoleon*.

Even more remarkably Watts fitted two pairs of diagonal tie plates over the iron upper deck in positions which suggested that they were holding the unarmoured extremities onto the central citadel. Such plates were required under Lloyds' Rules for wooden-hulled merchant ships, but they had no purpose on an iron ship. As D K Brown RCNC has stated, in his paper for the Royal Institute of Naval Architects, they establish that Watts did not fully understand the structural use of the new material.

This conservatism in the detailed design had a very good purpose. *Warrior* was, in overall concept, the boldest step ever taken in warship evolution. As with Walker's first ironclad corvette, design novelty was restricted; this had the same purpose, to prevent the failure of any other elements from ruining the experiment. Though none of the individual elements in *Warrior* were innovatory, their amalgamation into one package was.

WARRIOR AND HER CONTEMPORARIES

To appreciate the full significance of *Warrior* it is essential to consider her alongside her contemporaries. The total concept was novel, and greatly in advance of the mere sum of parts. When *Warrior* was first commissioned, the most powerful ships in British service were the last generation of wooden battleships. The three-decker 120-gun *Victoria* and the two-decker 100-gun *Duncan* were the culmination of ten years of dramatic development sparked by de Lôme's *Le Napoleon*. They were very powerfully armed with 6in solid shot and 8in shell guns. In this respect they completely outclassed the far smaller *Victory*. This increase in size had been made possible by a revolution in structural design begun by Sir Robert Seppings and continued by John Edye, Deputy Surveyor 1832–56. *Victoria* and *Duncan* marked the end of the line for wooden battleships. *Gloire* carried the line into the ironclad age, but her designer admitted that she was a dead end. Unable to match Britain's lead in iron shipbuilding de Lôme relied on a timber hull, constructed in the same way and very similar to that of the wooden battleships, to carry her armour. Her iron upper deck provided some additional strength, but the wooden hull allowed for no real subdivision. *Gloire* was also armed after the fashion of the wooden battleships. Like *Warrior* she carried 34 guns on the main deck, but these were badly crowded in the French ship and fired through very wide embrasures that weakened the armour scheme and exposed the gunners. The guns were 6.4in rifled muzzle-loaders, although they proved inferior to the British 68pdr smooth bore as armour piercing weapons.

As a seaboat *Gloire* left much to be desired, rolling badly and therefore providing a poor gun platform. Several half sisters of *Duncan* were converted into ironclads and proved superior to her in most respects. They demonstrated that *Gloire*'s only claim to fame was that she brought armour into the line of battle: otherwise she was not an inspired design. Despite the exaggerated hopes of the French and the absurd fears of the British, *Warrior* was a far better ship. *Gloire* was constructed in an attempt to overturn British mastery of the sea. *Warrior* demonstrated that the hope was unreal. By taking naval architecture into the industrial age the French played into the hands of Britain, already the leading industrial nation.

If *Gloire* was the inspiration for *Warrior*, her actual design had very different origins. The American Navy had abandoned the line of battle ship, and in the 1850s

Warrior and her contemporaries

	Guns	Date	Crew	Length (oa) (ft)	Breadth (ext) (ft)	Length/ Breadth	Draught	Displace- ment Tons	Engines ihp	Coal Tons	Speed Knots	Height of main deck ports (ft)
Victory	100	1765		186	52		21 6					4.5
Howe	120	1860	1000	260	60	4.3/1	25 10	7000	4564	550	13.0	8
Duncan	100	1858	930	252	58	4.6/1	25 6	5950	3428	520	13.0	8
Orlando	40	1858	600	336	52	5.8/1	21 6	5643	3617	850	13.0	9-10
Gloire	40	1860	570	255 6	55 9	4.7/1	27 10	5630	2500	665	12.5	6.25
1st Project	26	1858		280	58	4.7/1	23 3	5600	3200		10.0	10
2nd Project	26	1859		280	58	4.7/1		6096	3600		12.75	9
Warrior	36	1861	707	420	58 4	6.5/1	26	9137	5267	800	14.08	9

Black Prince as completed for service, with the reduced bowsprit, heightened funnels and side heads on the bulwark between the funnels. From the narrow hull top band it would seem that this is an early photograph. *CPL*

built a series of very large steam frigates, the *Merrimac* class. In response Walker had outlined the remarkable *Mersey* and *Orlando*, the longest, largest and most powerful single-decked wooden fighting ships ever built. Despite the most careful design, by Isaac Watts, and the best construction methods, these ships were unequal to the strains imposed on them by their engines. They demonstrated that the outer limits of wooden construction had been reached. To build a longer ship iron was essential, and this was evident to Walker. The need for a longer ship arose because *Orlando* was not the equal of a line of battle ship at close quarters, and lacked any margin of speed to keep at a distance and use her heavier guns. *Warrior* rectified all the faults of the *Orlando*, and by adding armour that was considered invulnerable over 400yd, established a clear tactical doctrine.

Being ships with a single covered gundeck, both *Gloire* and *Warrior* were classed as frigates, but *Gloire* was not a frigate. The French had always intended her for the line of battle, specifically in the Western Mediterranean and English Channel. She was therefore fitted with a light rig as built that would have done little to reduce her use of steam and keep her small bunkers filled. *Warrior* was intended to be an ocean-going cruising ship, her full rig and hoisting screw were fitted to allow for long passages under sail. They provided the strategic mobility. Furthermore *Warrior* was not designed as a battleship, and was never properly called one during her active career. As a descendant of *Orlando*, *Warrior* was conceived by Walker as a supplement to the line of battle ships, specifically to counter the new French ships.

In this respect *Warrior* symbolised the collapse of the old tactical doctrines of the Napoleonic Wars, which called for battleships and frigates to have clear and distinct functions. Frigates were cruising ships for fleet reconaissance and the defence of trade. They were not intended to take part in fleet actions. The striking success of the large American frigates in the War of 1812, ships almost as big as the standard British line of battleship, and subsequent outsize American frigates, culminating in the *Merrimac*, encouraged a blurring of the two types. This in turn created a hybrid heavy frigate class in the Royal Navy, where it lacked a clear tactical function. *Orlando* was not a line of battle ship, her armament was ill conceived for this role, and yet she was too large and costly for cruising and reconnaissance, the true roles of a frigate. This confusion had grown up in a period of peace, and it took the hard school of war to demonstrate the folly of the battleship-frigate hybrid. *Warrior* was originally also a ship without a clear purpose, beyond countering *Gloire* although the rapid disappearance of the line of battle ship left her and her type as the capital ships of the era.

As a fighting ship *Warrior* was far superior to everything that had gone before. It is often claimed that she could have sunk every battleship then afloat with impunity. This is an exaggeration, but it does reflect something of the giant leap that she effected in warship design. With her superior speed, armour and long range guns *Warrior*, well handled, could have destroyed any single wooden ship in short order. *Gloire*

Comparative sheer profiles to demonstrate the growth of the wooden
warship in the decade preceding *Warrior* and the close design
relationship between *Warrior* and the wooden frigate *Mersey*.

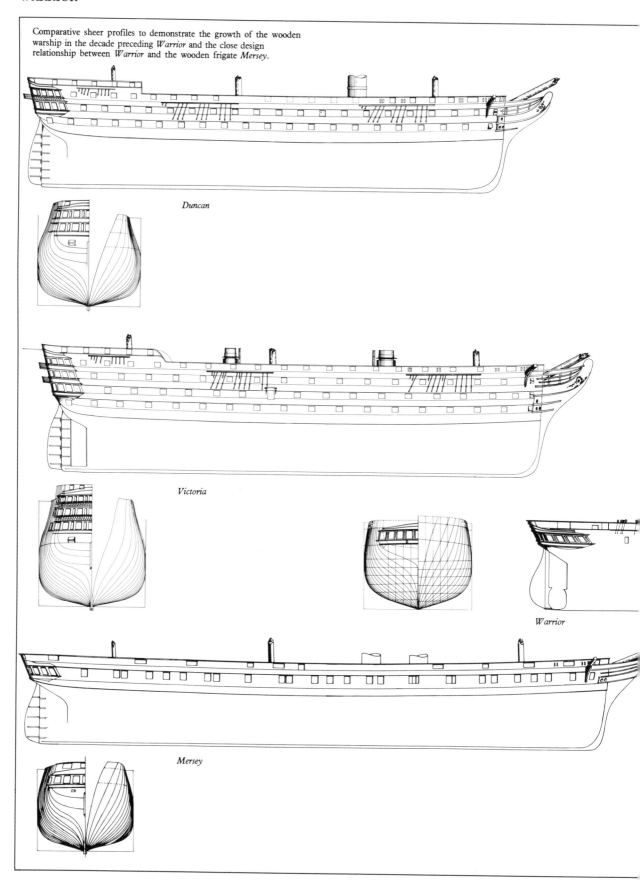

Duncan

Victoria

Warrior

Mersey

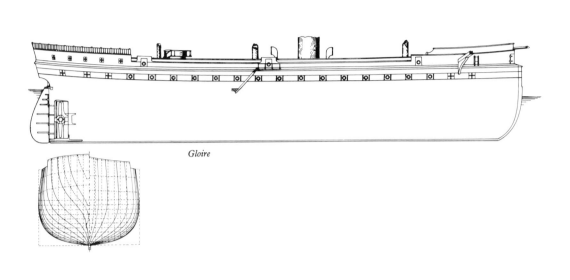

Gloire

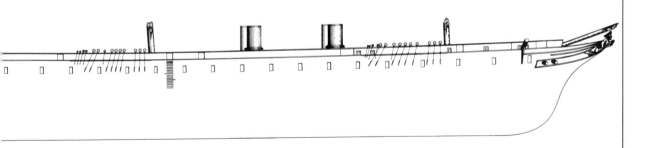

The steady growth in the size of the wooden warship in the eighty years after the completion of *Victory*, 1765, resulted in little more than 20ft on the keel. The first true steam battleships added another 20ft, while *Victoria*, designed only eight years after *Agamemnon*, was a further 30ft longer. This expansion required a substantial increase in the level of iron reinforcement, especially the massive 5in × 1in section diagonal riders that strapped the lower hull into shape. Similarly the stern was supported by an increasing amount of structural ironwork, to counter the strains set up by the propeller. The *Mersey* class took all these developments to the extreme. The experiment failed. The *Mersey*s were not significantly faster than the *Duncan*, or *Victoria*, and lacked the hull strength to support their powerful machinery. *Orlando* crossed the Atlantic in heavy weather and reached Plymouth with many of her seams wide open. The high cost of maintaining such ships must have played a large part in their early sale.

Note the similarities between *Gloire* and *Duncan* in terms of hull form. The greater spacing between the gunports of the British single-decked ships and their close design relationship reflect their common design role. *Warrior* was an iron-hulled armoured *Mersey*; both were frigates. *TED WILSON* would have been a more troublesome opponent, but her overcrowded battery, less effective guns and wooden hull should have given *Warrior* the edge. However it should be stressed that *Gloire* was never intended to act alone; she was an ironclad version of the line of battleship. *Warrior*, for all the apparent similarities, was a very different ship. It was hardly surprising to find that she was not at her best when constrained to follow the evolutions of a fleet.

AESTHETICS

Perhaps the least novel aspect of *Warrior*'s design was her appearance. In profile she was no more than an enlarged *Orlando*, and only the absence of her predecessor's single white band ever disguised the fact. By abandoning the frigate strake along the main deck (only *Defence* and *Resistance* among the ironclads were ever painted in the old style) *Warrior* achieved a degree of aesthetic novelty. However, the new paint scheme, all black with a thin white boot top and buff masts and funnels, was a complete success. Hitherto all warships of the mid-nineteenth century had been painted with a white strake along each covered gun deck. Only transports, like *Simoom* (see p12) had been painted in un-relieved black. After *Warrior* all this changed; not for nothing were capital ships of the late 1860s referred to collectively as the 'Black Battlefleet'. The new paint scheme had a menacing air of latent power, re-emphasising the effect produced by her size. The same basic scheme was continued until 1904.

Among the ironclads Ballard, who served aboard several of them, gave the palm for majesty of appearance to *Warrior*'s half sister, *Achilles*, as a three-masted ship. It would be hard to disagree. *Warrior* looked more than a little outdated alongside *Achilles* and the *Minotaur* class. Yet as the sole survivor of her kind, and seen outside her age, *Warrior* has a very pleasing appearance. It must be emphasised that this is the style of the 1850s, not the 1860s; she is in this respect an iron copy of her wooden predecessors.

By contrast *Gloire* made no concessions to contemporary views on elegance or majesty. She was a practical design and lacked any aesthetic refinement. Alongside *Warrior* she was a small, low and ugly ship. The French had been noted in earlier years for the elegance of their ships. In the ironclad era they abandoned style, concentrating on the exaggerated expression of military qualities. Their designs of the later nineteenth century were hideous.

CHAPTER TWO
In Service

CONSTRUCTION AND CONFUSION

The order for *Warrior* was given to the Thames Ironworks Company, successors to Ditchburn and Mare on 11 May 1859. Their tender, to build the ship for a price of £31.50 per ton on the old Builder's measurement (approximately two-thirds of the modern displacement) had been the lowest received from the eight firms invited to tender. *Warrior* was laid down on 25 May on the east bank of Bow Creek at the point where it joins the Thames. on the same day the tender of John Penn & Sons of Greenwich for the engines was accepted.

As C J Mare, Thames Ironworks had built several large iron screw steamers for the P & O Line, the 5500-ton *Himalaya* being the largest, although another dozen of between 1800 and 2800 tons were built in the 1850s.

During the Russian War the firm had built several warships, including the floating batteries *Meteor* and *Thunder* and some gunboats. The firm's reputation for quality workmanship had been established long before *Warrior* was ordered, and played a decisive part in securing the opportunity to tender for the contract.

When *Warrior* was ordered it was intended that she should be launched in eleven months and completed for sea in another three *ie* by July 1860. These dates were hopelessly over-optimistic, and reflected Walker's concern to complete the ship at the same time as *Gloire*,

Warrior at Plymouth during her first commission. She has been fitted with the short bowsprit, which ends just above the figurehead. The funnels, but not the steam pipes, have been raised. Compare this with a post-1873 view to emphasise the changes in the ship and the paint scheme. *CPL*

Defence, one of the quartet of unsatisfactory reduced derivatives of the *Warrior* design, forced on Walker by Somerset and Paget. They were greatly inferior as fighting ships, but offered major advantages in cost, economy of manpower and the ability to use docks outside the British Isles. *Defence* carried the full rig seen here only between 1864 and 1866, before and after that she was barque rigged. *CPL*

As a wooden ship *Gloire* should have taken at least three years to build; any less and she would not last long on account of dry rot. However the French were prepared to take this risk. Laid down in March 1859 *Gloire* was launched on 24 November and completed in August 1860.

While an iron ship could have been built more quickly, at least in theory, various design alterations to *Warrior* and the sheer novelty of the undertaking, created problems. Much of this delay can be attributed to Pakington's concern to outclass *Gloire*. Rather than building a British version of the French ship he favoured something superior; this also encouraged the trend toward an iron hull.

Warrior was officially named on 5 October 1859, although she was not launched until 29 December 1860. The use of the name 'Warrior' for the new ship was also significant. Only one ship had carried it before, a long lived and justly famous 74. The new ship was ordered only two years after the old one had been demolished. Sir John Pakington performed the ceremony while six tugs pulled her down the frozen ways, a most inauspicious start. *Warrior* finally completed for service only on 24 October 1861. The delay gave *Gloire* the prestige of being the first sea-going iron-clad, and gave rise to a series of increasingly intemperate letters from the Surveyor's Department to the builders and some of the subcontractors. Walker's humour could hardly have been improved by widespread public reports that *Warrior* would not fulfill the hopes placed in her, or the lack of direction evident on the new Board of Admiralty. The problems encountered during construction, many arising from Admiralty prevarication, caused the Thames Ironworks to make a considerable loss on the contract. They were awarded £50,000 to keep the firm solvent.

In June 1859 Lord Derby's Tory Ministry was replaced by the Liberal Government of Lord Palmerston. The result of the change at the Admiralty was to throw Walker's careful policy out of the window and replace it with a multiplicity of developments. The first sign of a crisis of confidence came when the second ironclad, *Invincible*, later renamed *Black Prince* to avoid confusion with one of *Gloire*'s sisters, was not ordered until October. Palmerston was in favour of regaining a decisive edge in wooden ships and only keeping pace with the French in ironclads. His First Lord, the Duke of Somerset, had no concept of naval policy and took advice from all manner of amateurs, especially Palmerston. This dramatically reduced Walker's influence over construction policy.

Somerset had suggested rationalising construction policy by discontinuing the construction of wooden

battleships; Palmerston's reply of 25 September 1859 makes interesting reading:

First as to the number of Line of Battle Ships which we ought to have, reckoning Two Deckers and Three Deckers as one class; now we must remember that we might have to encounter not only the French Navy, but the combined navies of France and Russia and that the chances of our having to do so would be much increased if it were well known that by reason of a Great Inferiority in numbers of Line of Battle Ships, we were unable advantageously to cope with the Two navies combined. But the French will soon have nearly as many screw Liners as we have, and the Russians are steadily recruiting their Baltic Fleet by Line of Battle Ships moved by screws. I should say therefore that although we want more large Frigates and more gun-boats, we ought not to discontinue the building of Line of Battle Ships.

A similar reasoning would apply to the opinion held by some, that long and heavily armed Frigates are better than Liners. If indeed such Frigates can be so coated with Iron as to be shot-proof at a moderate distance they would no doubt dispose of a Liner not so protected; but has the result of experiments led us as yet to the conclusion that any form of Iron coating would stand a well directed broadside? It is not enough to find that iron coating will stand a single shot; it might resist one shot and yet be shivered by the Blow of Twenty or Thirty shot at a time or in rapid succession striking the whole side of the coated ship. These are all questions of detail, to be settled by the opinion of good naval judges and by the result of experiments well conducted: but that which seems indisputable is that we should add largely to our naval force in order to put us in a condition to be known to be able to cope with any hostile force which might array against us; bearing in mind moreover that we have beyond sea possessions to protect, as well as our own shores to defend.

A confused First Lord receiving such a letter from the Prime Minister can be excused a little hesitation. Somerset continued work on the two-deckers. Palmerston was wrong about armour; it had already been demonstrated beyond question that it worked. As for 'good naval judges' the Surveyor had proved that he was the best man to answer all these questions, and yet he was increasingly ignored. Further ramifications of Palmerston's confusion can be seen in his letter to

Achilles in 1893. Little altered by her years of service she is still driven by the original Penn Trunk engines. Of note are the light, anti-torpedo boat guns along her topsides, also the steam pipe on her after funnel has been shifted, like *Warrior*'s, to the front of the funnel. *IWM*

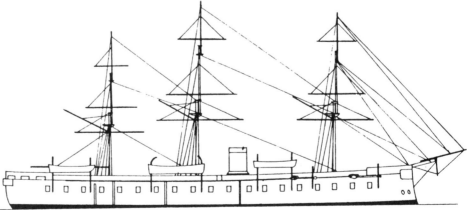

The first French iron-hulled ironclad, Audenet's *Couronne*. Delayed, like *Warrior*, by alterations to her plans she was to be completed after the British ship, even though laid down before. She was little more than an iron *Gloire*, and had no claim to any originality. Like *Warrior* she gave good service as a hulk, finally being sold in 1932. *CPL*

Gladstone, the Chancellor of the Exchequer of 25 November:

> I have received the inclosed from the Duke of Somerset, and I think we ought to authorize him to take the steps which he proposes to take. The French are making great progress in the construction of iron plated ships and if we do not in some degree keep pace with them we shortly find ourselves standing to a great disadvantage. I think the Duke right in proposing to build iron-plated ships of a smaller size and therefore less expensive than the two which were begun by the late government. There are some doubts whether this iron-plating would resist the heaviest shot delivered at a short distance but it will certainly stand any shot beyond 4 or 500yds, and ships so armed would therefore beyond those distances have an immense advantage over ships not protected in the same manner.

The origins of the idea lay with the Political Secretary to the Board, Captain Lord Clarence Paget; the explanation for its success lay entirely in the realm of finance. Walker objected to the plan on the grounds that smaller ships would not be capable of matching *Warrior*'s speed, which would leave them hostage to any large force of wooden ships they might encounter, and prevent them from acting effectively with *Warrior*. Furthermore iron ships would have longer lives than wooden ones, and, if built with a low speed, would quickly become obsolete, useful only for harbour defence. Under pressure in late 1859 he had Watts draw up the *Defence* and *Resistance*, reduced versions of *Warrior* specifically for 'Channel and Home Service'. They were followed a year later by the improved *Hector* and *Valiant*. These four ships justified everything Walker had claimed. They were not even an economic proposition. Later commentators, following Nathaniel Barnaby, Director of Naval Construction 1875–1885, have given *Defence* a military value only one quarter that of *Warrior*. *Hector* was rather better, although a poor seaboat, but both classes were slow, weakly armed and of limited endurance.

Warrior cost £357,291; *Defence* cost £237,291 and *Hector* cost £283,822. The smaller ships cost at least two-thirds as much as the larger one, but offered only a quarter to half the value. Later even smaller ironclads

were built. They were all failures, unable to combine the speed, endurance, protection and firepower required for a front rank ship.

Having been generally ignored and forced to build inferior ships which he considered thoroughly misguided, it can hardly have come as a surprise that

Walker resigned on 7 February 1861. His position had been designated that of Controller a year earlier. He had hitherto enjoyed the confidence of his political superiors, and, being very sensitive to criticism, soon tired of the thankless task of attempting to stem the confused flood of naval opinions that his political

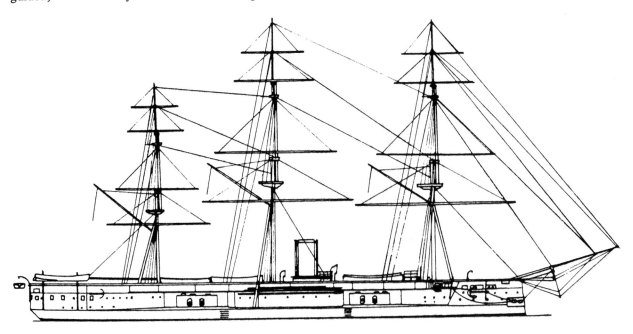

Cowper Coles' *Captain* of 1870. This unstable and over-masted monument to the folly of public opinion capsized off Cape Finisterre on 7 December 1870 after only a few months' service. *CPL*

The *Monarch* of 1869 was the first ocean-going turret ship. The two turrets can be seen under the hurricane deck on either side of the funnel. She was designed by Reed to meet the public demand for turret ships, and proved far superior to the design of the turret pioneer Cowper Coles. *CPL*

Bellerophon, as completed in 1866. This ship marked a complete break with the long fine-hulled frigate type that Walker and Watts developed. Edward Reed's design was more battle orientated, having heavier guns, thicker armour and better manoeuvrability, largely due to her short hull. This sacrificed the speed, endurance, stability and number of guns that had made the *Warrior* type such important ships. Reed also introduced his 'bracket frame' construction system with this ship. It offered a considerable saving in hull weight, from a more sensible layout of the hull framework. *CPL*

masters called a naval policy.

Walker was a remarkable man; perhaps the most talented naval officer to hold an administrative post in the nineteenth century navy. The wooden steam battlefleet, the Russian War flotilla and *Warrior* all stand to his credit. At the same time he had a major influence over strategic policy and the general administration of the navy. The thirteen years he spent as Surveyor/Controller spanned an epoch remarkable in British naval policy-making. His clarity of thought, experience and courage were to be sadly missed in later years.

WARRIOR AS A WARSHIP

Warrior was effectively ready for action in June 1862, after alterations principally reducing the size of the bowsprit to make her less bow heavy. The apparent defect of a lack of buoyancy forward had been noticed as soon as the ship went to sea. It was argued that her V-hull form and hollow bow lines provided insufficient lift to keep the bows up, ensuring that she often shipped green water over the bow, pitched and was generally wet and uncomfortable on the upper deck. Only a better design of bow could have prevented this. *Achilles*, by abandoning the heavy and useless knee and substituting a built-up forecastle was a dry ship. In fact the low beakhead was almost certainly the cause of the problem.

The other weak points of the design were the rapid fouling of the hull, the exposed steering gear and poor manoeuvrability. With an iron hull the dramatic buildup of marine growths was inevitable. There was no effective method of prevention, only the cure of regular docking. To maintain her speed, the most costly feature of the design, *Warrior* was docked on average every ten months during her first two commissions. The real problem was that only three docks existed that could take her, at Portsmouth, and in emergency Southampton or Liverpool. As a result lengthy overseas service was out of the question, at least until new docks

Despite her low freeboard the *Devastation* of 1873 was the first successful ocean-going turret ship. By sacrificing masts she could be made stable enough for the heaviest seas, although she was necessarily rather wet. She was the ancestor of the twentieth century battleship. *CPL*

The last of the frigate-hulled broadside ironclads, *Northumberland*. Her design, originally as one of the *Minotaur* class, was recast by Reed during construction to take account of the latest developments in artillery. This gave her a smaller number of individually heavier guns and a reduced armoured area on the main deck, similar to *Achilles*. Her other claim to novelty was the larger conning tower, seen between the after pair of masts. During her 1875 refit the second and fourth masts were removed. Unlike *Warrior* she and her two half sisters were slow sailers, with five masts or three, and made more use of their rig as a gymnasium. *CPL*

had been prepared. Walker had accepted this limitation, and always intended that the ironclads should be kept in the Channel. *Warrior* and *Black Prince* never served outside the limits of the Channel Fleet, although *Achilles* and the even longer *Agincourt* were sent to the Mediterranean in the late 1870s. Walker's successor, Captain Sir Robert Spencer Robinson, adopted the original logic of the design, treating the six long broadside ships as a powerful strategic reserve, based in home waters and for long periods in reserve or dockyard hands as an economy measure.

The lack of protection to the steering gear was the greatest fault in the original design. *Warrior* could have been disabled by a single unlucky hit, but even this would have been only temporary. This weak heel was corrected in her half sister, *Achilles*. Many amateur navalists thought that the concept of leaving the extremities unarmoured was even more serious. Palmerston expounded the layman's view in a letter to Gladstone of 21 July 1861. The purpose of this letter was to secure additional funds from the belligerent Chancellor by criticising the products of the previous administration.

The French ships with one exception, the *Couronne*, are built of wood like ordinary ships of war and are coated, most of them the whole of their length, some not quite to the end of their bows or quite to their stern, with iron. The

Black Prince during her first commission. The Royals are set, to make a display in harbour. *CPL*

Couronne is built like ours with an inside shell of ¾in of iron like a packet or a merchant ship, and outside of that first a wooden skin of about 2ft, and then an iron covering of 4½in. The consequence is that the part which is iron cased will resist ordinary shot, and the part which is not cased will be pierced by ordinary shot just as an ordinary ship of war would be; a hole being made in the wood which is easily stopped up by a wooden plug driven into it, and if a shell pierces the wooden end and bursts within, there are strong partitions closing in the iron cased parts, within which the crew will have retired to work the guns within the protected part and not much damage will have been done.

Warrior's first Captain, Arthur Cochrane, third son of the famous Lord Cochrane, tenth Earl of Dundonald. WPT

A contemporary print of the Bermuda Dock, showing Warrior in the dock, without caissons. While it is doubtful if Warrior was ever in the dock, it does indicate the size of the load she and Black Prince had to tow across the Atlantic. WPT

But our iron cased ships built on the model laid down by Pakington's Admiralty are in my opinion sadly wrong in principle. They consist like the Couronne of an internal skin of ¾in of iron; but this skin is not protected all the way from stem to stern – the middle part has like the Couronne, or I believe I ought rather to say that the Couronne has like them, over the iron skin a coating of teak wood 18in or 2ft thick, and outside of that an iron casing 4½in thick. But this

protection does not extend the whole way from stem to stern as it does in the Gloire, and I believe in most of the other French ships; and on a considerable part of the side of our iron ships towards the bow and towards the stern consists of nothing but the thin iron skin of ¾in of iron. My belief is that if the Gloire or one like her were to lie alongside of one of ours of equal force, the Gloire would before many broadsides had been exchanged, have smashed to pieces those parts of our ship Warrior, Black Prince or other, which consists only of this ¾in of iron. It is true that the protected part is shut in at each end by a strong partition supposed to be shot proof, and it is alleged that as the crew would in action be all withdrawn within the protected part no essential damage would be done by the smashing of the fore and after part of the ship. And it is said that all that part of the fore and after portions thus unprotected, which are under the water line, and which might be struck by shot, are divided into compartments by waterproof partitions so that only one compartment at a time could be filled by water. But this seems to me a very unsatisfactory arrangement; if the fore and after part unprotected by casing were shattered away the ship would become a mere box floating on the water, and if several of the watertight compartments were pierced by shot, and filled with water, the ship would by the additional weight of the water sink deeper and become what is called waterlogged and would be comparatively unmanageable. The reason why this manner of construction was adopted was, that our Admiralty people thought that if the armour extended the whole length of the ship, the bow would plough too deeply into the water, and the ship would be too heavy and would not carry her guns high enough out of the water, to admit of her portholes being left open when the sea was rough. I have repeatedly and strongly remonstrated with the Duke of Somerset against this pasteboard construction of our so-called iron ship of war; and the iron cased ships henceforward to be built will be so shaped in their Hulls as to have buoyancy enough to bear being iron-plated along their whole length from stem to stern.

I have entered into this long detail to shew that our nominal approximation to equality with the French towards the end of the summer of 1862 will have concealed under it a real inferiority of quality in our iron cased ships – and this seems to me to render it the more important that we should lose no time in adding to our numbers and improving the quality of the ships so to be added.

After inspecting Warrior for himself Palmerston revised his harsh judgement, but still used the 'pasteboard ends' to press for more ironclads. Considering Gloire to be a better ship reflected a profound ignorance of the concept of watertight subdivision which had been substituted for armour at the extremities. After a decade of complete waterline belts this system was reintroduced when armour became too heavy for any ship to carry overall. Walker's original idea, influenced by Scott-Russell, had been entirely correct. Warrior would not have become waterlogged even if her ends had been penetrated, because, as practical experiments demonstrated, these spaces contributed little to her buoyancy.

In service Warrior was condemned more often for her poor steering than any other single failing. This made her a danger to her consorts in a fleet, and the fact

Warrior as she appeared about 1875, while Guardship of the Portland Division of the Naval Reserve and Coastguard. As a result of her refit she has a modified forecastle and bowsprit. A poop deck has been added and a new charthouse provided just forward of the mizzen masts. The funnels have been replaced. The funnels have full length steam pipes, that on the rear funnel has been moved to a position before rather than abaft the funnel. This is the simplest method of identifying the date of any *Warrior* photograph. The turret ship *Thunderer* can be seen over her bow. Note the blackened figurehead. *NMM*

Warrior in drydock at Portsmouth, during her 1872 refit. The new, longer bowsprit is in place, but housed inboard and not yet rigged. Note the new embrasure in the bow on the upper deck, to provide ahead fire. The foremast is still wooden. Note the small number of shores needed to dock an iron-hulled ship. *IWM*

that she had only one minor collision during her career reflects great credit on her officers (see chapter 7). This unwillingness to answer the helm was a feature of all the long ironclads, and only partially alleviated by the introduction of steam steering gear. Some older Admirals went so far as to suggest that *Defence* was a better fighting ship because of her greater handiness under sail. This reflected a natural conservatism and the reluctance of the Admiralty to provide expensive fuel for ships fitted with masts and sails.

The positive points of *Warrior*'s design were more numerous. Overall she was the most powerful warship in the world throughout her first commission, thereafter *Achilles* usurped the crown. The combination of speed, armour and firepower in all weathers gave her a marked superiority over *Gloire*, which was effectively disarmed in heavy weather as her gun ports were too close to the waterline. This demonstrated the wisdom of Walker's decision not to imitate the French development, the simple course, but to attempt a far better ship. In this Pakington's support was essential. No other nation attempted ironclads of *Warrior*'s dimensions, and it was not until the 1890s that such long ships were again built in Britain.

After 1864 *Warrior* rapidly slipped down the ranks of the ironclads. *Achilles*, *Bellerophon* and *Monarch* all introduced supposedly better ideas in protection and armament. Only in the speed of the original frigate concept did *Warrior* remain unsurpassed. As rearmed

in 1867 with four 8in and twenty-eight 7in muzzle loading rifles, *Warrior* was still a very powerful ship but her armour was no longer invulnerable. In 1867 the Controller used her lack of a complete waterline belt to press for further new construction. While he admitted that she was a fast and well-armed ship he had essentially reduced her to the second rank.

In 1870 the first mastless capital ship, the turret ship *Devastation*, was under construction to carry four 12in guns and 12in of armour. *Warrior* had been left far behind by the ironclad revolution that she had helped to start. By then her early prestige had gone. Her silhouette gave her an appearance of premature obsolescence alongside the more recent ships. With no war service and no great disaster, such as the *Captain* tragedy, to keep her name to the fore she was soon forgotten. Being an expensive ship to keep in commission and unsuitable for overseas duty she spent the larger part of her front rank years either in the reserve or the dockyard. By contrast *Achilles* was, as late as 1879, regarded by many as among the finest ships in the Navy, while *Minotaur* carried the Flag of the Channel Fleet into the 1890s.

THE CHANNEL FLEET

When *Warrior* was completed the Royal Navy had only one serious rival: the French fleet, based at Cherbourg and Brest. Consequently *Warrior*, as a front rank ship, spent her entire active career in the Channel Fleet. She rarely went further afield than Lisbon. During her first commission she was the most powerful warship in the world, the most potent symbol of British prestige and an object of universal interest. As the first ship of a new

generation she was subjected to rigorous trials, both of her own qualities and in comparison with her wooden predecessors. Rear Admiral Smart took her round the coast of Ireland, flying his flag in the two-decker *Revenge*. His conclusions were generally favourable. Then, after *Black Prince*, *Defence* and *Resistance* had joined the fleet Rear Admiral Sir Sidney Dacres, with his flag in the two-decker *Edgar*, took the entire fleet on a cruise round Britain, between July and October 1863.

The twelve-week Round-Britain flag-showing cruise of the Channel, Squadron, 1863

When this cruise began the *Warrior*, a unit of the Squadron, had been a fully worked-up ship for only about a year, and was still the last word in naval architecture. She was the centre of attention wherever the Squadron anchored.

11	July	Depart Spithead
12–14		The Downs
14–19		Yarmouth Roads
23–28		Sunderland
29–		
4	August	Leith
7–11		Cromarty
12–18		Kirkwall
18–21		Sheltering from gales in Inganess Bay (Orkneys, north of Hoy Sound).
26–31		Moville (for Londonderry)
1–8	Sept.	Greenock
9–13		Carrickfergus (for Belfast)
14–25		Liverpool
26–		
1	Oct.	Dublin (Bay)
3		Arrive Plymouth Sound (end of cruise)

12 ports of call (11 ports of visit and one of shelter) in 12 weeks, during which the *Warrior* had literally tens of thousands of visitors aboard.

Warrior at the end of her sea-going career, as Guardship of the Clyde District, 1881–3. During her 1879 refit at Portsmouth she had received steam steering gear, a belated attempt to cure her very poor helm response. *NMM*

Table showing the size of Warrior's crew as commissioned in 1862

Deck Officers	42
Warrant Officers	3
Seamen	445
Royal Marine officers	3
Royal Marine non-commissioned officers	6
Royal Marine artillerymen	118
Engineers	10
Stokers and Trimmers	66
Total	695

Captain: Hon Arthur A L P Cochrane
Commander: George Tryon (the man responsible for, and drowned in, the *Victoria* disaster of 22 June 1893).
Master: George H Blakely
First Lieutenant: Henry B Phillimore
Second Lieutenant: Joseph E M Wilson
Third Lieutenant: George F H Parker
Fourth Lieutenant: Henry L Perceval
Fifth Lieutenant: Noel S F Digby
Captain of Marines: Henry W Mawbey
First Lieutenant of Marines: Herbert Everitt
Second Lieutenant of Marines: Francis H E Owen
Surgeon: Samuel S D Wells
Assistant Surgeon: William J Asslin
Chief Engineer: William Buchan
Second Chief Engineer: William Glasspole
Chaplain and Naval Instructor: Rev Robert N Jackson

The purpose of this cruise was to reassure the mercantile community by showing off the latest hardware. In this respect it was a complete success. However both Admiral Dacres and his Flag Captain were far from impressed with the squadron sailing of the two large ironclads.

Earlier this year the same four ironclads had been deployed to Lisbon, as a diplomatic gesture toward the Northern States, which had become increasingly hostile towards Britain during the course of the American Civil War. In the event of trouble these ships would have been sent across the Atlantic to reinforce Admiral Milne at Bermuda. The move to Lisbon was a subtle form of gunboat diplomacy. *Warrior* was later involved in keeping Northern and Southern warships from coming to blows in Southampton Water and at Gibraltar. However all this had little to do with the real purpose of the ship: to act as a deterrent to France.

The Vernon Torpedo School complex at Portsmouth 1900–1923. *Warrior* is serving as the floating workshop and power plant for the two wooden ships that flank her, the two-decker *Donegal* and the three-decker *Marlborough*, which is showing signs of hogging. The combination of pole masts, a single funnel and the frigate strake have reduced *Warrior* in comparison with her consorts, which are in fact one third shorter. Note the connecting walkways. *WPT*

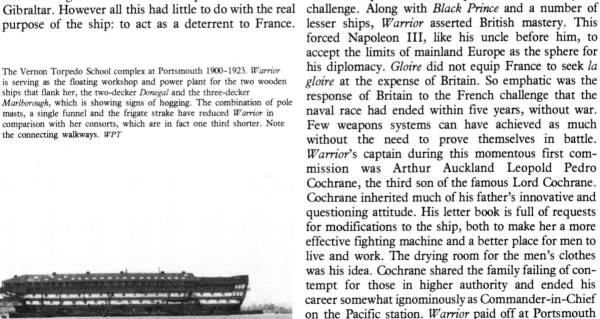

Unlike her sister *Black Prince* had a long period of service as a Training ship. In this capacity she took part in the Spithead Naval Reviews of 1887, 1889 and 1897. In 1896 she was sent to Queenstown in Ireland as a stationary training ship, but ended her days alongside the last wooden battleship, *Howe*, as part of the Impregnable Training establishment at Devonport. She was sold in 1923. She is seen here at the 1887 Review. *CPL*

Warrior's effect on France, where some dreamed of invading Britain, was profound. After 1861 the French challenge petered out while Napoleon rebuilt his Army. None of the French ships completed before 1870 were in any way equal to *Warrior*. Almost all were wooden-hulled and constructed of unseasoned timber. This meant that they did not last long, became obsolete even sooner and rapidly declined in military value. Just as Pakington had intended, *Warrior* was so superior to the French ships that she emphasised the futility of challenge. Along with *Black Prince* and a number of lesser ships, *Warrior* asserted British mastery. This forced Napoleon III, like his uncle before him, to accept the limits of mainland Europe as the sphere for his diplomacy. *Gloire* did not equip France to seek *la gloire* at the expense of Britain. So emphatic was the response of Britain to the French challenge that the naval race had ended within five years, without war. Few weapons systems can have achieved as much without the need to prove themselves in battle. *Warrior*'s captain during this momentous first commission was Arthur Auckland Leopold Pedro Cochrane, the third son of the famous Lord Cochrane. Cochrane inherited much of his father's innovative and questioning attitude. His letter book is full of requests for modifications to the ship, both to make her a more effective fighting machine and a better place for men to live and work. The drying room for the men's clothes was his idea. Cochrane shared the family failing of contempt for those in higher authority and ended his career somewhat ignominiously as Commander-in-Chief on the Pacific station. *Warrior* paid off at Portsmouth on 22 November 1864 and was taken into the Dockyard for a refit.

After her three year refit at Portsmouth, *Warrior* was at first intended to be the Flagship on the Coast of Ireland, a reserve role reflecting the economies hoped for by the Government. However she was eventually recommissioned for the Channel Fleet under Captain Henry Boys. This second commission was rather less interesting. *Warrior* was no longer the most powerful ship afloat, the public soon transferred their esteem to the five-masted *Minotaur* class, which were for twenty years the layman's idea of a warship. The only significant episodes of this period were the collision with *Royal Oak* (see chapter 7) in 1868, and towing out the Bermuda Dock, 1869.

THE BERMUDA DOCK

British interests in the West Indies had a long history. Several crises with the United States, both before and during the Civil War, convinced the Admiralty that a major base was needed to support a fleet on the North America and West Indies Station. Halifax in Canada was available, but during the 1860s the opinion of Admiral Milne, Commander-in-Chief 1860–4 and First Sea Lord, 1866–8, was decisively in favour of Bermuda as the main base for the squadron.

The first requirement for a naval base was, and is, a dry dock for the maintenance and repair of the ships. However the local stone at Bermuda was considered too porous for a normal dry dock. Therefore a floating dock, another product of the new iron age, was ordered in 1866 and laid down by Campbell, Johnstone & Co of Silvertown North Woolwich. This novel structure was launched on 3 September 1868 and named *Bermuda*. Finally completed in May 1869 the dock was 381ft oa, 330ft between caissons; 124ft extreme width, 84ft between sides. Overall depth was 74ft 5in, inside depth

53ft 5ins. Light draught was 11ft 2in, or 50ft when lowered for docking. Total weight was 8200 tons, excluding the caissons, which weighed 400 tons and were sent out separately. The plates were $\frac{5}{16}$ to $\frac{5}{8}$in. The cost of the dock reached almost £¼ million, a large sum and all but two-thirds of the cost of *Warrior*; as a result a great deal of care was taken to ensure that it arrived in one piece.

Commissioned as HMS *Bermuda* for the voyage, in case she had to put into a foreign harbour, the dock had a crew of 82 under a Staff-Commander. Six tugs towed it from Stangate Creek on 23 June, before handing over to the ironclads *Agincourt* and *Northumberland* at the Nore. The paddle frigate *Terrible* was tied up astern, to serve as a rudder.

This curious squadron reached Porto Santo in Madeira on 4 July, where *Warrior* and *Black Prince*, under Captain Boys of *Warrior* took over, *Terrible* remaining astern. The dock reached Bermuda on the 28th and entered the harbour the following day in the charge of three smaller warships. *Warrior* and *Black Prince* returned directly to Plymouth. They had towed the dock in tandem, across the Atlantic at an average of 4.7 knots. With the dock in place iron-hulled warships could be used in the West Indies. The dock lasted until the second decade of the twentieth century, before being sold to a German firm shortly before World War One. After some preliminary dismantling they attempted to tow it away, however the remains were driven ashore in squall at Spanish Point and have remained there ever since.

INTO THE RESERVE

Warrior's second commission with the Channel Fleet ended in August 1871. She then spent four years at Portsmouth under refit: being fitted with a poop deck, a longer bowsprit and a steam capstan. The underlying

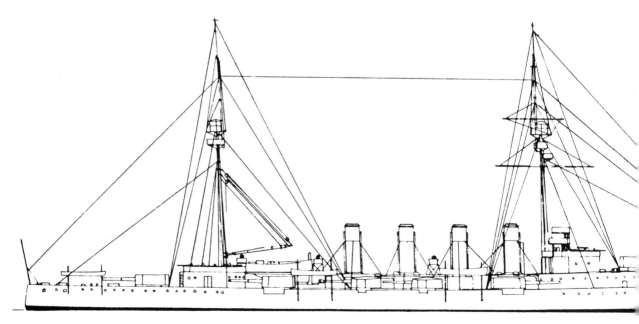

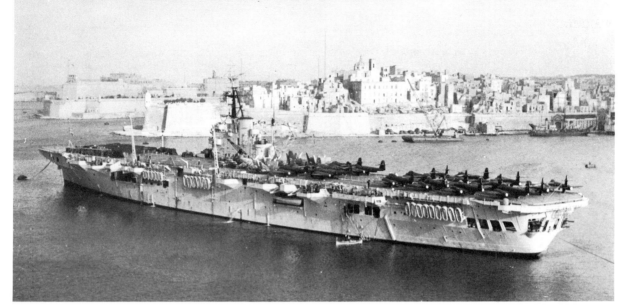

reason for such a long period in dockyard hands was the reduced need for first class ships, and the corresponding political drive for economy. The defeat of France and the collapse of the Second Empire in the Franco-Prussian War of 1870–1 had left Britain without a serious rival at sea. The continued value of *Warrior* was shown by the fact that she was reboilered; almost all of her wooden-hulled contemporaries were allowed to linger for a decade with worn-out boilers before being scrapped. Being built of iron *Warrior* was a better long-term investment, and justified some expenditure.

On the completion of her refit *Warrior* went into the First Reserve. As a modern and powerful ship, but not one required for the Channel Fleet and too large and costly for any other station *Warrior* was used by the Royal Navy Reserve and Coast Guard. The United Kingdom was then divided up into nine coastal districts and a major warship was stationed at a port in each of them. With a nucleus crew of full time ratings and specialist Petty Officers these ships were easily filled up with Royal Naval Reserve seamen in the event of war and could be ready for action in a matter of days. In peace time the ships of the first reserve were manned for an annual cruise, but otherwise their time was taken up with enlisting and drilling the RNR men, overseeing the Coastguard and acting as Guardship for their Home Port. Gunnery Drill at sea occurred every

The armoured cruiser *Warrior* of 1906, a 14,000 ton ship with 69.2in and 47.5in guns, capable of 23 knots. These ships were rendered obsolescent even as they were completed by the introduction of the larger, faster and more powerful battlecruiser. This *Warrior* was a highly regarded design. She foundered as a result of heavy gunfire damage on 1 June 1916, the day after the Battle of Jutland. *CPL*

Warrior of 1946, an 18,000 ton light fleet aircraft carrier. She served in the Canadian Navy until 1948 and in 1958 was sold to the Argentinian Government, serving as Armada Republica Argentina *Independencia* until 1971. Seen here at Malta on passage to Korea in early 1951 with a cargo of RAF Gloster Meteor fighters. *CPL*

The French Ironclad *Solferino* completed in 1862. This two-decker was a far better fighting ship than *Gloire*. With her sister *Magenta* she introduced the ram into the battleline. With 50 guns and good stability these were the only true battleships of the ironclad era. By the time Reed had built the double-banked *Sultan* and the *Audacious* class there were so few guns mounted that their purpose was to reinforce ahead fire, not the broadside.

Dupuy de Lôme was forced to build two-deckers to carry more guns than *Gloire* because a longer wooden hull was not practical. The British response was the *Minotaur*, 50 guns on a single gundeck. This was a cumbersome demonstration of the value of iron hulls. *IWM*

quarter, while the annual cruise of five or six weeks took place under the control of the Admiral Superintendant of the Naval Reserves.

The merits of the systems are apparent. Nine powerful ships were in commission, but with a cheap nucleus crew. In this way they were nearly ready for service, but cost much less in manpower and stores. Their Captains also controlled the RNR and Coastguard, drilled the reserve seamen and advertised the Navy. This period was the high water mark of British sea-

Warrior being towed across Portsmouth harbour, some time after the end of her service as a part of the *Vernon* establishment. *WPT*

Warrior, profile of inboard works.

power, combining unrivalled naval mastery with reduced estimates.

Warrior's eight summer cruises were largely uneventful, although on the first, when she was flagship, *Iron Duke* rammed and sank *Vanguard* off the Coast of Ireland. Admiral Sir John Tarleton was retired the following year. The 1878 cruise began with a mobilisation caused by the Russian War Scare – it was feared that Russia intended to seize Constantinople and the British Government was determined to resist. However the Russians backed down when a squadron under Admiral Hornby anchored off the city. During the crisis *Warrior* was the second flagship, flying the flag of Admiral Boys, who had been her Captain.

Within three years she was anchored at Kronstadt for a ceremonial visit by the Duke of Edinburgh.

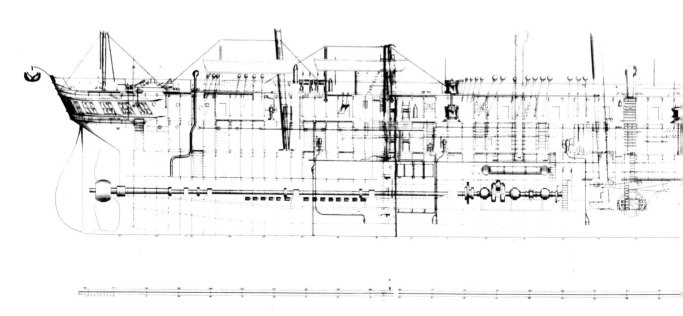

Warrior's eight Summer Cruises with the First Reserve Squadron, 1875-1882.

1875	29 July–9 September	Round Ireland, *Warrior* Flagship, *Vanguard* sunk
1876	13 June–23 July	Gibraltar, etc
1877	2–31 August	Vigo, etc
1878	3 July–3 August	Russian War Scare Mobilisation. Bantry Bay
1879	3 July–7 August	Gibraltar, etc
1880	7 July–13 August	Bantry Bay, Vigo, etc
1881	15 June–29 July	Copenhagen, Kronstadt, Kiel
1882	16 June–24 July	Gibraltar, etc

A total of 296 days seatime, averaging 37pa

Warrior was originally commissioned to relieve *Achilles* at Weymouth, for the Portland division. In 1876, 1878 and 1880 she was temporarily reattached to the Channel Fleet, the only front line formation in which she ever served. In April 1881 *Warrior* exchanged stations and crews with *Hercules*, Guardship of the Clyde District. Her new area comprised the north and west coast of Scotland, along with the Hebrides and Orkneys. Finally on 31 May 1883 she turned over her role and crew to the armoured cruiser *Shannon* at Portsmouth. This ended her sea-going career and her service as a warship.

THE YEARS OF HARBOUR SERVICE

After paying off at Portsmouth and de-storing, *Warrior* passed into the material service. She was now unmanned, receiving only occasional visits from the ship minders. Although amusingly classed as an Armoured Cruiser, *Warrior* was in reality little more than a hulk reduced to her lower masts and unarmed. That she was allowed to deteriorate was hardly surprising in view of her obsolescence. In military terms *Warrior* had become just as much of a liability in comparison to the latest ships as the wooden sailing ships had been when she had been launched. *Black Prince* served out these years as a training ship, and as such was present at the Spithead Reviews of 1887, 1889 and 1897. *Warrior* was too shabby for public display.

Although there was no further thought of using *Warrior* as a regular warship, conversion into a stationary guardship was considered in 1894, but her size and age made this unattractive. *Achilles* was sent out to be the stationary flagship at Malta in 1902, but she was in much better order than *Warrior*. By 1900 *Warrior* was

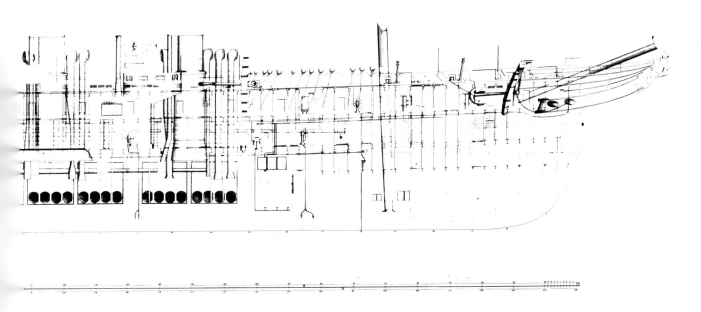

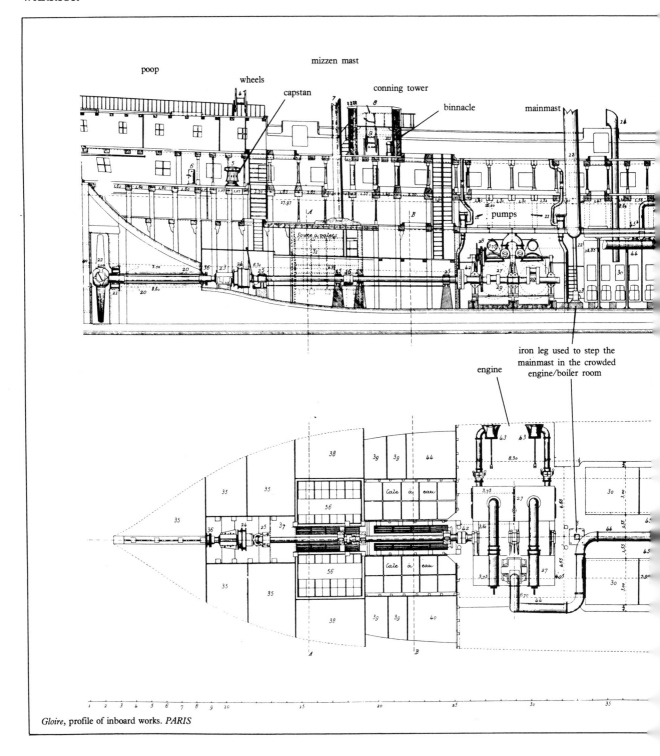

Gloire, profile of inboard works. *PARIS*

quite literally a hulk and no longer even worth mentioning on the Navy List. Yet she did have a value. The size, and especially the internal volume of the early ironclads made them very attractive for harbour service.

Many of the Navy's specialist training establishments used outdated warships as a combination of school and barracks. In 1900 most of these ships were the wooden types that *Warrior* had condemned to premature obsolescence. They were increasingly cramped and like all large wooden ships very unhygienic. From May 1901 to July 1902 *Warrior* was used as a hulk for torpedo stores. Thereafter she served as the depot ship for the Portsmouth Destroyers, flying the pennant of the Flotilla Captain. It was probably at this stage that her engines and boilers were removed, along with

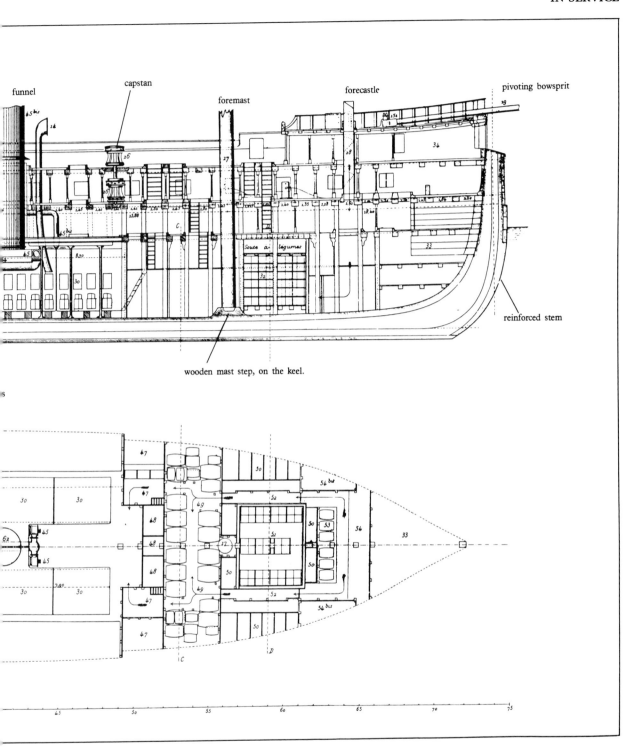

funnel

capstan

foremast

forecastle

pivoting bowsprit

wooden mast step, on the keel.

reinforced stem

several other warship features. Modern watertube boilers were installed to provide the power needed for the Depot ship role.

Between April 1904 and September 1923 *Warrior* served as the floating workshop and powerhouse for HMS *Vernon*, the Naval Torpedo School. The wooden steam battleships *Marlborough*, 120, and *Donegal*, 100, made up the remainder of the unit, the three ships

being a conspicuous feature of Portsmouth harbour. Further indignities were gradually heaped on the old ship. Her name was taken for a new armoured cruiser, sunk at the Battle of Jutland in 1916, and she was re-named *Vernon III*. It was during this period that an opening was cut in the aft armoured bulkhead on the lower deck to allow for the most effective use of the space. This work, carried out with hand drills and cold chisels, must have been an arduous business. The boiler room was used as a machine shop and quickly became unrecognisable. Externally the addition of a white frigate strake, in keeping with the paint scheme of her wooden consorts, with the loss of her topmasts reduced *Warrior* in scale. She now shared much with her long departed wooden precursor *Orlando*, and could easily be mistaken for a wooden ship.

For all the indignity of *Warrior*'s new role it did have the saving grace of preserving the ship. At the end of World War One there had been massive sales of obsolete warships. When *Vernon* went ashore, in 1923, the demand for scrap had fallen off. The Admiralty declared the ship redundant in March 1924, and by a Memorandum of 2 April 1925 offered her for sale. There were no takers.

Reprieved from destruction, *Warrior*, having resumed her original name on 1 October 1923, was taken in hand on 22 October 1927 for conversion into a mooring hulk for oil tankers at Pembroke Dock. She was towed to Pembroke between 13 and 15 March 1929 by the naval tugs *St Clears* and *St Mellons*.

Warrior continued in her new role at the Llanion Oil Fuel Depot for another fifty years. Periodic dry docking at Devonport and Milford Haven ensured that her condition was monitored, not that the hull showed any signs of deterioration. In World War Two she was used as a Depot for motor minesweepers. Another new *Warrior* was given her name by an Admiralty Order of 27 August 1942. The Light Fleet Aircraft Carrier *Warrior* was sold to Argentina in 1958 and renamed *Independence*; she was taken out of service in 1971. *Warrior* herself was renamed Oil Fuel Hulk C77, and never resumed her original name, which has been borne by the Fleet Headquarters at Northwood since the early 1960s. Even now *Warrior* has to carry the suffix (1860). Yet once again the old ship had a value beyond her scrap price and remained afloat.

The most remarkable aspect of *Warrior*'s career has been her survival into an age when her true significance has allowed her to be preserved. As a depot ship and then a hulk she found roles that preserved her from the breakers yard when many more modern ships were sold. This survival was never more than a happy accident.

CHAPTER THREE

Reconstruction

The reconstruction of HMS *Warrior* has been an unprecedented task. No previous ship restoration has involved so much work and so many people, or been compressed into such a brief time scale. It must be emphasised that the project has been a learning process on many levels, producing a much greater understanding of the problems involved as the ship has progressed.

The *Warrior* project has had many unique features: firstly, the ship was not to be restored at the intended point of display – indeed, when the process began there was no clear decision on where the ship would be located. In contrast, the *Great Britain* was placed in the Great Western Dock from the outset, and work on her progresses as fast as funds allow. *Victory*, the first and most famous of the preserved ships, has become a fixture at Portsmouth, her masts being stepped into the floor of the dock; she is also blessed with what amounts to be a permanent labour force.

BEFORE HARTLEPOOL

During the 1960s the idea of preserving *Warrior* was considered by a variety of interested parties. Despite several visits to the ship at Llanion Cove no real progress was made, because the Ministry of Defence still required a berthing facility. However continued service did mean that her condition was continually monitored, by docking.

In 1967 the first solid proposal for the future of the ship came from the Greater London Council. They were seeking a focal point for a proposed yacht marina at the new town of Thamesmead, just down river from Woolwich. They stressed *Warrior*'s London connections. Nothing concrete resulted, and the Ministry still would not consider parting with pontoon C33. In early 1968 HRH the Duke of Edinburgh assembled a distinguished group of individuals at Buckingham Palace, including the then Director of the National Maritime Museum, Frank Carr, and John Smith, then Member of Parliament for Westminster. This group discussed the formation of a National Maritime Trust to preserve historic ships; *Warrior* was, understand-

ably, a specific example. In August the Duke of Edinburgh visited the ship. Finally, in 1969, the Maritime Trust was formed.

The Maritime Trust made considerable progress in its first years with the preservation of smaller vessels, but the most significant event for *Warrior* was the dramatic rescue of her mercantile counterpart, the *Great Britain*, from the Falkland Islands. This indicated a much wider public interest in old ships than had been anticipated, and a willingness to take on seemingly impossible tasks.

One man suitably impressed was John Smith who, as Chairman of the Manifold Trust, was the major supporter of the Maritime Trust. The Manifold Trust is a grant-making charitable body set up by John Smith in 1962. It is mainly concerned with environmental causes, particularly with the preservation of buildings and ships – indeed Manifold has been by far the largest private source of money for the preservation of ships, especially warships.

London-based attempts to preserve *Warrior* were remodelled around the Borough of Newham's scheme to put the ship in the Royal Victoria Docks. As she had been built within the borough this project did have a certain attraction, but the funds needed to renovate the ship were never made available. All this time the Maritime Trust kept up their interest in *Warrior*.

Finally in March 1976 it was announced that the Llanion Oil Fuel Depot was scheduled for closure with effect from 1 April 1978; *Warrior* would thus be released from her long years of demeaning servitude. In order to secure the ship for the Maritime Trust it would be necessary to ensure a backer with the substantial funds, estimated even then at £3 million, needed to reconstruct *Warrior*. On 12 June 1979 it was announced in the House of Commons that *Warrior* had been given to the Maritime Trust. Their successful bid had been based on the commitment of the Manifold Trust in 1977 to put up the bulk of the money. This was vital because the Maritime Trust understood the difficulty of raising sufficient funds to do justice to this project without a major backer. They had learnt this

The old Custom House at Hartlepool, the administrative centre of the project. The ship lay only 100yds away. *AUTHOR*

with their experience of RRS *Discovery*. *Warrior* was officially handed over on 20 August, with the contractual proviso that the Maritime Trust should use their best efforts to preserve and restore the ship.

OWNERSHIP

During reconstruction, the ship underwent three titular changes of ownership. The Maritime Trust thought it would be more efficient, and effective from a fund raising point of view, if the vessel was reconstructed under a single ship trust, their wholly owned subsiduary Ships Preservation Trust, in line with the *Great Britain* Project and HMS *Belfast*. SPT would be supported by Manifold and every effort would be made by the Trust to find other backers through a public appeal.

However, the contractor chosen to carry out the work at Hartlepool proved unsatisfactory, and, sooner than move the ship once again, Ships Preservation Trust (SPT), with Maldwin Drummond as Chairman, took over direct responsibility. Tom Dulake, who already had considerable experience in restoration, albeit it in a different field, agreed to watch over spending of the Manifold Trust's money. Manifold's financial involvement became steadily greater, and when by 1982 no other major donor had appeared, it was felt

46

Warrior as she arrived at Hartlepool, seen here in early 1980. *DAVE MORRELL*

that control of the project should pass to Manifold, Tom Dulake becoming Managing Director of SPT with the responsibility of guiding the restoration.

The final alteration of ownership came in 1985 when the SPT was renamed the Warrior Preservation Trust; a name more closely linked with the purpose of the Trust. The controlling interest of Manifold, and the take-over of the SPT reflected the lack of significant public or government support, other than that offered by the Manpower Services Commission and those groups and individuals mentioned in Appendix II. This has meant that Manifold has provided 70% of the total cost. In the wake of this unforeseen development, financial constraints have played a major part in limiting the progress of work. The need to stay small created problems for all concerned but the success in overcoming these difficulties can be seen by all who visit the ship.

HARTLEPOOL

Nine days after being handed over to the Maritime Trust *Warrior* was towed out of Milford Haven by the mercantile tug *Hendon*. After an uneventful tow the two ships reached Hartlepool late on 2 September. *Warrior* was temporarily berthed in the Union Dock on the following day. She was finally moved to the Old Coal Dock on the 7th, in readiness for the reconstruction.

The reason why the ship was taken to Hartlepool requires some explanation.

When the Maritime Trust secured the ownership of *Warrior*, it was realised that special arrangements would have to be made and a non-tidal, alongside berth found. The Director of the Maritime Trust looked everywhere and, in particular, along the northeast coast where there were both the right facilities and the right shipbuilding skills. Hartlepool was chosen.

It was also seen as important to obtain grants from the EEC, the government and the British Steel Corporation which was running down. This could only be secured if there was an ongoing commitment beyond *Warrior*. To achieve this, a link was forged between SPT and a small contractor specialising in building replica locomotives. Their small work force would be reinforced by the large pool of unemployed skilled labour.

Before the ship could be placed alongside the Old Coal Dock for work to commence the berth had to be dredged clear, at a cost to the project of some £35,000. The annual mooring fee started at £18,000 and had risen to £25,000 in 1985. After the ship had been secured alongside, work actually commenced on 22 October when Foreman Stan Morrell with two shipwrights and five labourers went aboard. Shortly afterwards the Old Custom House some two hundred yards away was acquired as a base for the project. Both the ship and the building required a considerable amount of basic work before any real progress could be made. *Warrior* had to be made safe, accessible and watertight – not an easy job on a ship with four decks each of nearly 16,000 sq ft. Nothing was available: tools, gangways, lights all had to be found. Similarly the Custom House had to be fitted to serve as an office, and all the necessary equipment installed. The original staff of the Drawing Office, Bill Stevenson and Keith Johnson, had to obtain drawing boards and materials before they could start work. Similarly Jean Bartram, the Personal Assistant, had to create an administrative structure to control the project and fit out the offices.

The first two years' work on *Warrior* was dominated by the need to make her a safe place to work. Safety rails, gangways, ladders, lights and fire extinguishers all had to be installed before the reconstruction could start. During this period the workforce expanded slowly. Following the dismissal of the contractor in early 1980 several of the original staff who had left earlier were invited to return when Ships Preservation Trust took over.

As the end of the reconstruction approached the choice of Hartlepool was revealed as being a mixed blessing. The Coal Dock had none of the facilities normally associated with work on large ships, namely covered working spaces and heavy dockside cranes. The cost of the berth, even with a covenant from the port authority, was far too high and could never have been matched by the tourist revenue. However, the local workforce have carried out a complex task with great skill and application. They have made *Warrior* a monument to the industrial skills of the area. Furthermore considerable outside assistance has been available, to help with large scale and series production of replica parts.

DECISIONS

At an early stage in the reconstruction the influence of the Manifold Trust was used to lay down the guidelines of the project. First the ship should be restored, as nearly as possible, to her condition when she first entered service in 1862. Secondly the ship should be restored to last for another 20 years without the need for any further major work. Finally nothing was to be done that would prevent future generations from reconsidering the issue afresh. Lost items were to be replaced, but nothing should be added to the structure which would damage the surviving fabric.

These aims dominated the subsequent efforts of the workforce, until in mid-1984 a time scale was imposed: *Warrior* was to be ready to move down to her new home at Portsmouth in September 1986.

The decision to restore her to her 1862 appearance was a simple one to take. During her first commission *Warrior* had been the world's most powerful warship. Once *Achilles* was commissioned in 1865, *Warrior*'s pre eminence had been lost forever. Her later career had contained nothing of note that would justify rebuilding her in a modified condition, unlike *Victory*. From this decision all the research efforts could be concentrated on the specific period of that first commission. Although *Warrior* was not greatly modified while in service there were significant changes to the armament, the poop deck and the addition of steam steering gear.

The second decision affected the quality of materials to be used, and the nature of the work. Twenty years is the average life of a modern warship. The significance of this decision is apparent in the areas most exposed to damage, the upperworks and upper deck, where the finest timbers have been used. During the reconstruction it also involved the removal of all decayed or im-

The stern of *Warrior* soon after arrival at Hartlepool. She still carries the poop deck. The different condition of the wooden and iron areas can be seen, some of the mizzen cabin plates are still in place. *DAVE MORRELL*

The upper deck showing the poop, the recently stripped deck and the damaged bulwarks. *DAVE MORRELL*

perfect timber and the careful selection of new materials that could co-exist with the old.

The initial deadline for the ship to be moved to Portsmouth proved to be slightly optimistic and in early 1986 it was decided to delay this by six months. This would be entirely beneficial to the progress of the reconstruction, and provide some relief from the growing pressure to hurry work on the ship.

MANAGEMENT AND DECISION MAKING

When Manifold placed *Warrior* with SPT, solely to control the project, there was no management structure. There was no expertise available within the organisation to run a small shipyard, although the experience gained from the conservation of historic buildings for the Landmark Trust did prove valuable. Before the Manifold takeover a workforce had been built up under the direction of the first Project Manager, the late Ray Hockey. This team was retained by SPT after the contractor had been dismissed; thereafter both sides had to adjust to the new situation. The experience of the workforce had been in large shipyards, lately as a part of the British Shipbuilders group. As a result they were familiar with a management that could provide higher direction based on a knowledge of the industry. Not only was this not possible, but the *Warrior* involved very different constraints on working practices to those in effect during the construction of a new ship. Before ill health forced him to retire, Ray

Hockey was able to get the project onto the right lines, taking over the vital middle management role. Both management and workforce had something to learn.

Before this process could be carried through, there was some confusion. The central task of clearing the concrete off the upper deck proved to be a pivotal act. Once that work began, many other decisions had to be taken and the project took shape, pushed along by Manifold.

Thereafter the roles and responsibilities of the two diverse bodies became more clearly defined; the middle ground of executive decision making was occupied by both sides, according to their experience. As the project moved into the reconstruction stage the positions of London and Hartlepool were much better understood. The SPT, through regular Board meetings and the weekly visits of Tom Dulake, held the final power of decision, and were responsible for funding and the overall momentum of the work. At Hartlepool the second Project Manager, Bill Stevenson, and the Ship Manager, Stan Morrell, were responsible for the daily running of the project: the labour force and co-ordinating supply with the seasonal nature of the work and the available labour. This was a considerable expansion of responsibility and initiative. The success of the reconstruction is in no small part due to the development of management skills at Hartlepool, able to transform policy into wood and metal.

RESEARCH

Before the dirty hulk that arrived at Hartlepool in 1979 could begin to be transformed into something approaching her former glory it was necessary to establish *exactly* what that 'glory' had been. This required a great deal of research. *Warrior* and her contemporaries had never been studied in the type of detail that would be required to reproduce the long-dismantled masts, engines and guns, let alone the innumerable small details that made her a working warship. This information would have to be recovered from a variety of surviving sources and then transformed into plans which the craftsmen could use to work from. The process of research has close affinities with detective work.

With *Warrior* the research can be divided into two mutually supporting areas. The ship herself was a vital source of information. Long-empty bolt holes, parts of bulkhead fittings, the gunports and even gaping holes all helped to indicate how the ship had been fitted originally. Furthermore the results of all research carried out off the ship could always be checked against the existing structures to ensure its accuracy. Research work was carried out in London, using the extensive public collections of the National Maritime Museum, the Science Museum and the Public Record Office, backed up by work around the country in private sources, notably the memorabilia of *Warrior*'s first Captain.

Among the Government and Admiralty Papers, those which were of the greatest value were the detailed drawings of *Warrior* showing the fittings, the layout of the decks, the dimensions of the missing items and the function of long-empty spaces. The Sheerness Dockyard Book contained many drawings of detail fittings of the period, several directly attributed to *Warrior*. These were especially useful for upper deck fittings such as the skylights and gratings, bulwarks and hammock nettings. To assist this process all known photographs of *Warrior* were assembled. Many were enlarged to show individual points of detail, often with astonishing clarity. The basic problem was that *Warrior*'s fittings were typical of the period, and were therefore never recorded in any depth. This forced the team to consider evidence from other sources in an effort to build up a complete picture of the ship. In some areas evidence was easily obtained. In others, notably the guns, an enormous effort and prototype replication over a period of a year was necessary before the final design of the gun carriages could be decided.

As a result of the early start to work aboard *Warrior* there had been little time available for research, although Manifold had argued that this should be done before any work was begun. Once the project was under the direct control of SPT a more rational approach developed.

The problems created before the SPT took over ensured that research could never get ahead of the work in hand. This created pressure, which was only partially alleviated by the breathing space provided during the lengthy process of stripping the deck. Research was still forced to adopt 'hand to mouth' tactics. If a year had been available for research before the ship was moved

then much of the evidence could have been assembled, correlated and assessed in time to start work with a clear idea of what was required. Once the work had started it would have been necessary to dismiss the workforce if the research effort were to catch up. This SPT was unwilling to do. Other restoration projects without the time limits of *Warrior* have a considerable advantage in this respect.

When the Drawing Office staff were assembled they had no material to work with, and had to concentrate on what the ship could tell them. Even when the first research data reached Hartlepool it was not always very helpful. It proved necessary to create a *Warrior* archive which contained *all* the evidence, however unimportant it might at first seem. In this way the Research and Drawing Office staffs have been able to carry on effectively, without the constant uncertainty about the completeness of their sources.

Research has been a team effort, involving a large number of people both inside and outside the Project. Members of the Drawing Office staff visited the major collections in the South of England, as well as other

The upper deck from the bow. Anything less like the final product is hard to imagine. *DAVE MORRELL*

The stern viewed from the recently erected mizzen mast. Note the skylight gratings, anchors and the propeller lifting well cover. The bulwarks are still in need of repair. *WPT*

restored ships, in an effort to assess just what was available. This work has been backed up by professional research and several interested individuals. Captain John Wells, the researcher and historical advisor, as well as author of a history of the ship, provided valuable material, and most significantly located the Cochrane Memorabilia in Northern Ireland. This major source was generously purchased by the Royal Naval Museum, Portsmouth, only a stone's throw from the final resting place of *Warrior*. Other outside help of great value came from the late John Moore, who made the first collection of archival material related to the ship, and Richard Tomlin who had written a paper on the engineering aspects of the ship. Richard continued to assist the project, especially once the replication of the engines had begun.

At Hartlepool the Design Office team at first led by Bill Stevenson and, during the last 18 months, Keith Johnson, were responsible for the translation of research material into production drawings. Their

technical discussions were assisted by Master Mariner Captain Walter Brownlee, seconded from Cleveland Local Education Authority, in 1981, and from September 1984 a full-time member of the staff as Ship's Historian and Research Co-ordinator. He assessed the research material as a trained Historian, assisted by a seaman's eye and the ship herself, still the basic text of the research effort. During the project Walter established a reputation among the workforce for showing an interest in any discovery aboard the ship, however minor it might seem. This combination of nautical experience and historical interpretation helped him to prepare working papers on the items required to complete the ship. These then formed the basis for discussion, before the Design Team translated ideas onto paper and the workforce recreated the next piece in the task.

The team at Hartlepool were initially confused by the weight of evidence available, and the sheer number

51

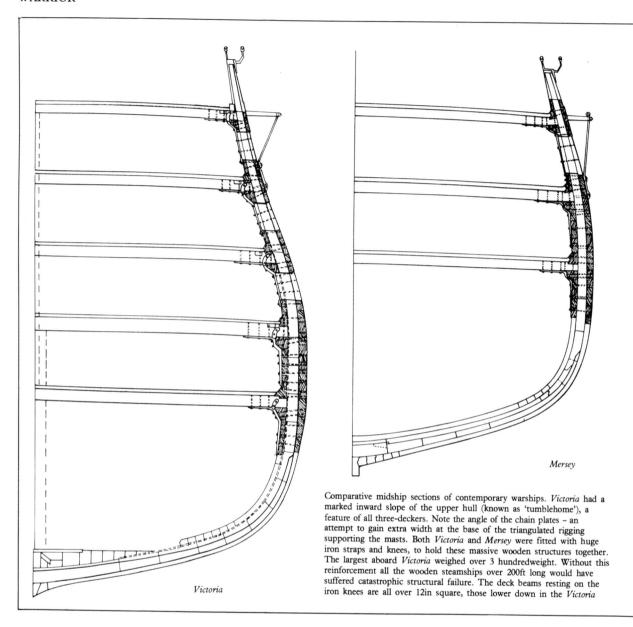

Comparative midship sections of contemporary warships. *Victoria* had a marked inward slope of the upper hull (known as 'tumblehome'), a feature of all three-deckers. Note the angle of the chain plates – an attempt to gain extra width at the base of the triangulated rigging supporting the masts. Both *Victoria* and *Mersey* were fitted with huge iron straps and knees, to hold these massive wooden structures together. The largest aboard *Victoria* weighed over 3 hundredweight. Without this reinforcement all the wooden steamships over 200ft long would have suffered catastrophic structural failure. The deck beams resting on the iron knees are all over 12in square, those lower down in the *Victoria*

Mersey

Victoria

of 'expert' opinions. Their difficulty was solved by Roderick Stewart, the man behind the long term restoration of the wooden sailing frigate *Unicorn* at Dundee. Having visited the ship, members of the team were greatly impressed by the thorough and uncompromising attitude that he displayed. His advice was to consult all the available sources, never to accept defeat and to trust their own judgement. This paid dividends with such spectacular items as the 68 and 110pdr guns. It was widely reported that no examples of either type had survived, yet by a combination of persistance and good fortune perfect guns were located and used to construct replicas.

The obvious solution to the problem of selective and irregular research data was to hire a full-time professional researcher. From early 1983 Antonia MacArthur, based in London, was appointed to locate *all* material relevant to *Warrior* and sent it to Hartlepool. Further she was often directed to specific areas to meet the demands of work in hand on the ship. It took her a considerable time to convince all concerned that research data was not a commercial product freely available to be bought off the shelf ready sorted, nor could it be treated as a basic functional process to be turned on and off at will. The best research is a form of detection involving a building-up of cross references, the pursuit of any hints and the development of a 'feel' for the subject. Where no previous work of a sufficient depth has been carried out it was necessary to follow any number of leads. Often synthesis only arises after a great deal of interlocking work. The material was not organised in a way that makes access easy. Often related

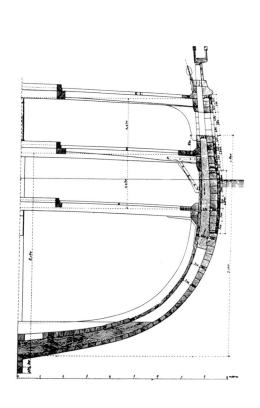

Gloire

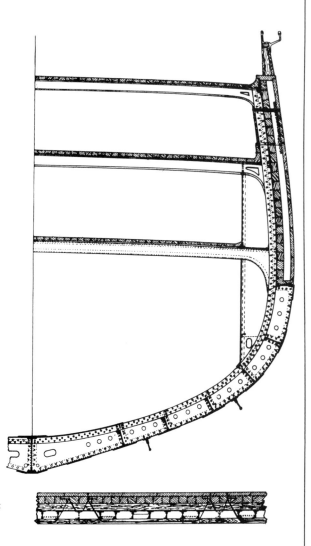

being 16 × 17in. The extra space provided by *Warrior*'s iron beams and integral bracketing played a significant part in creating a more spacious deck head.

Gloire demonstrates several affinities with the British wooden ships, but her iron knees are similar to the brackets of *Warrior*. Note the step in the armour just above the waterline and the dead eyes carried inside the bulwarks. The latter feature emphasises the low priority given to the rig aboard French ships. Within five years the British had followed this example.

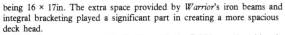

Warrior

collections are divided up in a quite abitrary way, causing major problems. As an example, the plans of *Warrior* and all other British warships of her era are held at the National Maritime Museum. The paperwork that accompanied and explained these plans was held at the Public Record Office.

Once the material had been acquired it had to be assessed in the light of the evidence aboard the ship. This final stage had to be carried out at Hartlepool, and was undertaken by Walter Brownlee long before he joined the staff of the SPT in September 1984.

It is important to note that *Warrior* was not restored exactly as she was built. The cost factor alone made this an unreal ambition. The replica items had to be re-drawn for modern construction and modern materials. This did not mean that appearance or durability could

be sacrificed, as the decision to restore for twenty years without major work showed.

FUND RAISING

With a project involving as much money as *Warrior*, some £6.5m to date, every possible source of assistance has been considered. Appendix II provides full details of the funds provided for the project. The fund-raising process has involved a full-time fund raiser, Tony Bridgewater, based at the WPT's London Head-quarters. He approached many companies and such bodies as the Tourist Board and the National Memorial Heritage Fund for grants and obtained sponsorship in the form of goods, services or information from public, commercial or private sources.

The results have been disappointing and few donors

have been found. This is in part due to the wish of those involved with the Warrior Project that the ship should not be over-exposed to publicity too soon. They have also rather shied away from the normal fund-raising practice of assembling a body of eminent persons to head a general appeal. Apart from a few publicity coups, such as the display of the figurehead at the 1983 Boat Show, little has been done to catch the eye of the media in the way that *Great Britain* and *Mary Rose* were advertised. The result will be a more dramatic entrance. The huge distance over which *Great Britain* was recovered, and the televised suspense of the *Mary Rose* salvage could not overcome widespread public disappointment at the incomplete state of both ships. *Warrior* will reach Portsmouth effectively complete, and from the first day she will be a major draw for tourists in the city, a publicity triumph and a visual delight.

WORKFORCE

The greatest single contribution made by Hartlepool to the success of the *Warrior* project came in the shape of the labour force. The human resources of the area, a pool of unemployed men and women with the skills required by the job, and any number of people willing to work for a year on the MSC Community Programme were vital. These people and their enthusiasm for the ship have made *Warrior* what she is today. Just as she was once a testament to the quality of London labour she is now a tribute to the skills of Hartlepool. Those intimately involved with the project all refer to this human dimension.

Aboard Ships' Foreman and later Ship Manager Stan Morrell had selected and directed the labour force. From the very beginning of the work, back in October 1979 when there were only seven men, he had the responsibility for creating the workforce. The team was built up as the work progressed; new jobs called for extra men with new skills. The very nature of the work called for a return to long-abandoned working methods, and for shipwrights experienced with wood. Only older craftsmen, primarily in the over fifty age group who could be expected to have experience with an adze, helped to lay and caulk a large wooden deck and used a caulking mallet. The recent decline in local shipyard work ensured that many of these men were, before *Warrior*, almost resigned to the prospect of never working again. From the upper deck of the ship they could see the sites of the four local yards, where most of them served their apprenticeship, and reflect on the curious turn of events that brough them back to work. The same policy of selecting men with experience and application was followed in all the craftsman positions. The results show for themselves

Warrior photographed from overhead in May 1982. Note that the port side sponson is still in place. The upper deck is largely cleared down to the plating, allowing the camera to point up the diagonal tie plates at the forward end, crossing between the first two hatch covers. *WPT*

the value of this recruitment policy – there is no substitute for experience.

The first two years of the project involved clearing the ship of the filth and accretions of eighty years service as a hulk. That this took so long might appear surprising until the size of *Warrior* and the large numbers of compartments is taken into account. Furthermore it was not possible to use more labour until much of this initial cleaning had been completed. As *Warrior* was gradually converted into a place of work the restoration proper could begin. It was then possible to take on more specialist craftsmen. When the concrete upper deck was lifted and the iron structure below made watertight it was possible to work on the main deck during wet weather without getting soaked. This was an important step, allowing more men to be taken on in the knowledge that they could be kept busy in all conditions. The recruitment rapidly gathered pace from late 1982, both full time staff and those employed under the MSC.

It is clear from the table that the MSC played a significant role in carrying out the reconstruction in seven years. By late 1985 over two-thirds of the labour force were employed through the Community Programme. This meant 52 weeks work for those who have had at least one year unemployed. Some have been hired for specific skills required by the project. Others, often also skilled, have been happy to work as labourers, painters or security guards. Several have later been transferred to the full-time staff at the end of their 52 weeks; others have had their period extended. More recently a separate scheme has been set up specifically to deal with the replication of the engines.

The MSC schemes involved some of the staff in additional bookwork, and direct liaison with the MSC, through the Hartlepool Job Centre. However, by allowing so many local people to work with *Warrior* the Community Programmes have helped to establish the link between the ship and the town. Additionally the funding provided by the MSC has allowed extra labour to be taken on when the project reached the stage where it was most needed. The *Warrior* scheme was con-

Table showing Labour Force working on Warrior Project, late 1985

Description	WPT Ltd	CP Scheme 1 (Ship)	CP Scheme 2 (Engineering)	Total	% of Total
Management	3			3	
Supervision		7		7	5
Technical/Research	5*	3*	1*	9	6
Accounts/Wages	2	1		3	
Administration		2		2	
Secretarial	1	2		3	
Stock Control		1		1	
Shipwrights	6	10		16	11
Platers	3		2	5	3½
Joiners	3	2		5	3½
Welders	3		4	7	5
Burners/Caulkers	3	1	2	6	4
Drillers	1	2		3	
Painters	1			1	
Labourers	13	24	4	41	29
Ship's Guide	1			1	
Apprentices	4			4	
Riggers		3		3	
Rigger's Mate		4		4	
Cleaners	1	4		5	
Security Guards		10		10	6
Fitters			2	2	
Electrician	1			1	
Wood Machinist	1			1	
Total	52	76	15	143	
% of Total	36	53	11		

* includes Engineering Technical Staff

Another overhead view, this time from September 1985. The upper deck is now planked over, the masts are up, the sponson is long gone and the conning tower has been installed. The dockside buildings have also grown with the progress of the work and the increase in the labour force.
WPT

sidered to be a showpiece by the MSC. The whole-hearted co-operation of the local branch created a healthy and cordial relationship. The resultant degree of flexibility smoothed out some of the problems created by the nature of the work and the scheme. In all some 21% of the work on *Warrior* while she was at Hartlepool was attributable to the MSC, along with considerable extra funding. The completion of the project in seven years reflects the added weight provided by the scheme. It played a vital role in accelerating the work once the management had been settled and the initial clearing operation completed.

As Project Manager Bill Stevenson stressed, the *Warrior* has a great significance for the Hartlepool area as a source of employment. In the long term it will provide an impetus for development, as well as being an advertisement for local skills.

THE NATURE OF THE WORK

The reconstruction of *Warrior* was no ordinary task; the work involved, and the skills of the men who carried them out, belonged to the 1860s rather than the 1980s. In the shipwright crafts, such as relaying the deck, building new bulwarks and caulking, the working practices required had long been abandoned in mainstream commercial shipbuilding. Wooden decks were last fitted in the early 1960s. Since then timber has become too expensive for such applications. However the craftsmen selected for the work were able to call on their experience to tackle these tasks. The main require-

ments were for a good eye, manual dexterity and physical strength, all directed by a practised mind. While the bulk of the work was carried out by older craftsmen, a few young apprentices were able to learn some of these virtually lost skills, helping to preserve them for another generation.

The shipwrights who worked aboard *Warrior* all admitted to a renewed pleasure in their work, and a resurgence of the pride a craftsman feels in a job well done. *Warrior* provided a stimulating variety of jobs, and the example left behind by the long-forgotten workers from the Thames Ironworks inspired the admiration of the men of the North East.

Other skilled tasks were also affected by the unusual demands of the job. The carpenters had to return to the working practices of the era, when labour was cheaper than materials. The welders and platers quickly discovered that uniting wrought iron with steel by the arc welding method is an awkward business calling for great care and some practice. Similarly the riggers had to adjust to the demands of working on a ship; all their experience had been gained ashore and much had to be reconsidered.

Much of the work aboard *Warrior* was physically demanding. With no dockside lifting gear available most items, except the masts and figurehead, had to be carried aboard the ship up the gangways. The debris of *Warrior*'s long career came off the ship in the same way. Some items, such as the railway chairs used as ballast, and the 30ft long 8in × 3in deck planks were awkward as well as heavy. All the craftsmen mentioned this as one of the less pleasant aspects of the job, although they admitted that they felt fitter and stronger as a result. Elsewhere the construction of the gun carriages, working the greenheart timber for the bulwarks and shaping the 14in timbers for the waterbar all involved heavy physical work, combined with the need for accuracy.

Inside the ship, especially below the main deck, the work of cleaning and painting every inch of the exposed ironwork created a particularly unpleasant environment. Using needle guns to descale the plating involves noise and debris on the grand scale. Consequently the labourers had to be equipped with ear protectors, helmets and faceguards. Furthermore some compartments were so small that they were difficult to get into, let alone work in. With such a large ship and so many separate compartments it was no surprise that up to 38 men were involved in this unenviable task for over three years. Almost all were employed under the MSC Community Programme.

Despite, or perhaps because of, these physical demands a tremendous team spirit developed at Hartlepool. The men came to love the ship and worked with great enthusiasm. Everyone in the team helped to raise the tempo of the project from mid-1984, and maintained an impressive rate of progress as the *Warrior*'s time at Hartlepool came to an end. Those closely involved with the management of the work attribute the increase in tempo to several other factors. Firstly, the completion of the clearing stage, which allowed more men to be taken on and real 'progress' to be made. Secondly, the installation of guns and cooperage and mess equipment on the main deck, which created the right atmosphere. Thirdly, the erection of the masts, which made the most dramatic change, while at the management level the final structure was at last adopted, making for a more smooth development toward the ultimate object of completion. Observers off the ship felt that the motivation of the craftsmen reflected the decision to move the ship in 1987, they wanted to finish the job before the ship went South. Many of them expressed doubts about the ability of anyone else to complete the work. This was not a matter of unthinking arrogance, but an honest reflection of the craftsmans' pride in his work, both individually, and as part of a team.

Part of that pride reflected the ever-changing mental demands of the work aboard *Warrior*. Every task required a change of method and involved some experimentation. This constant change was a stimulus to the labour force, supplementing their technical skills. The

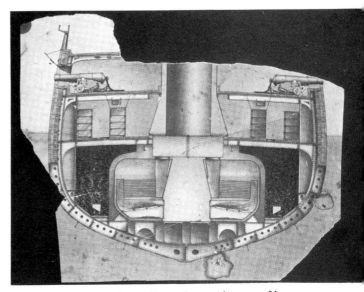

This section through *Warrior* was discovered among the papers of her first Captain. It shows the operation of the boilers, the seamen's bag racks, and the main deck 68ps. *WPT*

The upper deck skylight gratings, showing one half in place. The wooden grating allowed the men to use all of the deck, without the danger of falling into the Captain's cabins below. *WPT*

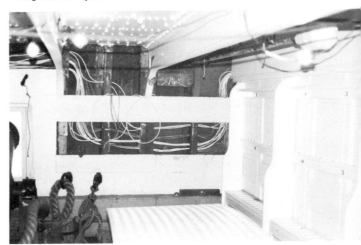

Aft on the starboard side of the citadel, September 1985. This view shows how the electrical installations were wired in behind the deck cladding. Also in view are the racks for the seamen's Enfield rifles. *AUTHOR*

shipwrights admitted that the only dull jobs were those that involved repetitive series production of such items as the mess furniture and the production models of the gun carriages.

One factor often forgotten by those who never visited Hartlepool in the winter was the influence of the weather. Winter in the North East can be long and very cold. All work on the upper deck depended on mild weather, and, as this could not be guaranteed, other arrangements had to be made to keep the workforce busy. Once the ship was watertight it was possible to shift the labour force onto the main deck, or into the steadily growing number of sheds on the dockside. In one shed the woodworking machinery was installed, while another housed the burning and welding operations. However this need to prepare alternative work to take account of the weather imposed an additional administrative load on the management team at Hartlepool, hampered continuity of work and made it necessary to keep additional materials in stock. The advantages of a modern covered shipyard are obvious.

Similar delays resulted from the regular opening of the ship to the public over the weekends of the tourist season, April to September. In the early days, while the ship was being cleared, it took the small workforce a full half-day on Fridays to make the ship safe for visitors. The safety rails, gangways and barriers then had to be dismantled on Monday, ready for work to begin again. This was done to allow the public to see the work underway. Many people returned time after time to see the progress being made.

OUTSIDE HELP

Despite its large scale the *Warrior* project was not self contained. A great deal of valuable support came from the local area, particularly businesses and Technical Colleges, that were prepared to manufacture items to designs provided by the project. A sample would include: Billingham Industrial Training Centre, where the two Rodger's pattern stern anchors were made up in sheet steel; Hartlepool College of Further Education, which made the massive tiller yoke that arcs around the propellor well, along with many smaller items, often in large numbers; The Cleveland Combined Council of Churches Unemployment Programme, a charitable body, located in the right hand annexe of the Old Custom House which provided jobs for local unemployed youth and turned out much valuable work for *Warrior*. This has been in the area of series production of small scale artefacts, such as ram rods, buckets, powder cases, pistol racks shot and shell, rifle slings and many other such items. Without these pieces the reconstruction would appear incomplete. Yet by taking on the work the CCCUP has allowed the SPT staff to concentrate on the major items, while it filled in the detail. While the funds of the CCUP have come from the MSC, the sponsoring Churches and the Charles Heyward Trust for the Unemployed, materials

The main deck, February 1982. At this stage only preliminary clearing
had been undertaken, while the upper deck was made watertight.
Everything on this deck would have to be repaired, replaced or painted.
DAVE MORRELL

The main deck, November 1982: the first items of mess furniture, the
table, bucket, hammock and mess rack have been tried in place. The deck
is being lifted in the most damaged areas. On the left one of the remote
spindles for the lower deck Downton pumps can be seen. *DAVE MORRELL*

Cleaning out the double bottoms below the wing tanks. In the smaller compartments the rail chairs have been installed as ballast. *WPT*

One of the lower deck watertight doors, before cleaning. Note how the spindle is turned from the main deck. *WPT*

for all work connected with the ship were provided by the SPT. In this way the experience has been mutually beneficial: *Warrior* gained many necessary artefacts, while the CCCUP was able to offer the unemployed of the area meaningful work with suitable materials.

This pattern has been repeated all over the Hartlepool area; work on *Warrior* offered trainees valuable experience and the added interest of real work with a visible end product. Too many apprentice schemes end up as technical exercises with no end result, and therefore of little relevance to those taking part. *Warrior* provided a focus for such work, to the benefit of all concerned.

During the reconstruction two registered charitable groups were formed to promote and support the ship. The Hartlepool-based 'Friends of the *Warrior*' was established shortly after the ship reached the town. Their contribution was primarily in the area of local publicity, providing guides for tourist parties and manning the souvenir shop. The voluntary labour of this group saved the project team much time and helped to foster links with the town. The Portsmouth-based '*Warrior* Association' was formed in July 1983, to work in conjunction with the Hartlepool group, and prepare for the arrival of the ship at Portsmouth. It proved particularly successful at fund raising and promoting the ship in the South of England.

SUPPLIERS

The regular and reliable supply of materials is vital to the success of any large scale work. This depends on good stock control, and the co-operation of the suppliers. With the *Warrior* project many suppliers were, at first, reluctant. They found it difficult to take the idea of rebuilding an old ship seriously; it was not a real job, merely a folly that was bound to fail. Being asked to supply at cost was a further disincentive. These attitudes made some unwilling to tender, while others were alarmed by the prospect of working for a charity. Further problems arose simply because many of the materials required for the work aboard *Warrior* were outside the normal line of commercial business, high grade timber for the upper deck being an excellent example. Speeding up the project in mid-1984 helped to overcome some of these difficulties, but as the work at Hartlepool neared completion the work was always threatened by late delivery or short supply. This also placed an extra burden on purchasing.

Fortunately the suppliers became more amenable as the ship progressed, and many became aware of the publicity value to be gained from making a contribution to the project. This had always been stressed, as the need to make the money available go as far as possible was a governing factor. When it became clear that *Warrior* would become a celebrity the advantages no longer needed to be emphasised.

PREPARING FOR DISPLAY

The object of the restoration of *Warrior* was to save her

An artist's impression of *Warrior* at Portsmouth. *Victory* can be seen to the left, while the Royal Naval Museum lies in between the two ships. *WPT*

in the hope that the public would share the enthusiasm of the projectors and hopefully generate the funds to keep her afloat. Like all archaeological sites the ship that left Milford Haven was perfectly comprehensible to the enthusiasts. They needed no masts, engines or guns to appreciate the scale and significance of the first iron-hulled ironclad. However the the general public would certainly have found the grimy, cluttered hulk an unattractive proposition for a paying visit. Reconstructing the ship has provided it with a visual power that cannot fail to bring the interested layman aboard. It is this mass audience, from all over the world, that will provide the revenue to maintain the ship in the future. Here again the *Warrior* project has differed from other large scale work on ships. The *Great Britain* for example progresses only as fast as the incoming funds allow.

All this might seem obvious, but it is worth stressing for one major reason. In order to make *Warrior* function as a public exhibit certain compromises had to be made. These were limited by the decision taken very early in the project that there should be no unsightly, intrusive and cluttering onboard displays.

As a public exhibit, *Warrior* is affected by fire regulations. Before any large number of people could be allowed on board, several safe exits had to provided and illuminated, and fire doors installed. In addition fire alarms and television monitoring were needed for the security of the public and the ship. Obviously *Warrior* never had any such installations when she was built. They have been added as she was reconstructed, in order to minimise their visual impact.

The demand for several exits and escape routes for the public was the most difficult requirement to meet. It ran completely contrary to the design philosophy of the ship which was to reduce the number of openings to a minimum, especially those between the central citadel and the unprotected bow and stern below the main deck. The aft 4½in bulkhead had already been cut through on the lower deck during *Warrior*'s term as the power station for HMS *Vernon*. The unpierced iron wall was clearly a nuisance of the highest order; it was cut through with hand drills and cold chisels, a massive job. The forward bulkhead remained intact, and may not have to be cut on the lower deck in the area of the long demolished forward magazine. Other additional openings will be less obvious to the untrained eye.

The electrical control cables for the alarms and

monitors, as well as the power and lighting installations had been positioned along the sides of the main deck before the cladding was fitted. It was therefore hidden from view in a very neat manner. All the control cables were concentrated in the Paymaster's cabin on the starboard side of the main deck. This will be the control room when the ship is in service, and consequently the Paymaster's large desk will be full of television monitors and alarms, but these will be covered unless required. Elsewhere only a few control boxes and modern electric fittings will be seen. The installation of electric lighting will, however, have the effect of making the ship seem smaller. When *Warrior* was built the only below deck lighting came from candles and oil lamps. They provided a dim light, along with a good deal of smoke and smell. The first Royal Navy warship with electric lighting was the battleship *Inflexible* of 1880. All these matters are minor when viewed in the context of the restored ship.

A less obvious requirement for modern display was the removal of more than one hundred layers of Victorian lead-based paint. In the 1970s lead-based paints were identified as a serious health hazard, consequently special arrangements had to be made for it to be removed, notably the use of breathing apparatus. Similarly unseen are the innumerable railway tie plates that fill the double bottom and wing passages. These serve as ballast to replace the weight of the original machinery, guns and coal. Without them *Warrior* would not float at the proper draught. Railway irons were selected for the job because they were available in large numbers and very easy to install. They have the additional benefit of interlocking and being portable, the latter being of no small consequence for all elements of the project.

The requirement for an effective control of the temperature aboard *Warrior*, for the benefit of the public, led to the glazing over of the gunports, a feature of her days as a hulk, being retained. The original ventilation system (see chapter 8) was restored and adapted to serve again. Electric motors keep up a constant circulation of air, and when necessary, provide warmth.

PORTSMOUTH

The choice of the proper site in which to display *Warrior* was a vital element in securing the long-term future of the ship. It was essential that she be brought to a position where a large viewing public could be assured. While there were a number of possible sites around the country, Portsmouth was always the favourite. The original contract with the Navy, under which *Warrior* was handed over, specified London or Portsmouth.

Already home to *Victory, Mary Rose* and the expanding Royal Naval Museum, Portsmouth was also historically suitable. As a Channel Fleet Ship, *Warrior* was based, and refitted at Portsmouth. She also spent many years there with the Vernon establishment. The run-down of the Dockyard emphasised the need for the city to find alternative sources of employment. One of the most obvious was to increase the tourist trade. Under the leadership of Councillor John Marshall, then Mayor of the City, Portsmouth Council actively canvassed for the ship, and, once she had been promised, spent £1½ million on the jetty and supporting facilities.

With the other attractions already in the Dockyard Portsmouth will now house the finest collection of historic warships anywhere in the world. This will benefit *Warrior* and the other exhibits. To organise and promote this unique centre the Portsmouth Naval Heritage Trust has been set up, with *Warrior* as an integral part of the whole. Another development under consideration is a Warrior Museum, similar in scope to that already established for *Mary Rose*. It would house some of the growing collection of artefacts and documentation that has been built up during the reconstruction.

CHAPTER FOUR
Hull and Armour

When *Warrior* arrived at Hartlepool she was little more than a hulk. Only her hull and armour survived to connect her with the once great ironclad. Before considering the restoration of the ship it will be useful to consider these two surviving elements.

IRON SHIPBUILDING

The Industrial Revolution brought about the wide spread use of iron. The superior qualities of this material for shipbuilding were initially appreciated on the growing network of canals. Iron barges were in use before the end of the eighteenth century. However the first really bold step came in 1821, when the ironmaster Charles Manby constructed an iron paddlesteamer, the *Aaron Manby*, and persuaded one of the most progressive officers in the Royal Navy, Captain Charles Napier, to take her direct from London to Paris. This voyage demonstrated the value of steam, and the subsequent career of the *Aaron Manby*, on the Seine, demonstrated the strength of iron ships. Despite often being aground on sandbanks she required no major work on her hull until 1850.

For all the qualities of iron its adverse effect on magnetic compasses prevented voyages out of sight of land for another sixteen years. In 1839 the Astronomer Royal, Professor Sir George Airey, published his work on the measures needed to insulate and correct the

Although HMS *Achilles* was built in drydock at Chatham Naval Yard, the design of the ship and the nature of the work were all but identical to those of *Warrior*. Like her wooden predecessors the work began with the keel and then extended from the centre section toward the extremities. The transverse frames were the first to be set up. The high level dockside trackway was set up especially for the construction of *Achilles*, the first iron armoured warship to be built in a British Royal Dockyard. The beams in place are the floor beams of the main deck. *NMM*

compass for service aboard iron ships. Basically he installed powerful magnets to counteract the effect of the iron. It reduced deviation to one degree or less. The direct result of this breakthrough was that I K Brunel, an engineer rather than a shipbuilder, changed from wood to iron for the hull of the epochal *Great Britain* at a late stage in the design process. Similarly the Honourable East India Company ordered the first real iron warship, the paddle gunboat *Nemesis*, from Laird's of Birkenhead, in early 1839. Under Lieutenant William Hall's able command *Nemesis* played a major role in the Opium War of 1841. She avoided the difficulties of a badly-adjusted compass and rapid fouling by operating on the Chinese Rivers. Here the marine growths were killed by fresh water and the compass was not required. More significantly *Nemesis* stood up very well to gunfire.

When Hall returned to Britain in 1843 he reported the performance of *Nemesis* to the Admiralty. This was the major influence behind the decision to build a large number of iron warships in the mid-1840s, beginning

Achilles a few weeks later. The frames have advanced to the turn of the bow. The shipwrights are standing ahead of the forward watertight bulkhead, approximately where the citadel ended on *Warrior*. Markings on the plates were made in the mould loft, where each was cut to shape, for the guidance of the workmen. Comparison with the preceeding shot shows how the 'U' shaped floor of the centre section is sharpening off into the 'V' section of the bow, to provide hollow lines of entry. Note the stem piece, set up well in advance. *NMM*

with the *Trident* of 878 tons, laid down in 1843. She was followed by the ill-fated *Birkenhead*. In 1845 four iron screw frigates were ordered. However the Admiralty became alarmed by the dangers of splinters demonstrated during the trials of the *Simoom* target. After a change of Government it was decided, in December 1846, to cancel the iron frigates. This proving too costly an option, they were converted into troopships, apart from the *Greenock*, which was sold into the merchant service. Other nations followed Britain's early lead in iron warships, notably France and the USA, but none were ever used in action. As Dupuy de Lôme commented, the iron ship programme of the 1840s had been entered into and then abandoned too hastily.

In the mercantile marine the success of the *Great Britain* started an irresistible line of development, despite the disasters to the *Royal Charter* and *Prince*. Even the Admiralty's threat to withold lucrative mail contracts from firms using iron ships did not stop P & O from building the *Himalaya* in 1852. For commercial purposes large iron hulls could be built stronger, more durable, up to 40% cheaper and with only 70% of the weight. Wooden shipbuilding went into a rapid decline in the ocean-going steamship class, although it hung on elsewhere for many years. During the Russian War the shortage of, and resultant high price commanded by,

shipbuilding timber encouraged the move to iron. Three floating batteries, the *Erebus*, *Thunderbolt* and *Terror*, were built with iron hulls. Inexperienced design made the system of fastening the armour to the hull suspect. However armour did solve the problems pointed out by the *Simoom* and *Ruby* trials of 1845–6.

Fouling remained insoluble. Special paints and chemical compounds of an unspeakable composition all failed to arrest the dramatic growth of marine organisms, and this problem has still to be given a total solution. While the hull of an iron ship could be regularly docked and cleaned the disadvantage could be tolerated. *Warrior* was docked on average every ten months during her first commission to preserve her speed, one of the main features of her design. As she could only be docked in home waters she was necessarily limited to the Channel in war or peace, except for brief cruises further afield. Walker realised this when he outlined the ship, and accepted the consequences. That he was prepared to press for such a powerful ship to be built, knowing that it could not maintain its speed outside home waters, reflected an overriding concern with the French Navy and the menace in the Channel. He must have hoped that suitable docks would be built elsewhere, but such things were outside his control. Overall the fouling issue demonstrated his determination not to compromise the design, even by reducing the spacing of the guns, to achieve a shorter ship. Later wooden-hulled, or wood-sheathed, ironclads were prepared for service in the Pacific and China seas where docks were scarce.

Fitting out. The 'A' brackets for the bowsprit are a nice detail touch. The pivot for the bowsprit can be seen; this would allow the use of the ram bow without wrecking the head gear. The anchors are already in position, along with the sponsoned side head on the starboard bulwark, just abaft the forebridge. The steam crane aboard ship might be connected with the installation of the machinery. The six flagstaffs indicate the original positions of the bowsprit, the four masts and the jackstaff at the stern. They have been installed so that the ship can be dressed up for her ceremonial 'floating out', a substitute for the launch ceremony for dock built ships. *Achilles* was floated out on 23 December 1863. This photograph was taken very shortly before that event.

In the next dock the old 84-gun two-decker *Bombay* is being fitted out for service as flagship on the South American Station. She was to be destroyed by an accidental fire off Montevideo on 22 December 1865.

Out in the Medway the sheer hulk lies ready to install *Achilles'* masts. *NMM*

Cautious hull design denied *Warrior* the extra carrying capacity that iron would have allowed. However, internal subdivision and a partial double bottom, in addition to the great increase in strength and durability, gave an ample demonstration of the value of iron. An excellent illustration of this point can be seen in the docking procedure adopted for wooden and iron ships. The wooden ships had to be supported in dry dock by a forest of timber shores, to prevent bulging and distortion (see the *Caledonia* photograph on p75). Iron hulls need far less timber, and even that was purely to keep them upright in dock. This structural weakness of wood was a major factor in the brief lives of many wooden ships. Once the structure began to move all manner of corruption crept into the ship. All wooden

A third photograph from the same vantage point. The stem piece has now been taken into the hull structure. Note how the skin plating has advanced along the frame, almost in parallel with the upper deck beams. This view emphasises the fact that the bulwarks were built on after the iron structure had been completed. *Warrior* had her knee bow built ahead of the stem, but *Achilles* was finished at this point, with a slightly outward sloping stem. Another watertight bulkhead can be seen just behind the stem. *NMM*

Warrior showing details of the upper deck.

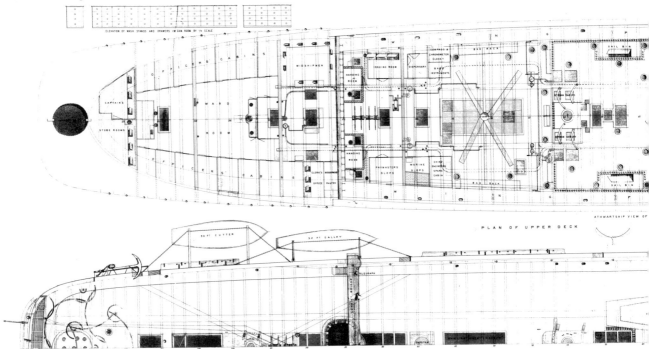

ships went out of shape to a degree as soon as they left the stocks. This affected their speed, by spoiling the hull lines conceived by the designer.

When considering the rise of iron shipbuilding it is interesting to note the pivotal role played by non-specialists, especially engineers from other disciplines, Brunel, Manby and many others helped overcome the prejudices of the age with their faith in iron as the best material for all requirements.

CONSTRUCTION

The physical act of constructing Warrior was largely conditioned by the limits of contemporary technology. It began with the fabrication of the keel plate and the setting up of the frames, before the hull plating was attached. The design and structure of the hull was in many ways no more than a modification of wooden ship practice of previous centuries, with iron plates and rivets substituted for plank and treenails. The small size of the available plates made substantial framing essential. The Contract Specification (Appendix III) provides a full description of contemporary practice. It must be borne in mind that there had been no significant experience of building warships in iron, so Warrior's structural design reflected experience with merchant ships. After Warrior and her broadside descendants, naval architects began to alter the structure of the iron ship to meet the requirements of carrying ever heavier weights of armour, machinery and artillery.

The formation of the Institution of Naval Architects, (since 1959 the Royal Institution) brought together designers and constructors to discuss their work. This had the effect of forcing the pace of advance. It was

dominated by men with a reputation for forward thinking: Edward Reed, later Chief Constructor in succession to Watts, Reed's successor Nathaniel Barnaby and the great self-publicist John Scott-Russell. Reed was, with some inspiration from Scott-Russell, to make the first great structural advance with his 'bracket frame' system for the ironclad Bellerophon.

Warrior's iron hull, while it marked a major shift in naval construction policy and was the second largest yet built, after the Great Eastern, was not of itself remarkable. The general layout of longitudinal frames with strong transverse angle irons and girders was an example of the best practice of the era. The strength of the design was not based on theoretical models of stress but practical experience with other iron ships, with the conservative additional emphasis of the Surveyor's Department. This over-strong design was reflected in the hull's low carrying capacity. Watts could not be expected to produce an innovative iron structure at short notice, and he had to rely on mercantile practice. This was because success had to be guaranteed, no risks could be taken with the hull design, which might threaten the total package.

The frames were on average 44in apart (although there were variations) and the longitudinals up to 113in where the hull plating was 1⅛in thick, or 60in where ⅞in plating was used, notably on the outer plating of the bottom. The latter was not overly well supported, bearing in mind its low initial strength. As a transverse framed design based on wooden shipbuilding Warrior placed too much strength in the massive athwartships frames, and insufficient in the longitudinal structure. However the massive over-design of the ship prevented

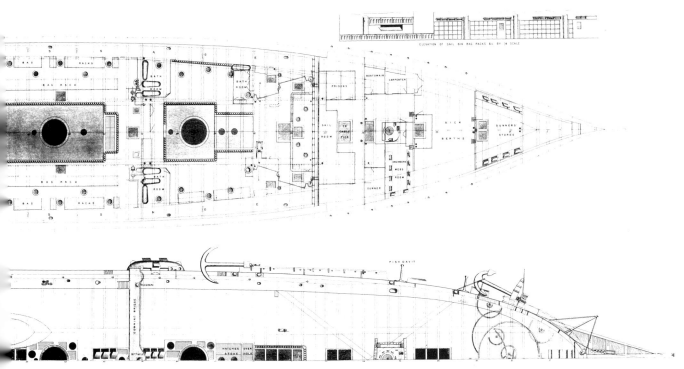

her from showing any signs of weakness. What it did not do was make the most effective use of the tonnage. If any further proof is needed that Scott-Russell did not design *Warrior* the structure provides it; Scott-Russell was far in advance of the methods used in *Warrior* in his own ships, including the earlier *Great Eastern*.

Weight making up the displacement of *Warrior*

Hull			4970
Armour	Iron	950	
	Timber Backing	355	1310
Armament			340
Equipment			850
Machinery			890
Coal			850
			9210

WARRIOR'S ARMOUR

The reason why 4in or 4½in iron plates were specified for the armour of the early ironclads lay in the available technology of the 1850s. In 1854, when Thomas Lloyd suggested the 4in plate as armour, he knew that this was the thickest continuous iron slab that could be rolled or hammered with the existing machinery, and even that was a recent development. In 1859 4½in was practical, and it was selected for *Warrior*, instead of the 4in plate of the first ironclad project and the floating batteries, largely because of reports that *Gloire* had plate of that thickness. Plates thinner than 4in were often tried, in the hope that smaller warships could be

armoured, but they did not provide any effective protection.

Earlier attempts to devise iron armour had foundered on the weakness of plates thinner than 4in, and of thicker plates built up from a laminate of thin strips. The combination of the Russian War, Napoleon III's vision, Lloyds' practical approach and the advances in rolling and hammering technology was fortuitous, although armour itself was probably inevitable.

The armour for *Warrior* was designed in detail following the *Erebus* and *Meteor* trials. The 4½in plates were to be bolted to the ⅝in skin plating of the iron hull through 18in of teak, composed of two 9in baulks laid crossways – the whole to be recessed into the side of the ship, leaving the external surface of the armour flush with the hull plating of the unarmoured areas. Each plate was 3ft wide and 12ft long. It was held in place by double nuttled bolts every 18in. During the construction of the ship the horizontal joint faces of the plates were ordered to be made to interlock on the 'tongue and groove' principle, like floorboards. To this end the plates were modified with 1½in tongues which locked into a groove on the connecting plate which had a 1½in supporting lip on either side of the groove. This was complicated, expensive and consumed a fair proportion of the time by which *Warrior* failed to meet the contract delivery date. The object of the exercise was to provide mutual support between the plates, which could not be made any larger. During one of the trials it had been observed that the joints between the plates were a weak element, and might be suspect if struck by several shots.

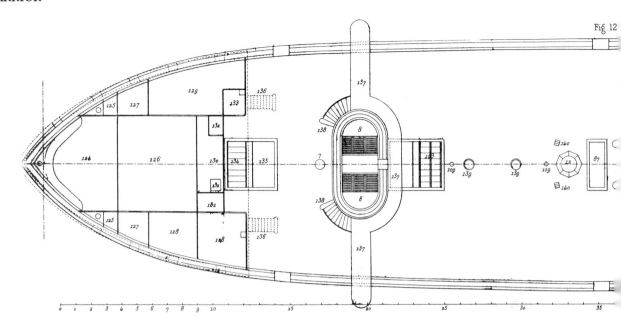

Fig. 12

Upper Deck of *Gloire PARIS*

Plan of the main deck

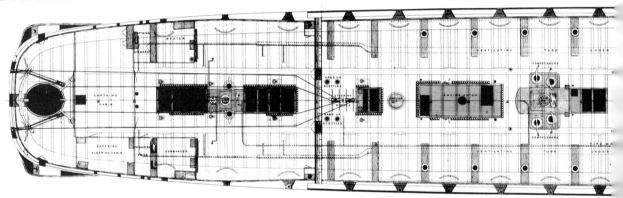

Just as *Warrior* was completing, in January 1861, the War Office set up a Special Committee to investigate the use of iron as armour, on land and sea. This body, composed of naval and military officers, shipbuilders and scientists carried out a very detailed study of the manufacture and properties of iron. To conclude their work they devised a series of gun versus armour trials. They had already concluded that rolled or hammered soft wrought iron was the best material. Therefore the trials concentrated on how the 4½in plate should be mounted to achieve the best results.

The first target was an iron frame with the armour bolted directly to it, similar to the iron floating batteries. The target failed after very few shots had struck it, but only because the bolts broke. The armour and the iron frames were still in good condition. Finally in October 1861 a target was built to represent a 20ft by 10ft section of *Warrior* with a gunport in the centre. The plates used were manufactured by Thames Iron-

works and were identical to those aboard *Warrior*. Lacking adequate rolling mills Thames relied on hammered plates. A mixture of two-thirds London scrap and one-third new puddled iron from Milton in Yorkshire was used. The scrap was cleaned, and any paint burnt off before it was rolled into 5in bars. These were laid crossways with the new iron, also in 5in bars, and then forged together. The resultant plates were hammered down to 4½in with a 4 ton blow Nasmyth steam hammer. It was claimed that this process produced a more uniform armour than rolling. Even if this was not true the resistance of the Thames plates was only bettered by those of Palmer's, the Jarrow shipbuilders. The bolts, 1½inches thick and fitted with locking nuts, were countersunk to prevent the heads being struck by shot.

At a range of only 200yds this target was hit by 29 projectiles of between 68 and 200lbs, totalling 3229lbs. None penetrated, even when three 200pdr shot were

rd.

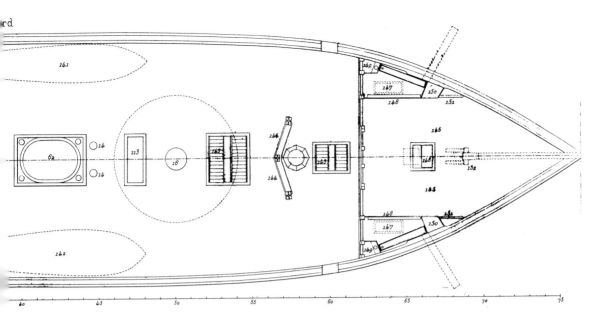

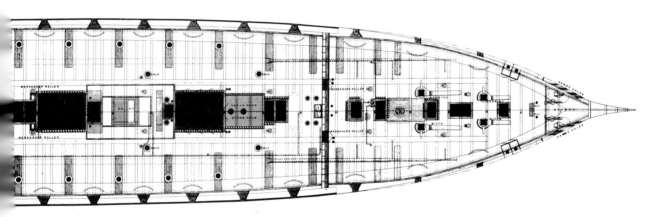

fired in salvo. One bolt was damaged and a 3in dent formed in one plate. The Committee was able to report that no previous target had stood up to such a battering. However, they criticised the tongue and groove joints, which they considered were likely to transmit shock between plates, and would also make the replacement of damaged plates extremely difficult. The practice was then abandoned. The results obtained from testing the *Warrior* target just as the ship was completing obviously had no influence on her design, apart from confirming the general soundness of her protection. It was intended to provide information for future developments, although it also served to point up the folly of designing new systems without proper trials. Overall the *Warrior* target proved the excellence of the basic design, and the ability of a well-supported 4½in plate to resist any weapon then in existence at point blank range. This was far more than the original projectors of armour had hoped for, and demonstrated

the value of experiment.

The value of wooden backing had been realised long before this trial, but even afterwards the manner in which it contributed to the strength of the system was not understood. It was thought that the wood provided a flexible support for the plate, allowing it to flex under impact. Recently D K Brown has established that the wood did not support the armour in any meaningful sense, but served to damp out tensile shock waves which would otherwise travel along the length of the bolts. It was these shock waves that caused unbacked targets to fail, by breaking the bolts. Clearly this was undesirable, and had been noted earlier. The French adopted a very different system for their ships. The plates were attached to the wooden hull, which doubled as the backing, by a number of large screws. While the concept was repellant in engineering terms it served the intended purpose and stood up well in exhaustive trials.

Fig 1

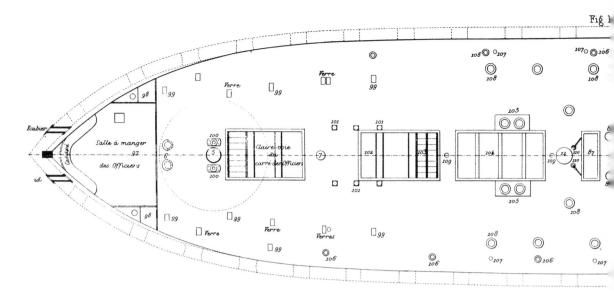

Main Deck of *Gloire*. PARIS

Plan of the Lower Deck

Fig 14

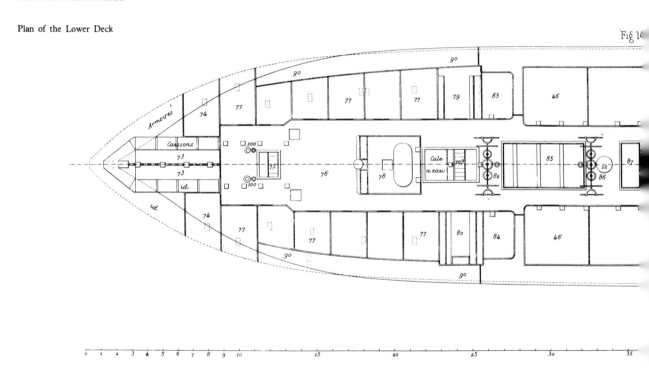

More has been established about the armour itself in the course of the reconstruction. Some plates were removed from the port side of the ship when she was converted into a jetty, in order to fit a sponson. These plates were left aboard the ship and have been used for trials. The longitudinal and perpendicular strengths were found to be as expected for wrought iron. However the impact resistance varied dramatically with alterations in temperature, something that was entirely unexpected.

Resistance of Warrior's armour to impact

Temperature (in degrees centigrade	0	15	40	100
Absorbed Energy (in joules)	11	17	24	26

(I am indebted to John Bird of ARE, Dunfermline for the results of his work).

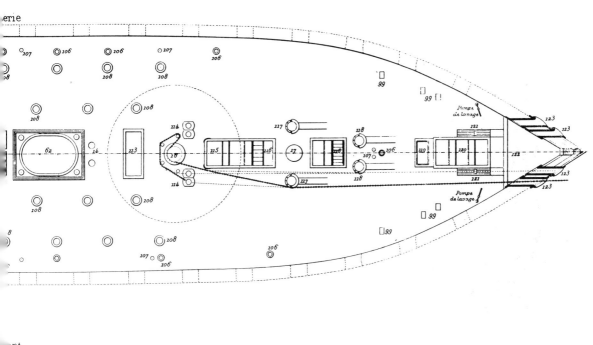

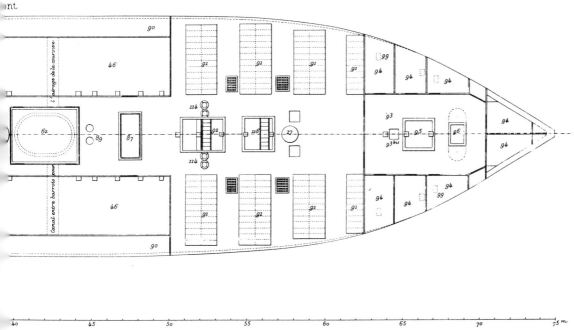

The variable performance of wrought iron armour in trials, and the success of unarmoured ships, such as the *Nemesis* in China, can now be explained. Wrought iron becomes increasingly brittle at low temperatures. As a result the date of each trial, and the state of the weather become matters of real significance in understanding the hesitant advance of armour.

The unarmoured portions of *Warrior* were no better protected than the 1845 iron frigates, indeed *Simoom* had 10in backing inside the hull plating which was far superior to the unbacked shell plating of *Warrior*. However the hull was subdivided by four bulkheads ahead of the central armoured citadel and two behind. Flooding in these compartments would not have seriously affected *Warrior*'s fighting performance. However the 'Achilles heel' of the design, the unprotected rudder head, was a real source of weakness, and one that needed to be rectified. Under the machinery spaces there was a partial double bottom, and alongside there were watertight wing passages, although the latter had

Royal Oak fitting out in drydock at Chatham, early in 1863. Originally a 90-gun two-decker of the *Bulwark* class she was lengthened on the stocks and cut down into a 36-gun armoured frigate. Note the large quantity of timber in the the foreground that has been removed during the conversion. As completed, *Royal Oak* was barque rigged, with no square sails on the mizzen mast. The fore yard is fitted for stunsails, the main yard is not, because of smoke and heat damage to the extra sails which made them an expensive luxury.

The track of the dockside steam crane can be seen starting by the capstan in the right foreground. *NMM*

too many doors low down to be entirely satisfactory. There were 92 separate sealable compartments. Watertight doors were fitted to the ship very shortly after she entered service, even if they were not envisaged in the original design. They can still be seen on lower deck, where they seal off the ends of the armoured citadel. The doors are closed by a T-bar from the deck above, which operates on the spindle of the ratchet.

With the exception of the rudder head *Warrior* was well protected, and capable of sustaining considerable fire without suffering any mortal damage. The unprotected main deck guns on the other hand were a liability and given the Royal Navy's philosophy would have proved expensive to man in action. Furthermore they had no means of receiving ammunition save from the citadel, and that required the armoured doors to be opened, ruining the whole concept of an armoured, sealed battery. The bow and stern chase guns were in a similar position. By contrast the reduced gunports (see chapter 5) were a great improvement over previous practice, and over *Gloire* where the embrasures were so wide, and so close together as to constitute a profound weakness to the armour scheme.

RESTORING THE HULL

Warrior's iron hull has lasted remarkably well, with very little wastage. It should survive another hundred years afloat. Before any significant work could be carried out inside the ship the upper deck had to be made watertight. However this was an enormous proposition, for *Warrior* was completed with an uninterrupted expanse of wooden decking on one level from bow to stern totalling over 16,000 sq ft. In many ways the upper deck was at the centre of the reconstruction, for once it had been finished the rest of the ship could be worked on. However this was a daunting prospect. Eventually Ship Foreman Stan Morrell and his team began the work, in May 1980.

At that stage *Warrior*'s upper deck was a confused mass of later fittings, crumbling bulwarks and old concrete. The wooden deck had begun to decay while at Milford, and large areas of it had been ripped up and replaced with concrete 6in thick. This had cracked and allowed water to reach the $\frac{3}{4}$in iron plating below. By the time the water reached the deck it was saturated with lime, from the concrete, forming a very corrosive alkaline solution. This penetrated the deck and formed stalactites on the deckhead below. The main deck was therefore a wet place. Other non-original fittings were less destructive. They included the light wooden poop deck fitted during the 1871–5 refit, a helicopter landing pad, modern derricks, a 1920s vintage lamppost and the fuelling sponson amidships on the port side. These curios from the career of a jetty were gradually removed during the following years, as and when necessary. The poop came down in January 1981, but the sponson remained aboard until June 1983.

The concrete decking was lifted with heavy road

drills during the latter half of 1980. This exposed the corroded deck plating, which had to be repaired, and the numerous bolt holes that had once secured the planking, elements of the rigging and fixtures on the deckhead below. All had to be noted and related to their original purpose. It would be well to know what went in each hole, and replace it before the deck went down. There was no great urgency to deal with the bolts because the deck itself needed extensive repairs. Additional craftsmen from the metalworking trades,

The steam crane revealed, with its primary load, one of the armour plates marked up and drilled ready for the port side (note the letter P). This 4½in plate, unlike those of *Warrior*, did not have tongue and groove edges. The tracks are a temporary fitting in this dock, which is alongside that where *Achilles* was built. *NMM*

The iron-hulled Russian War floating battery *Terror* at Bermuda with Admiral Milne's North America and West Indies Squadron in 1862-3. She still carries the light barque rig installed for the Atlantic crossing. Note that even this bluff little iron box carried a figurehead. Both *Terror* and the fleet behind her were in place because the British Government anticipated trouble with the Northern Government during the American Civil War. The other ships in harbour are three or four two-deckers, two or three large screw frigates, possibly including *Mersey* or *Orlando*, a paddle frigate and a harbour service hulk. *NMM*

impossible to obtain. Several suppliers were used, and one after another failed to meet delivery dates and provide the quantities contracted for. Irregular delivery was a constant hindrance to the work, until a regular source was found.

Before the timber was laid a latex compound provided by ICI was mixed and spread over the entire deck to a depth of 1in. This provided additional

Minotaur in drydock at Portsmouth. This view shows off to advantage her ram bow and fine hull lines. Note the small number of supports needed to keep her in position. *CPL*

welders, platers and burners, were taken on to seal the holes and fix new plates where necessary. By October 1981 a small section of the deck had been repaired and sealed, but in the absence of suitable timber and with the onset of winter attention had to be switched to the by now partially habitable main deck.

Timber for the decks proved to be one of the biggest problems the project had to face. The first consignment came from a demolished warehouse in Bradford. Although a large quantity was bought for only £10,000, it proved to be a questionable bargain. Three-quarters of the upper deck was planted, but at an uneconomic cost in the man-hours spent checking it for faults and nails. Subsequently adequate supplies of the proper close-grained Douglas Fir from Canada proved almost

weatherproofing and a smooth surface to fit the planks onto. Without this latex layer the underside of each plank would have had to be shaped to fit the deck, which had several irregular and uneven features. Another benefit was the reduction in the depth of planking required from 4in to 3in. With 16,850 sq ft of timber to find the cost saving was considerable.

The replanking process began in the spring of 1983,

One of *Royal Oak*'s sisters, the *Caledonia*, in drydock at Malta during her period as flagship of the Mediterranean Fleet. Note the forest of timber shores required to support her wooden hull. Compare this view with those of *Royal Oak. CPL*

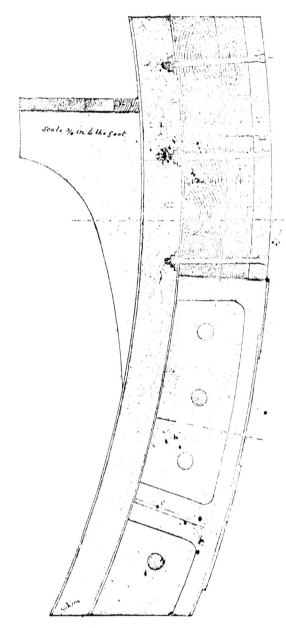

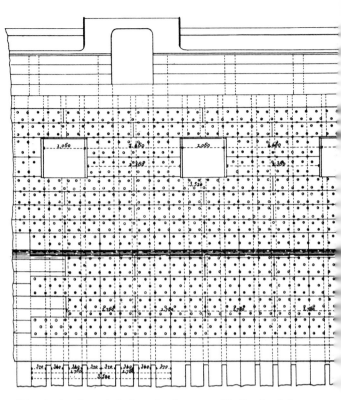

Gloire, showing the method of securing the armour. The French relied on a large number of screws to hold the armour to the hull. Note the large gunports, 2.060m square, far larger than those of *Warrior*. PARIS

The system of securing the armour to the hull of *Warrior*. Note the countersunk, double nutted bolts. The wood they pass through served to damp out any shock waves which might otherwise have broken them. Also note the overlapping hull plating below the armour. *WPT*

working forward from the stern. By November three-quarters of the deck had been laid. Before the actual planking could be fitted the water channel bars had to be installed and cut to shape. These timbers, bolted to the deck edge form a rounded water channel where the deck and the bulwarks meet. They direct any free surface water into the scuppers, keeping the gently arched deck, clear of water. As *Warrior* was prone to shipping water over her bow, the original water bars had seen much service. The replacements were formed from 12in by 14in section baulks of pitch pine 12ft long. Once fixed, these timbers were cut to shape by hand, using an adze. This was one of many jobs that called for

The 4½in armour plates removed from *Warrior* during her conversion into a jetty. They show clearly the interlocking tongue and groove edges, designed as a reinforcement, but later abandoned. *AUTHOR'S COLLECTION*

November 1981, new deck plates being installed around the stump of the mizzen mast. Where the original plates had been badly corroded by the alkaline solution created by the old concrete, replacements were cut and welded into position. *WPT*

November 1982, one of the new hatch coamings being bolted into place. With the water bar these formed the edges of the deck, and had to be fixed before the work could be completed. Note the bronze rail supports at the corners of the coaming; these are new castings. *WPT*

skill and experience in long-abandoned working methods. At the same time the hatch coamings along the centreline of the ship were bolted into place. These also served to divert water, this time to keep it from running down the hatches and into the ship.

The first stage in planking was to fix the bolts into the deck plating. After the latex compound could be spread and finally the 8in by 3in 20ft long planks were carried aboard the ship, positioned parallel to the axis of the ship, marked and drilled to take the bolt. Then the plank was ready to be secured and the bolt hole could be filled up with a wooden dowel. The cover of the lifting well for the propeller was also planked in this fashion, but remains a separate structure with lifting rings.

July 1984, the last areas of the deck being laid. The ICI Latex compound is being spread to provide a smooth surface before laying the planks. *WPT*

The view from the newly erected mizzenmast as seen in September 1984. The deck now only requires a final sanding down, and the fitting of the racer plates for the upper deck guns. *WPT*

The deck timbers being bolted down. *WPT*

The water bar being cut to shape at the stern, an awkward task calling for skilled use of the adze. Note the newly finished bulwarks, and the remaining original material on the right hand side. *WPT*

When the deck had been bolted down it had to be made watertight in the old manner, to prevent water getting between the planks and causing rot. Balls of oakum were prepared for the task. Oakum was always made of tarred hemp or manilla rope that had been unpicked. This was a tedious and slow process, particularly hard on the fingers and thumbs, and as a result, it was often used as a naval punishment. Although not used as a punishment aboard *Warrior* in the 1980s, preparing oakum remained an unpleasant task, even if new rope of the required diameter was bought for the job. Once ready the oakum was hammered into the seams using a special caulking iron and mallet. Caulking effectively fills up the gaps between the planks. As the process had not been in common use for twenty years before *Warrior* required caulking, there was a distinct shortage of the proper tools. However the Hartlepool Harbour Authority and a local businessman, the late Charles Dickens, were able to loan the necessary items. After the oakum has been forced home the seam was filled up with hot pitch, a mixture of tar and coarse natural resin from pine trees. This process was known as 'paying'. The awkward seams around the hatch coamings and against the water bar, called the 'devil's seams', gave rise to the expression 'paying the devil' to describe yet another process

The shipwrights caulking the larger part of the deck in October 1983. The unusual caulking mallets and balls of oakum can be seen. *WPT*

aboard the *Warrior* that called for a steady hand and a good eye. Even though the oakum had been tarred, unless the seam was sealed with pitch it would eventually become filled with water and the oakum become rotten. The pitch prevents any water getting into the seam.

By November 1983 fully three-quarters of the deck had been planked and caulking was well underway. A mild winter, very much the exception in the North East, allowed work to continue, principally permitting the hatch coamings to be installed. The whole process was effectively complete on 14 September 1984, four years after it had started. The deck still required planing down, but that was left until after all the other work on the upper deck had been completed.

The other large scale project on the upper deck was the refurbishment of the bulwarks, the 5ft high wooden wall that enclosed the deck. Large parts of this structure were still in place, even if they looked decidedly second-hand. However, once the restoration began it soon became clear that patching up the original woodwork did not offer the degree of durability called for by the original conception of the project. Consequently the rotten timbers were taken out and replaced by a series of rectangular steel frames, supporting a cladding of greenheart timber. This wood was the most durable of all those in modern day use but it had disadvantages. It was very hard to work, blunting saws and drills with uncommon rapidity. However the project secured a large stock from a recently closed sawmill at a very reasonable cost.

As the new bulwarks were of little importance to any other aspect of the work aboard *Warrior* they were built

The new bulwarks being installed. The original wooden structure had been bolted onto the top of the iron hull. Almost all were either badly damaged or too rotten to retain. The steel frames were clad with greenheart timber to provide a suitable alternative, which was all but indistinguishable from the original. *WPT*

The stern of *Warrior*, September 1985. Work is just starting on the outboard planking of the bulwarks. The platform and safety rail have been temporarily welded onto the hull for this work, and for the following task, fitting the mizzen chain plates. The fine underwater stern lines of the hull are exposed while the ship is high out of the water. Note the plug scuttles. *AUTHOR'S COLLECTION*

up alongside, but subordinate to, the main outdoor task of relaying the deck. The more easily accessible inside surfaces were finished long before the outside, which required the use of a pontoon at the stern and all along the starboard side.

Unlike her wooden predecessors *Warrior*'s bulwarks were largely unpierced. At the bow and stern there were several ports for the chase guns, on the broadside only four smaller guns and the companion ways served to break up the line. Earlier frigates had, by contrast, mounted almost half of their armament on the open upper deck. Above the bulwarks were the hammock nettings, a further 2ft high, and when in service filled with over 1000 hammocks, each man having two. Quite why all this heavy structure should have been built of wood when a much lighter iron bulwark could have been designed is open to some conjecture. The only advantage of wood was its greater resistance to splintering, yet in action *Warrior*'s upper deck would have been almost empty as it was largely unarmed and the sails would not be used.

During her time at Milford Haven *Warrior* lost the end of her beakhead, and some of the upper strake of armour on the port side went even before she left Portsmouth. Both had to be replaced. The last eight feet of the beak were snapped off when the tanker MV *Warlaby* crashed into *Warrior* in 1976. That there was already some thought of saving the ship was shown by the action of recovering the lost portion, and strapping

it to the deck. Replacing the beakhead would be an essential part of the reconstruction, for its purpose was to carry the figurehead.

The original section was hammered straight and then used as a pattern for the construction of a steel replica. The new beak was installed aboard the ship, using a mobile crane on 10 July 1981. The detailed fixing was complete by the end of the month. The figurehead was not to come aboard for several years.

The section of armour that had been removed back in the 1920s was replaced by a section of 1in steel plate. This work encountered the same problem as refitting the beak. Welding steel to wrought iron is a tricky operation. By 1983 this was realised and the new 'armour' went aboard without any major hold-ups. It can still be seen from close up, the surface of the steel being rather more smooth than the original iron below.

Below deck the process of clearing, cleaning and painting was rapidly advanced once the upper deck had been made weatherproof. This allowed the damaged areas of the main deck, most of it in fact, to be replaced and the internal cladding renewed. Only after this process had been completed would it be possible to display the guns in their true environment. With that the main emphasis of the project shifted from saving the existing structure to recreating long-lost items.

A model of the midship section of *Warrior*, showing the layout of the decks, the engine platform and the watertight wing passages. The hull was built up from small sections in much the same way as preceding wooden ships. *SCIENCE MUSEUM.*

CHAPTER FIVE
Guns

The purpose of a warship is to carry and use (it must not be assumed that the two are always synonymous) an armament. When *Warrior* was built that could only mean artillery. Before *Warrior* the most powerful warships had been the wooden steam battleships. The largest of these mounted between 100 and 130 guns on two or three gun decks. These guns were the famous 32pdr 6in solid shot gun, and 8in shell firing guns. Some ships had a single 68pdr 8in solid shot gun at the bow, to provide chase fire. However the philosophy behind the armament was to develop the greatest possible weight of fire on the broadside, especially at close range. Ships armed in this fashion,

albeit with smaller guns, had been the mainstay of British seapower for two hundred years. They fought in fleets, normally arrayed in a line of battle, one behind the other. *Warrior* was not conceived as a battleship. She was intended to act as a frigate, using her high speed to keep clear of the battle line. She was accordingly to be armed with a smaller number of guns, initially 40 68pdrs. In this respect she followed the *Orlando*, which carried 28 10in shell guns and 12 68 pdrs. This armament was originally intended for

The restored gundeck, with the breech of a 110pdr and three 68pdrs. *WPT*

A 110pdr Armstrong rifled breech-loading 7in gun mounted on an upper deck slide and pivot carriage. This photograph is attributed to *Black Prince*, during her first commission. The racer plates fitted into the deck allowed the gun to move between the various ports around the quarter. *NMM*

A replica of the 110pdr gun on a main deck carriage. Note how the breech rope passes through the carriage, in the absence of the cascabel loop found on all contemporary muzzle loaders. *WPT*

effective fire at longer ranges. It was inspired by the armament of the American *Merrimac* class frigates. However, by the time *Warrior* was designed the emphasis had shifted to armour penetration, and for this task only the 68pdr was considered. In trials the effect of individual shots from the 32 and 68pdrs was in the ratio of one to five. The armament of *Warrior* therefore developed approximately twice the effect against armour as that of the 120-gun *Howe*.

Introduced in 1846 the 8in 68pdr was the last and largest of the cast iron smooth bore muzzle-loading guns, although merely an expansion of the 32pdr 6in gun, but weighing 95cwt, as opposed to 56cwt for the smaller weapon. It established a tremendous reputation during the Russian War for durability, range and accuracy. Even the French had to swallow their Gallic pride and beg the War Office for details. Aboard *Warrior* the original intention was to mount 38 guns on the main deck, and two on pivot carriages on the upper deck to cover the bow and stern arcs of fire, and allow for long-range chase action. The single calibre armament was the ultimate expression of Walker's practical approach to the demands of gunnery. It would simplify the magazine and battery arrangements.

Walker's practical approach also ensured that these large and heavy weapons were mounted with enough space between them to allow for easy working. Aboard line of battleships 8ft 6in was given between the centres of each 32pdr; *Warrior* would have 15ft. This wider spacing, a feature of the *Mersey*, and even more so the *Orlando*, would make the guns more efficient in battle. However on the negative side of the balance it would also make for a ship of unprecedented length, limiting her to docks in the British Isles. Later it provided the space on the battery deck to allow the much heavier 7 and 8in muzzle loading rifles to be installed, without being overcrowded.

While *Warrior* was completing the Armstrong breech-loading rifled gun was adopted by the Board of Ordnance for land and sea service. Initially 10 of the 100, later 110pdr 7in guns, and 4 of the 40pdr 4.75in guns were added to the warrant in place of 14 68pdrs. Soon afterwards it was discovered, to the great surprise of all concerned, that the new gun was significantly inferior to those it replaced. In September 1861 a prototype turret, installed aboard the Floating Battery *Trusty* defeated the new gun. The Select Committee on Ordnance, embarrassed by this discovery, ordered that no more 110pdrs be placed aboard *Warrior*, or any other ironclads. In the event only *Warrior*, *Black Prince*, *Defence*, *Resistance*, *Hector*, *Royal Oak*, *Achilles*, *Prince Consort*, *Caledonia*, *Enterprise* and *Pallas* ever carried the gun, and none were allowed to rely on it as their sole heavy armament.

The fortunes of the Armstrong were now firmly set in a downward path. It had been intended that *Warrior* and her descendants should be rearmed throughout with the new gun. However they met with increasing opposition both from conservative officers, who did not trust the ratings to keep such a complicated weapon effective, and from advocates of Joseph Whitworth's polygonal system of rifling. When Vice Admiral Kuper's Squadron bombarded Kagoshima, on the coast of Japan, on 14 August 1863, the 21 Armstrong guns mounted in his ships suffered 28 accidents in firing only 365 rounds. These were almost entirely confined to the imperfect breech mechanism. Furthermore their shooting was considered erratic, the very thing that rifled guns were supposed to avoid. Inaccurate shooting resulted from the lead-coated shells which rapidly fouled the rifling. Once this had occurred the shells would not spin, and therefore gained no benefit from rifling. In fact the early promise of the small guns had not been matched by the larger weapons. Attempts to build them in steel failed; only 5 were so constructed and all the wrought iron guns, coiled or solid forged, were reckoned to have flaws. By early 1864 the 110pdr had been officially withdrawn from British naval service. The 40 and 20pdrs, suitably modified, were retained for another two decades. A combination of overconfidence and bad design armed the first ironclads with a weapon that failed to match the performance of the gun it should have replaced. *Warrior* and her contemporaries would all have been much better served by a single calibre battery of 68pdrs.

As if the presence of an inferior gun were not enough they were arranged on the main deck in a haphazard way. This would have created confusion in action. It was unnecessary and entirely contrary to the practice established by Walker during the 1850s. After he left the Constructor's Department, the lack of his professional logic and straightforward commonsense was noticeable. He would not have tolerated the armament carried by *Warrior* during her first commission, other than as a temporary expedient.

The general arrangements of the 40pdr Armstrong RBL 4.7in gun on the upper deck. Note the rear truck carriage. This gun introduced the 4.7in calibre into British service; it remained in use until the 1960s. *WPT*

A replica of the 68pdr smooth bore muzzle loading 8in gun, mounted on the rear chock main deck carriage. This gun has been fitted with sights and a firing hammer. *WPT*

When *Warrior* was rearmed the original folly was repeated. She was equipped with a combination of 7 and 8in rifled muzzle loaders on the main deck. If the 7in gun was adequate, which it was, it should have been carried throughout. If the 8in were sufficiently superior to justify the extra weight it should have been made universal. The only feature that the mixed battery offered that a single calibre would not improve on was confusion.

THE ARMSTRONG BREECH MECHANISM

The breech-loading arrangement of the Armstrong gun was novel, but proved to be unsatisfactory in service. To load the gun the vent piece at the end of the barrel was lifted out. The shot and the powder charge could then be pushed through the hollow breech screw into the firing chamber. The vent piece was then replaced behind the charge and the breech screw tightened up, using the two handles to apply leverage. This system

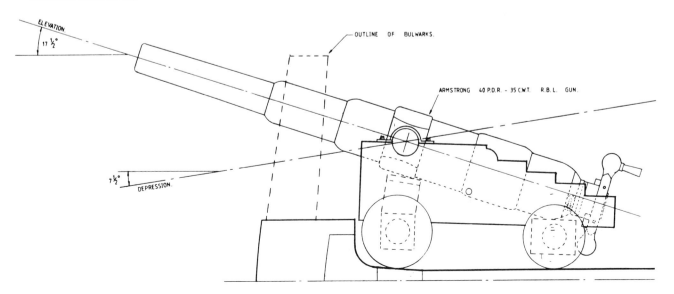

The upper deck of *Minotaur*. Men of the Royal Marine Artillery are preparing to fire a 9in muzzle loading rifle. This gun was slightly larger but otherwise similar to the 7 and 8in weapons with which *Warrior* was rearmed between 1864 and 1867. Note how the chains have been moved inside the bulwarks, to the inconvenience of all concerned, especially the guncrews. *CPL*

The breech block of a replica 110pdr, showing the lifting handles, firing hammer, breech face and the central firing point. This block was forced home against the rear of the barrel by the hand-turned screw thread. The resulting gas seal was at best imperfect, problems with distorted blocks were largely responsible for the early end of this weapon in naval service. *WPT*

failed to provide an adequate gas tight seal at the breech, or sufficient support for the vent piece. The breech screw provided no absolute closure, the gun crew could only tighten up as hard as possible. This naturally varied from crew to crew, and, as Kuper's Squadron demonstrated at Kagoshima, could be overlooked in the heat of battle. With this breech design, relying on the steel faced wrought iron vent piece as a gas seal, both the vent piece and the breech screw were subject to distortion. Later breech loaders used an interrupted screw with a definite closed position and an improved gas seal.

The 7in Armstrong gun was originally designed in 1859 for use by the Army as a siege gun. The muzzle velocity of 1150ft per second, while adequate for the original role, was hopelessly low for armour penetration. The first guns weighed 72cwt, but their recoil was considered too violent. Even so 77 of this type were

delivered to the Army between 1862 and 1866. Of the 82cwt naval guns, introduced in 1861, 914 were built: 255 by Armstrong and the remainder at Woolwich. Most were handed over to the Army before 1867 for use in the coast defences.

The failure of this new weapon highlighted the essentially divergent requirements of the two services with regard to heavy artillery, and the folly of leaving their procurement in the hands of a single, Army-dominated body. The Navy was not to take control of its own guns until Jackie Fisher was Director of Naval Ordnance, 1886–1891.

ATTACKING ARMOUR

Warrior was originally intended to carry 40 68pdrs, because these were the only available guns that had the potential to penetrate 4½in armour. No thought was given to smaller weapons. This provides further emphasis for the point that *Warrior* was designed to counter *Gloire*, and not to take a place in the line of battle.

After the initial trials new steel shot provided the 68pdr with a realistic armour-piercing capacity. Indeed French 6in plates were, because of inferior metallurgy, also vulnerable. This means that no ocean-going ships put into service by the French before 1870 could have stood up to the fire of a gun developed years before armour went to sea. No other nations, Britain aside, did any better. However armour could keep out any shells that a 68pdr could fire; only explosive shells could destroy a ship. Therefore ever larger guns were designed to throw a shell through armour plates of ever increasing thickness. After the disheartening experience with the Armstrong the Royal Navy returned to muzzle loaders. The 7in 6½ ton and 8in 9 ton muzzle-loading rifled guns issued to *Warrior* for her second commission were powerful, but inaccurate. However this mattered little in view of the very short ranges then envisaged for combat.

The power of British guns, and the strength of British armour, would have given *Warrior* a major advantage over *Gloire*. *Warrior* would have had the luxury of selecting the range, because of the 2kt speed difference. As a result *Warrior* could either close in for a short range broadside action, or hold off to make the best use of her superior qualities.

RAM

During the 1860s the tactical mobility provided by steam encouraged many naval enthusiasts to consider a return to the ancient practice of ramming. The dramatic success of the Austrian Admiral Tegetthoff in sinking the Italian ironclad *Re D'Italia* at the Battle of Lissa, 20 July 1866 was taken as proof of the point. Even before that the idea had been widely circulated that the new iron ships could 'run down' their enemies. *Warrior* was designed with a strong bow and keel to allow for such tactics, but her knee bow would have prevented the underwater contact that was vital to the successful outcome of a ramming. Furthermore *Warrior* and her descendants were so unhandy that they could never have *deliberately* rammed any ship that retained the ability to move under its own power. The slow and imprecise manner in which the long ironclads answered the helm ensured that they were hard pressed to avoid undesirable collisions. *Warrior* did hit *Royal Oak*, but her bow saved both ships from the worst effects.

After *Warrior* all ironclads were designed for ramming. *Resistance* set the style, and was known as 'Old Rammo' to the end of her career. However these fittings never harmed another enemy warship after Lissa; all they did was sink several major warships in accidental collisions. The British battleships *Vanguard* and *Victoria* were both destroyed by their squadron mates. Other navies suffered similar disasters. However in defence of the idea of ramming it must be recalled that the artillery of the era was so slow firing, inaccurate and generally ineffective that it made ramming seem very attractive.

THE BROADSIDE ARMAMENT

It is necessary to consider the whole broadside armament as a single entity, appreciating how the guns fitted in with their carriages, the gunports, the ammunition, the magazines and the vestigal fire control.

THE GUNS

Originally intended to carry 40 68pdrs, all but two of them on the main deck, *Warrior* and her armament altered even before she entered service. On 25 September 4 of the main deck guns were ordered to be replaced by 40pdr Armstrongs on the upper deck. These were almost certainly those from the extreme bow and stern, outside the citadel. The 2 chase guns were replaced by 100pdr Armstrongs by an order of 28 February 1861, and 8 of the main deck guns followed suit on 22 August.

When *Warrior* left the fitting out basin for Portsmouth she carried the following battery:
26–68pdr 95cwt guns
10–110pdr 82 cwt guns
 4–40pdr 32cwt guns
 2–20pdr 13cwt (These smaller Armstrong breech-
 1–12pdr 8cwt loading rifled guns were for boat and
           field gun service. They were mounted
           for use aboard the ship, but would
           have been of little value.)
 1–6pdr bronze muzzle-loading 6cwt brass gun for
           short range practice.

As *Warrior* was found to trim by the head, the four empty main deck ports were normally those at the bow, while the 40pdrs were all carried just abaft of the main and mizzen chains respectively. As shown on the plan prepared by Midshipman Murray the main deck 110pdrs were carried in the 3rd, 4th 16th and 17th ports on both sides counting back from the bow, not including the first two on each side which were not used as gun ports.

The 40pdrs were to have been replaced by Armstrong 70pdrs, but the 70pdr failed the proof tests and was never issued. As a result the 40pdrs were replaced by an improved 35cwt gun of the same calibre in late 1863. The only other significant change to the armament was the gradual shift to fitting pivot and slide upper deck type carriages on the main deck. This had not been completed when the ship paid off for her 1864–7 refit and rearmament, only having begun in October 1863.

THE 68pdr GUN

A cast iron smooth bore gun.
Nominal weight: 96cwt
Preponderance (breech heaviness): 10½cwt
Length: nominal (face of muzzle to base ring) 120in, overall 135.55in.
Diameter: at the base ring 27.76in, over the muzzle swell 18.65in, trunnions 8.12in (the trunnions were underhung by 2in).
Width: shoulder to shoulder between trunnions 23.68in, outside trunnions 36.68in.
Bore: smooth 8.12in, length 133.9in. The vent entered

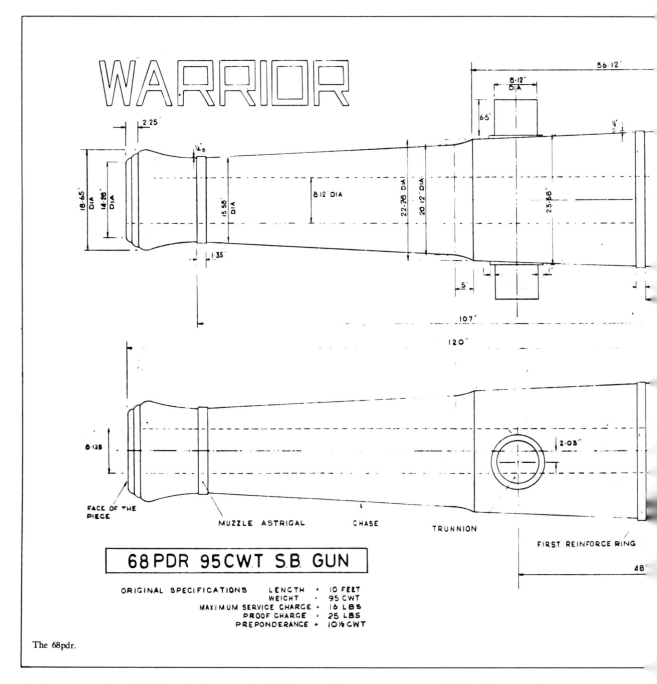

68 PDR 95 CWT S.B. GUN

ORIGINAL SPECIFICATIONS	LENGTH	·	10 FEET
	WEIGHT	·	95 CWT
	MAXIMUM SERVICE CHARGE	·	16 LBS
	PROOF CHARGE	·	25 LBS
	PREPONDERANCE	·	10½ CWT

The 68pdr.

the bore at a point 2.5in from the bottom (11.4in from the muzzle).

Shot: The spherical solid shot had a diameter of 7.849 to 7.925in and a nominal weight of 68lb (actual weight varied). Cast iron 67lb, chilled iron 69½lb, wrought iron 72lb.

Red hot shot: These could be heated in the ship's furnaces and then carried to the guns in special bearers. They were very dangerous when used against wooden ships.

Case shot: A cylindrical sheet iron case 7.82in diameter; filled with 90 8oz balls; total weight 50½lb; the case broke when fired, scattering the balls. Used at close quarters, especially against open boats.

Grape shot: 15 3lb balls in three layers held together by discs 7.4in and an iron rod. Separated when fired. Carried further than case shot. Used against small vessels; like case shot mainly intended to kill personnel.

Common shell: hollow sphere 7.925in, 2lb 9oz of gunpowder and a time fuze, weight 49lbs 10oz.

Diaphragm shrapnel shell: 341 balls and a 5oz bursting charge with time fuze, weight 60lb 13oz. Provided distant anti-personnel fire.

Both types of shell were fitted with wooden bottoms to stop them rolling in the bore, jamming the fuze against

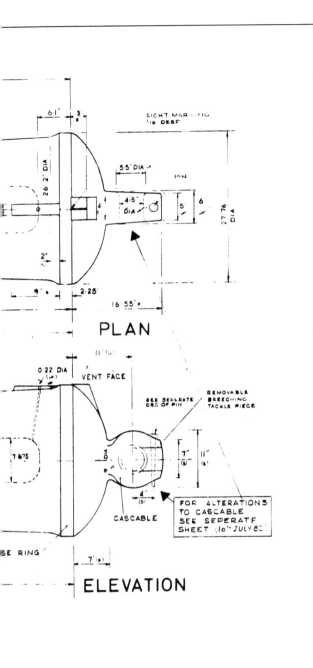

PLAN

ELEVATION

1.2in. Weight empty, 33lb, full 59lb.

Powder charges: flannel covered. Distant 16lb; full 12lb; reduced 8lb. Distant could only be used with solid shot and common shell. The charges were carried from the magazine in leather cases 17in long, 8.9in in diameter and weighing 6lb 6oz empty. With solid shot and a 16lb charge the gun ranged to 3200yd at 12° of elevation. Muzzle velocity was 1579ft per second. It took 12.875 seconds to reach the target.

THE 110pdr GUN

A built-up or solid forged wrought iron gun. Originally termed the 100pdr gun, until February 1862. After 1864 it was known as the rifled breech-loading 7in gun.

Nominal weight: 82cwt

Preponderance: 8cwt 3qtr 11lb.

Nominal length: 120in (face of muzzle to rear of gun, excluding breech screw).

Diameter: maximum 27.7in. At muzzle 13in, trunnions 8in.

Width: between trunnions 28in, outside trunnions 40in.

Bore: Rifled with a diameter of 7in across the lands.

Rifling: 76 grooves each .06in deep and .166in wide with a twist of one turn in 37 calibres, perfectly adequate for the low muzzle velocity.

Length: 99½in. Rifled portion 82.5in. Powder chamber 16in, diameter 7.2in. For 9in in front of the powder chamber the bore was of a larger diameter, forming a 'seat' for the projectile when it was rammed home.

Breech Screw: Two start thread with a pitch of 1.4in. Weight 5cwt 2qtr 18lb.

Vent Piece: Weight 136lb.

All shot and shell were ogival-headed and lead coated. Cylindrical case shot.

Solid Shot: 109lb 13oz to 110lb 14oz, 12.28 to 12.35 in long.

Common Shell: weight 105lb 10oz, bursting charge 7lb 10oz, 18.53in long.

Segment Shell: This was ogival-headed, two calibres long, lined with 112 3.3oz segments built up in layers. Cylindrical powder chamber in the centre. Weight 101lb 10oz, bursting charge 3lb 2oz.

Case Shot: as per 68pdr. 74 8oz balls 67lb.

Powder charges: distant 14lb (shot), 11–12in long 7.026in diameter, full 12lb (shell), 10–11in long, 7.026in diameter. In June 1863 the 14lb charge was withdrawn. In March 1865 the 12lb charge was reduced to 11lbs.

With solid shot and the 14lb charge the gun ranged to 4000 yards at 11¼ degrees of elevation. Muzzle velocity was 1150ft per second, a third less than that of the 68pdr. Little wonder the gun was ineffective against armour.

THE 40pdr GUN

A smaller edition of the 110pdr.

Weight: 32cwt.

the bore and causing an explosion in the gun. This wooden base had a hole in the underside to allow it to be used over a common shot, when the gun was fired with two missiles.

Martin's molten iron shell: A thin wall shell, reinforced at the bottom, carried molten iron and when broken, allowed this to escape, setting fire to any combustible material at hand. Introduced in 1860 to replace red hot shot, being easier to handle, safer and more effective. Wall thickness 0.5in, 1in at base, inside coated with 0.25in of loam. Diameter 7.86in empty, 7.875in full, the heat caused expansion. Filling hole

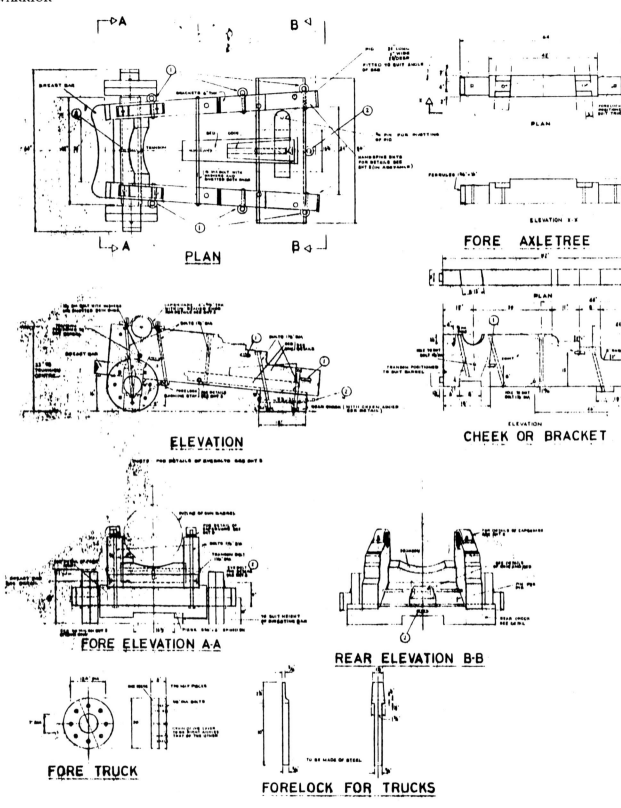

PLAN

FORE AXLETREE

CHEEK OR BRACKET

ELEVATION

FORE ELEVATION A·A

REAR ELEVATION B·B

FORE TRUCK

FORELOCK FOR TRUCKS

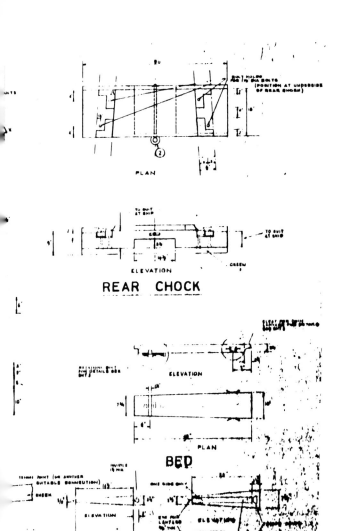

REAR CHOCK

BED

COINS

BREAST BAR

Constructional details and general arrangement of the 68pdr main deck carriage. The method used to reproduce these carriages was almost exactly the same as would have been used originally. *WPT*

Preponderance: 5cwt 1qtr 19lb.
Nominal length: 120in
Diameter of trunnions: 7in.
Diameter: maximum 16.438in, at muzzle 7.75in.
Width between trunnions: 17.875in. Outside trunnions 27.755in.
Bore: rifled. Diameter 4.75in across the lands, Length of bore 106.375in, of rifling 91.89. Powder chamber 13.5in, diameter 4.96in. Shot chamber 7in long.

Rifling: 56 grooves 0.06in deep 0.166in wide twist of 1 turn in 36½ calibres.
Breech screw: Single start square thread (changed to a buttress thread from January 1861) with a pitch of 0.9in.
Weight: 2cwt 1qtr 13lb.
Vent piece: weight 59lb.
Solid shot: 40lbs 13½oz to 41lbs 3oz. 10.28in to 10.3in long.
Common shell: 40½lbs filled 13.86 to 13.87in long, 2½lbs bursting charge.
Segment shell: 72 2.4oz segments, 13oz bursting charge, 39lbs filled weight.
Case shot: 37 8oz balls, weight 31½lbs. 10.15in long.

The only powder charge was the full or service charge, weight 5lbs, 10–10¾in long and 4.7–4.77in diameter. The leather cases were 6.75in diameter, 11.25in long and weighed 2lbs 4oz empty.

Range: shot or shell 3800yds at 10 degrees of elevation. In June 1863 Captain Cochrane requested that the 32cwt guns be exchanged for 35cwt pieces which had an improved breech. This gun used the same ammunition and produced the same ballistics. They were aboard by February 1864.

THE GUN CARRIAGES

The main deck guns aboard *Warrior* were mounted on a modified type of gun carriage, the rear chock type. These differed from the common practice of the wooden navy by replacing the two rear trucks (the small wooden wheels) with a large block of wood, the chock. To run the gun out a long handspike with a roller on the end had to be placed under the chock lifting loop, pivotted up and pushed.

These carriages had been copied from French patterns in use during the Crimean War and first issued for service aboard the Floating Batteries, although experimental types had been used before. They were found superior to the old rear truck pattern carriage in one vital area. When used with the most powerful guns, especially the new 32pdr of 58cwt the rear trucks cut into the deck of the wooden battleships, even 4in oak plank. This was because the new 32pdr had a reduced windage (the gap between the bore and the ball). This increased the violence of recoil, driving the edges of the truck across the deck. They cut into the surface very quickly. The 68pdr, which had yet to be mounted on the broadside would hardly be less damaging. The rear chock spread the load far better, having a greater friction surface and none of the sharp edges that the truck developed.

A further modification of the gun carriage came about because the Surveyor's Department wished to reduce the size of the gunports. In the past the gunport had been wide enough to allow the gun to train through an arc of 52 degrees (26 degrees each way). With a 68pdr gun this required a port some 3ft 10in wide. This was a large gap in the armour, therefore it was decided

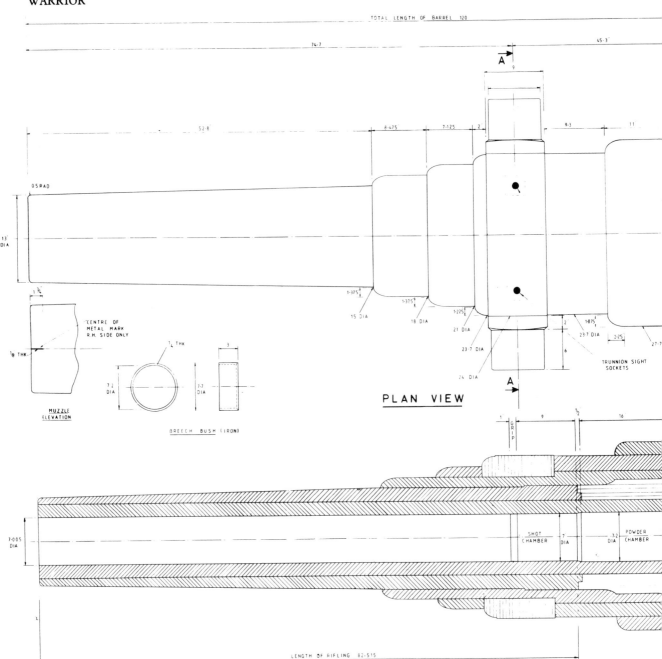

The 110pdr gun barrel, showing constructional details. *WPT*

PLAN VIEW

SECTIONAL ELEVATION

that the size of the port should be as small as possible. This was not taken until after *Warrior*'s ports had been built. If some method could be discovered to pivot the carriage near the sill the port could be made significantly smaller. The wide port was a legacy of the sailing age, when it was a substitute for manoeuverability. Steam warships did not need or use such extremes, primarily because they made the guns less effective.

The solution was the directing bar. This was a wood and iron bar that connected to a pivot bolt set in the lower sill of the gunport. The gun carriage was cut to slide along the bar, under recoil, keeping in line. When the gun carriage was handspiked over it pivotted about the fighting bolt in the lower sill, much further forward than it would have done otherwise. As a result a port only 2ft wide and 3ft 7¼in high could be used. *Warrior*'s ports were modified to this form using

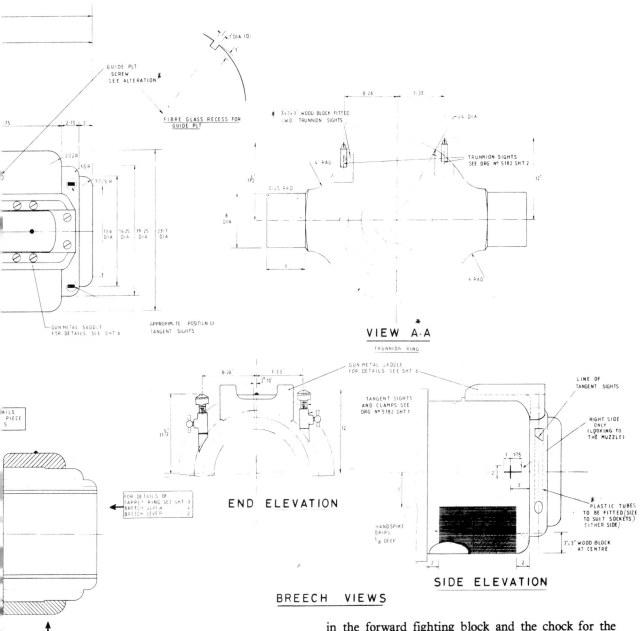

VIEW A-A

TRUNNION RING

END ELEVATION

BREECH VIEWS

SIDE ELEVATION

almost 9in of armour during her construction, causing some delay.

The design of the carriage and the assoicated gear was determined by a series of trails aboard HMS *Excellent* on 15 December 1860. The prototype installation had been built at the Royal Carriage Department. The trials resulted in some modifications, but the systems were ordered to be fitted aboard *Warrior* eight days before she was launched, using a modified carriage devised from the results of the trials.

The principle differences between the new carriage and the earlier rear chock type was the need to cut a slot in the forward fighting block and the chock for the directing bar. Provision was made for an elevating screw in addition to the normal wooden quoin, these were ordered to be fitted in 1862. The guns were fired flush with the ship's side, but being armoured there was no danger of fire.

Dimensions	68pdr	110pdr
Weight:	13½cwt 3qts	12½
Length, excluding breast bar:	77½in	64
Trunnion axis:	33in	35in
Diameter of trucks:	20in	
Maximum elevation:	15°	
Elevation for housing:	18°	20°
Maximum elevation with stool bed in place:	15°	

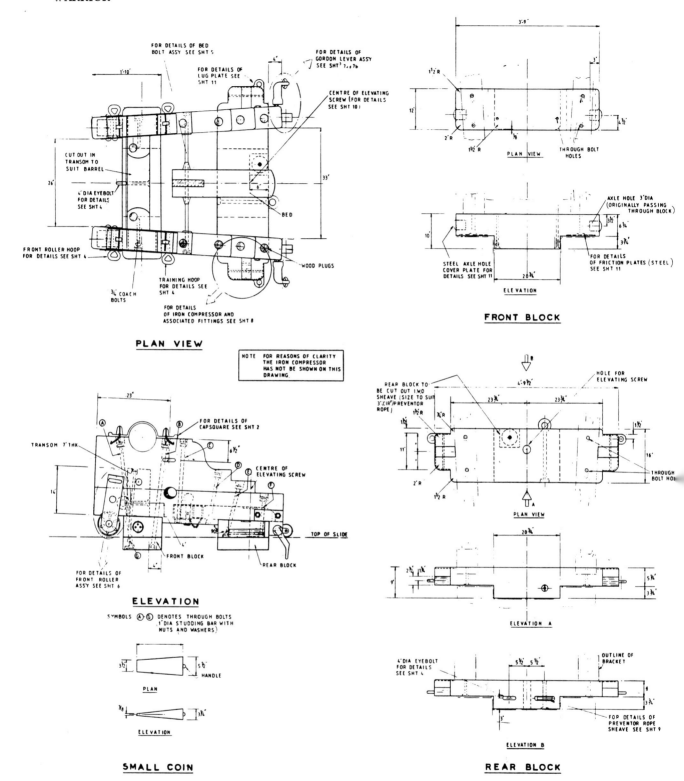

PLAN VIEW

FRONT BLOCK

ELEVATION

SYMBOLS (A)-(G) DENOTES THROUGH BOLTS
(1" DIA STUDDING BAR WITH
NUTS AND WASHERS)

PLAN

ELEVATION

SMALL COIN

REAR BLOCK

NOTE FOR REASONS OF CLARITY
THE IRON COMPRESSOR
HAS NOT BE SHOWN ON THIS
DRAWING.

With the large quoin this allowed between 1½° depression and 7° elevation. The small quoin gave 6° to 11° of elevation.

The gun ports had a lower still height of 18in, and an upper of 61¼in above the waterway. This would allow no more than 15° of elevation and 7° of depression, on the maindeck. Even in the design of such details there is irrefutable evidence of the frigate concept that lay behind *Warrior* and further links with *Mersey*. *Warrior*'s gunports were originally 42in square,

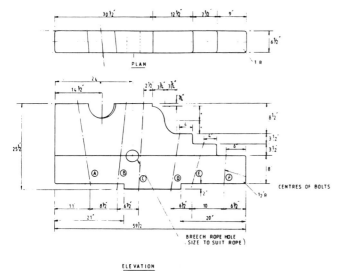

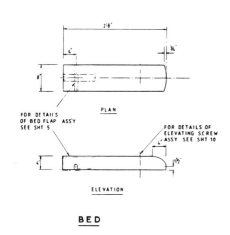

The upper deck sliding gun carriage for the 110pdr gun. *WPT*

although Walker had envisaged ports 46in square. *Mersey*'s were 44in deep.

Victoria's two lower gun decks were both 42in wide, and 33 or 35in deep. While *Warrior*'s ports were reduced to 24in wide by the new directing bar arrangement, they remained 43¼in deep. The purpose of this depth, 9–11in more than aboard *Victoria*, was solely to increase the elevation, and therefore the range, of the guns. *Victoria* was conceived by Walker for close range action in the line of battle, developing a massive concentration and volume of fire. *Mersey* had the opposite purpose of firing at long range. Her original armament had been envisaged as 50 68pdrs, but this was altered to include 10in shell guns, probably in imitation of the American *Merrimac*.

Warrior followed the pattern established by the heavy frigates. Her deep ports were not designed

casually, the concern to reduce width indicated a desire to minimise the exposure of unarmoured areas. Therefore the deep frigate ports were deliberately adopted by Walker as a part of his rationale for the ship. She was to fight at long range, avoiding the concentrated fire of wooden battleships.

Recoil was controlled by a 9in thick hawser passed through the cascabel loop and secured to 1⅝in breeching bolts on each side of the gun port. The gun muzzle was 44–48in inside the inner port sill when fully in. It was run out by side tackles, of 3in hemp rove through 10in blocks.

The directing bar was a substantial item, weighing about 5cwt with an iron hinge 3ft 9in long, as finally developed. The tail was 12–13in wide and the whole way 11ft long overall, enough to remain engaged with the carriage even when the gun was fully run in, the muzzle then being 7ft from the gunport.

A brass sweep plate or race was fitted under the trucks to allow the carriage to be traversed more easily, the trucks sliding on it, while the tail right forward was raised to lift the block off the deck to avoid it digging in.

The rear chock carriage with the directing bar was not an unqualified success. It added considerably to the physical effort required to traverse the gun. Further, when guns were fired with a considerable lee heel on the ship, it was found that the gun would often run out again before the slack in the tackle could be taken up. The carriage would then crash into the head block and shear off the fighting bolt or pivot. Also the whole arrangement required up to eight minutes to clear for action. Minor adjustments to training were equally troublesome.

Captain Cochrane and Gunnery Lieutenant Jackie Fisher proposed a solution to these problems – fitting the upper deck sliding carriage, suitably adapted to work from a strengthened fighting bolt, although these only allowed 12° of elevation as the trunnions were 2¼ inches higher. However *Warrior* only began to ship these mountings in 1864, and was paid off before they became universal. When rearmed an iron development of these mountings was installed to carry the heavier muzzle loading rifles.

The 110pdr main deck carriage was a modified version of that for the 68pdr. The major differences were that the breeching had to be run through the sides of the carriage in the absence of a cascabel loop and the whole structure had to be shorter to allow the breech mechanism to operate. Elevation was secured by a screw with a ratchet operated by a lever, but could not be used at extreme elevation.

The same pattern of directing bar was used. With the 110pdr it proved to be even less satisfactory. The breech loader was reloaded in the out position. Traversing the carriage was also awkward.

The two upper deck 110pdrs were mounted on sliding carriages with pivoting and revolving slides. These allowed the guns to be fought at a variety of ports at the bow and stern, and moved even in action.

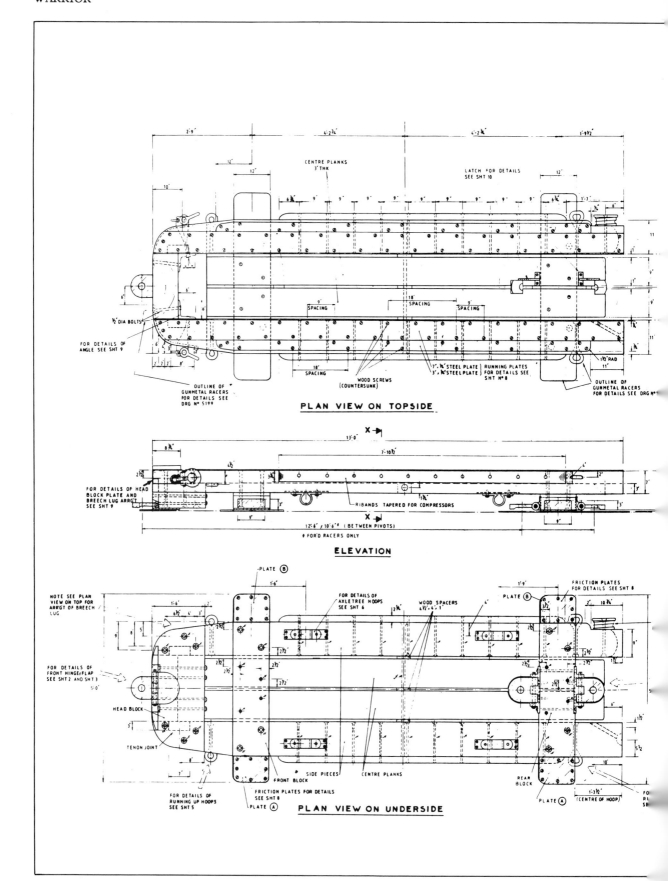

PLAN VIEW ON TOPSIDE

ELEVATION

PLAN VIEW ON UNDERSIDE

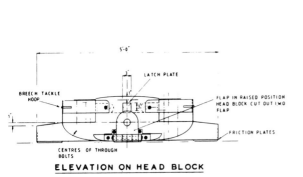

ELEVATION ON HEAD BLOCK

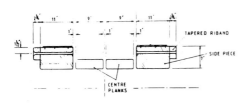

SECTION X-X

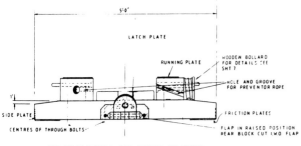

ELEVATION ON REAR BLOCK

The slide for the upper deck gun carriage. *WPT*

They had been developed for the early steamers, where a heavy bow fire was seen as a substitute for the reduced broadside caused by paddle wheels. As a result the type was far better developed than the main deck carriage with directing bar, introduced aboard *Warrior*.

In the effect the carriage was a main deck type with front and rear guide blocks substituted for the axles. These guide blocks spanned the slide, and the centres projected down into it, preventing any lateral movement. This was a control system for the recoil of the gun, essential to prevent the gun overturning under recoil, as the early carronades had done. Fore and aft movement was allowed by the rollers at the front and rear of the carriage. These could be lifted clear, at the rear, to allow the gun to house solidly. When the four rollers were down the gun was ready for use, and the recoil was arrested in the conventional manner by rope tackles, assisted by blocks outside the slide which worked on the friction principle. The carriage was different from the main deck type in weighing only 15cwt and having a length of only 64in.

Trunnion axles: 31in above the slide, 43in above the deck.

Elevation limits: Elevating screw in bed 4° depression to 6° elevation. As above but with the quoin inserted between the bed and the rear guide block, 1° to 11° depression. Elevating screw in rear guide book, 2° to 12° elevation. All the above elevation limits are approximate.

The 68pdr on a main deck carriage, showing the directing bar that pivotted on the fighting bolt on the gunport sill and allowed for a reduced gunport while retaining a significant arc of training. Note that the length allows the gun to recoil without becoming disengaged from the directing bar. A slot was cut into the base of the carriage and the rear chock to permit this. *WPT*

The 110pdr on the Upper Deck sliding carriage. *ERNEST SLAYMAKER*

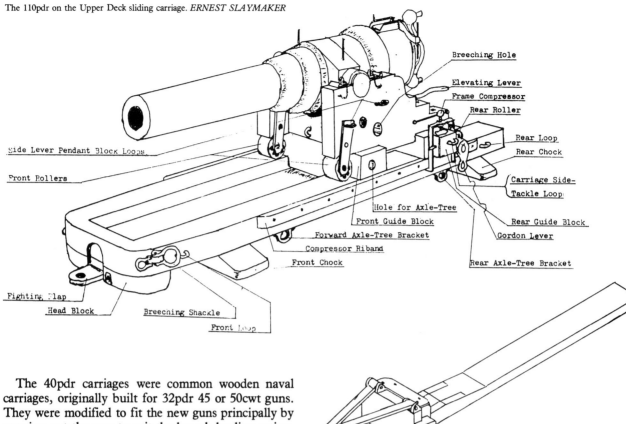

The 40pdr carriages were common wooden naval carriages, originally built for 32pdr 45 or 50cwt guns. They were modified to fit the new guns principally by opening out the rear to suit the breech loading action.

Weight: 8¼cwt

Rear of carriage to gun muzzle: 128½in

Trunnion axis: 32in.

Gun port sill: 12in

Maximum elevation with elevating screw: 4½° to 13°.

THE MAGAZINE

The structure of of *Warrior*'s magazines was typical of her wooden predecessors. It reflected long experience with gunpowder, the most dangerous substance aboard the ship. They were wooden structures built below the waterline; all internal fittings were of brass or wood, the only light that entered came through bull's eye glasses. The candle lamps were kept in a separate light chamber. No iron was allowed into the magazine, on account of the danger of a spark, and the men who worked inside were issued with felt slippers to walk on the lead-sheathed floor. In the event of fire the surrounding water tanks made it easy to flood. Here, in semi-darkness deep in the bowels of the ship, brave men, who did not suffer from claustrophobia, made up the gun charges. Ventilation was provided manually, using a special pump.

One improvement from the age of Nelson was to the

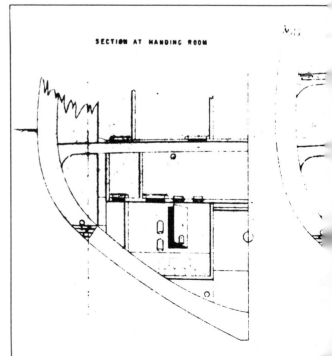

The later reinforced pattern of directing bar used aboard *Warrior* from 1863. *ERNEST SLAYMAKER*

SECTION AT HANDING ROOM

A section through the area of the magazine and handing up room, showing the special ventilating arrangements.

supply arrangement. Rather than sending the famous 'powder monkey' to run down to the magazine a hand-up system, based on French practice was fitted. The leather cartridge cases were filled in the magazine and handed out through a special 'Fearnought' canvas tube, again to avoid sparks. Beside the magazine was the hand-up area, from here the case was passed via the orlop and lower deck hand-up areas, to the main deck. The powder man would than take it to the guns. The charges for the upper deck guns and the main deck guns outside the armoured citadel were passed to the main deck and then through the armoured doors so the main deck did not remain sealed.

Modern systems for carrying ammunition from the magazine to the gun were no more than a mechanised version of this arrangement. Empty cases were dropped back to the lowest hand-up area via another canvas tube, and then back into the magazine. With four hand-up systems the two magazines were expected to keep up a supply of 60 charges per minute in action.

It is possible that a primitive signal telegraph operated by the gunnery officer on the main deck told the magazine crews which charges to load. The officer merely raised or lowered a rope, which was attached to a board carrying three panels of coloured glass set vertically. When the board moved across the beam of one of the lights, it interrupted it, signalling a change. A blue glass meant 'full' charges; a red glass 'reduced' charges while a plain glass with a large 'D' stood for 'distant' charges. If the indicator was hauled entirely clear of the bull's eye it meant 'cease fire'. In action this simple system avoided reliance on the human voice, and allowed the magazine to remain entirely sealed.

The ladder down into the handing up room, from the hatch on the lower deck. *DAVE MORRELL*

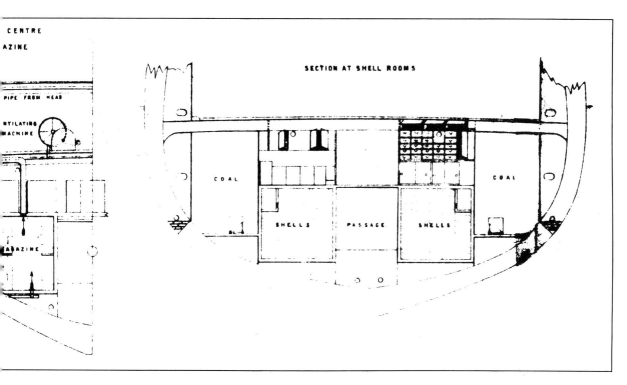

The after magazine door, before cleaning. Note the brass hinges and the low scuttle, this was used to return empty cartridges cases into the magazine, through a spark excluding canvas sack. *DAVE MORRELL*

The shelves of the aft magazine, before cleaning. Note the bull's eye glass. This would allow the magazine to be illuminated from the external light room, avoiding the need to have naked flames inside with the loose powder. *DAVE MORRELL*

Shot were stored in the iron garlands around the Main deck hatch coamings. Those were considered sufficient for any action. To replenish the garlands the crew had to open the central shot lockers, amidships abreast of the mainmast, and climb down. Bringing up each shot by hand was not an easy business. Shells were filled and fused in the shell rooms alongside the shot lockers. These were also set well below the waterline. They were hauled up to the guns by tackle when required. Red hot shot and later Martin's molten iron shells were brought up from the boiler room on special iron bearers carried by two men. Any attempt to fire full broadsides of these lethal projectiles would have been fraught with danger as large numbers of men ascended steep ladders with heavy and very hot shells. Perhaps this goes a long way towards explaining why they went out of favour so soon.

SMALL ARMS

When *Warrior* entered service small arms were still thought of as having an important place in naval battle, specifically in boarding. Cutlass drill accordingly formed a major part of naval life. The small arms aboard *Warrior* were rifles, revolvers, cutlasses and tomahawks. The 370 rifles were the Enfield 1858 pattern sea service muzzle-loading rifles of 0.577 calibre. This was an effective and accurate weapon, later much favoured by both sides in the American Civil War. They were noticeably shorter than the Army pattern, because service in boats made long barrelled muzzle loaders impractical. The 72 pistols appear to have been Colt's 0.36 calibre six shot revolvers of the 1851 Navy pattern. These were withdrawn from service in 1860, but the surviving pistols racks aboard *Warrior* are a perfect fit for this weapon. Therefore she might well have been the least major warship to be fitted with them. Cutlasses and tomahawks were of the standard type. The Marines were equipped with the curious yataghan bladed bayonets adopted by the French some years before, while the seamen's rifles had cutlass bayonets. A further distinction between Marines and seamens rifles lay in the finish of the sling: the 68 Marine rifles, white, seamen's rifles tan.

Although intended for shipboard use these small

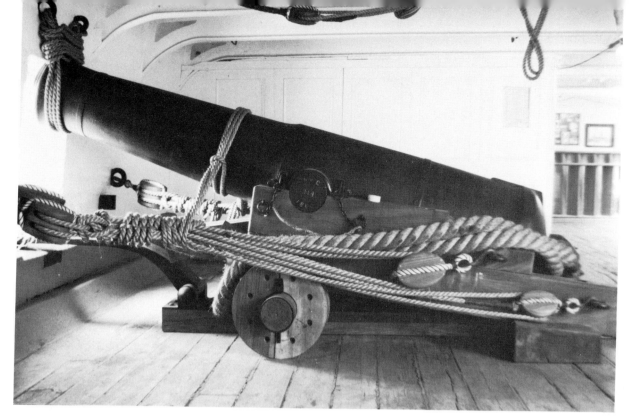

arms saw far more service off the ship in the Victorian period, either from boats in restricted waters or on land, assisting the army. British sailors and Marines served in every land campaign of the nineteenth century, especially as artillery men. Their activities in the Crimean War and Indian Mutinies were the stuff of legend. Even in the Boer War the Army relied on the heavy guns and ingenuity of the Navy.

As she never served outside home waters *Warrior*'s crew did not use their small arms. The ship took part in no wars, and she never fired any of her guns in anger. The enemy she was built against was, in the modern language, 'deterred' and would not risk war.

RESTORING THE ARMAMENT

Long before *Warrior* passed into the oblivion of harbour service her original armament had been removed. All trace of the 68 and 110pdrs was removed during the 1864–7 refit and larger weapons were installed. Having decided to restore the ship to her condition on entering service, it was necessary to replace an armament that was last aboard the ship 115 years before. This turned out to be no easy task, for a variety of reasons.

The guns originally fitted were transitional weapons. The 68pdr being the last of the old type was uncommon. The 110, being the largest example of an experiment that failed, was especially scarce. Few 110pdrs were made, and the chance of any surviving into the 1980s were slim. Initially the idea was to build up replicas in glassfibre from original drawings, as all the 'experts' consulted declared that no examples of either weapon were still in existence. Fortunately this advice proved to be incorrect, but only just, and both

The 68pdr housed for sea. *Warrior* was among the last capital ships to secure her main armament in this manner. *WPT*

The 110pdr gun as found at the foot of the War Memorial at St Helier in Jersey. It is the right hand gun, and is mounted on an army coast defence carriage. It bears a number from the sequence known to have been aboard *Warrior*, and might have been one of her original guns, before being turned over to the Army for coast defence. *WPT*

weapons were located by the project. Roderick Stewart had the same experience with the guns he required for the *Unicorn*, hence his advice to the team to keep looking.

Although more than 2000 68pdrs were cast between 1853 and 1861, none were on display. When an example did turn up it lay outside at the Woolwich Rotunda Artillery Museum unrecognised among a number of the slightly smaller 32pdrs. The gun had no

One of the four 40pdr gun carriages being built during the early months of 1986. Again traditional working methods were best suited to such a small production run. *WPT*

New gunport lids lying on the dockside, ready to be installed. The scuttle port in the centre was to provide some natural light on the main deck. *Author*

proof markings, indicating that it had never been issued for service, probably because of a structural flaw in the casting. The Rotunda very generously lent the gun to the project in January 1983. Once it had been cleaned and measured it was used to make a mould for the production of glassfibre replicas, each of which had been given a serial number and proof markings. The local firm of E&F Plastics, less than half a mile from the ship, then took over the production of the 26 guns required for the main deck. Recent improvements in glassfibre technology ensured that they are all but indistinguishable from the original, although far lighter. By mid-1983 one gun, aboard a prototype carriage and with all the necessary equipment for service, had been installed on the main deck. This helped to make the ship more comprehensible to visitors.

The 110pdr was far rarer than the 68pdr, and because of its complex built-up shape offered a greater challenge for replication. Fortunately an example in perfect condition was located in Jersey, bearing a serial number from the sequence known to have been aboard *Warrior*, mounted at the foot of the War Memorial in St Helier on a coast defence carriage. Following the visit by Project Manager Bill Stevenson and Draughtsman Keith Johnson the gun was made available to the SPT by the generosity of the States of Jersey. The gun arrived in Hartlepool in December 1983 despite being detained for a firearms licence. After cleaning and measuring, the moulds were made for working replicas, in which the breech mechanism could be operated, albeit without the precision of the original. E&F Plastics carried out this task with equal success. By later 1984 some of the ten replica guns were aboard *Warrior*, displayed on the main deck. After opening the breech and lifting out the vent piece it is possible to look along the barrel, and see the rifling. Clearly the original gun was in excellent condition, the barrel having been sealed.

One of these guns, mounted on a main deck carriage was sent to Portsmouth in August 1985. Positioned just inside the *Victory* gate of the Dockyard it replaced the figurehead as a taste of what was to come. Visitors to the other attractions of the Dockyard, *Mary Rose*, *Victory* and the Museum had to walk past the gun. The curiosity of small boys made it necessary to seal the breech mechanism, and close the muzzle, which many felt made an excellent litter bin. It was also used to help a local fund-raising effort to provide the cost of the gun, some £3000, and prepared and 18-man crew for demonstration, once *Warrior* reached Portsmouth.

The gun carriages were even more unusual. Only the first half dozen ironclads ever used the main deck type with rear chock and directing bar. Here there was no realistic chance of such a carriage having survived. Furthermore there appeared to be little concrete evidence as to the exact design. The need for accuracy was reinforced by the special design of the gunports:

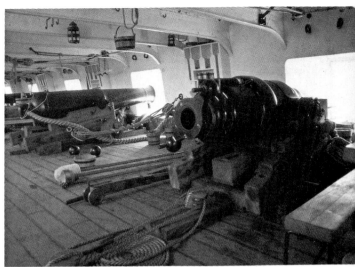

The gundeck of *Warrior* with a 110pdr and several 68pdrs. *WPT*

A mock-up of the main deck gunport lid, complete with the lifting chains. The lid, 1in thick and intended to be bulletproof, was raised by a block and tackle over the relevant gunport, what happened if the chains were broken is uncertain. *WPT*

only the proper carriages would provide the correct elevation, depression and traverse. After a major research effort the final figures for the all-important trunnion height were confirmed by the accurate scale section of *Warrior* found among the papers of her first Captain in Northern Ireland. After an experimental carriage had been built, providing interesting parallels with the original development of the type back in 1860, the 26 68pdr main deck carriages were put into production. The eight 110pdr main deck mountings were built later, being of a modified design. Although a few minor compromises were made, to ease the construction, the design drawings were very close to the original. Each carriage absorbed best elm costing £600, along with specially commissioned iron fittings and a great deal of labour by the shipwrights and joiners of the project. Apart from the use the power tools, notably woodworking machinery, they were assembled much as the originals had been, even down to the final rubdown with linseed oil.

These carriages, along with the mess furniture provided an excellent alternative to work on the upper deck during the worse of the North Eastern weather. However, once a few had been made, they did turn into a rather mundane 'production line' task losing the 'unique' feel that so much of the work aboard *Warrior* achieved. The upper deck sliding carriages, with the pivoted slides, and the 40pdr mountings, were all left until the deck had been completed. Each of the 110pdr mountings would have to be hand fitted to the exact shape and requirements of the finished deck. Once that had been done the sweep plates and racers would have to be laid where the carriage pivoted about the deck. The 40pdrs were a smaller task, and as a result did not get a high priority. It is hoped that at least one original gun will be obtained, if only to provide an accurate demonstration of how the breech system worked. All the research data required for these items was assembled, and the 110pdr mountings were produced during the winter of 1985–6, ready to be installed in the following spring.

When considering the armament of a ship, even one so basic as *Warrior*, it is essential to recall that guns alone do not make up an armament. Without the rope tackles to control their recoil and fire them, the ram rods and sponges needed to reload and clean, the sights, hammers, ammunition and even the primitive fire control arrangements, the guns would be no more than an interesting decoration. A ship's armament is a complete system.

Some of these items were relatively simple to reconstruct. The ramrods, sponges, worms, shot and shell, powder cases and blocks could all be turned over to the Cleveland Combined Churches Unemployment Programme for series reproduction. However, every single item had to be researched and redrawn before this could happen, just like the guns.

Other items required much thought. The ropework of the gun mountings will appear to the casual observer to be perfectly normal. This is not the case. All the rope used for Royal Navy tackle was specially made with a left-hand lay, the individual strands being laid up anticlockwise. Almost all rope is laid up right-handed, as are the fibres in the strands but left-handed rope was more pliable and was considered best for gun tackle. However the Navy noted that rope laid up in the same direction as the strands would soak up water more easily. Water-soaked ropes quickly became weakened, and when they were expected to control a six ton gun recoiling across the crowded deck this was a matter of no small concern. With a left-hand lay the rope was more durable. Period photographs all corroborated the evidence of Nares' *Seamanship* of 1862 on this point, once they had been printed properly (some of them had been reversed, which made the rope appear to be right handed). Once the desired rope had been acquired specialist riggers were taken onto the staff to fit the miles of tackle needed to complete the main deck.

The sights and hammers fitted to the guns were also transitional fittings, developed aboard HMS *Excellent* to meet the demands of the new, more scientific, gunnery. Replication involved detailed research, model making and even some calculation of the elevation required for longer ranges. These had to be marked on the rear sight along with the different charges, distant, full and reduced. The theme of early advances in modern gunnery was carried further by the fitting of concentration of fire lines and symbols on the deck head. Rather than firing a broadside at right angles to the side of the ship *Warrior* was equipped to train all her guns to strike the same point at a variety of ranges. This new development reflected the need to secure repeated impacts in order to penetrate armour. Previously gunfire had been intended to disable the crew, which could be best accomplished by striking every part of the battery deck. With ironclads penetration required more effort, hence the concentration. The combination of hooks and lines, with the directing bar underneath the gun carriage, made this type of fire a practical proposition aboard *Warrior*. Furthermore it also demonstrated the new tactical mobility offered by steam. A ship could now manoeuvre into position to attack the weakest point of the enemy, normally the unarmed stern.

Heavy wrought iron bars over the gun bay allowed the crew to dismantle the armament and remove it to the upper deck without the assistance of a dock. Several of these dismantling bars were missing when *Warrior* reached Hartlepool. They were replaced by new fabrications made using an original bar as a pattern.

The other major element of the armament, the ammunition supply, involved work lower down in the ship. Due to the nature of the project this was put off until the upper and main decks had been completed. On the lower and orlop decks the after hand-up areas had long been demolished, the whole forward magazine and associated gear had disappeared from the ship. The after hand-up areas left much evidence behind to indicate their exact dimensions, primarily in the form of bulkhead shadows on the deck and deck head. The lowest hand-up area and the after magazines, separated by the propeller shaft, were still intact. However they were flooded, by rain water not seawater. Being inaccessible and of no value for storage, the area had been ignored. As hanging magazines these structures had no

facility for draining, only for getting water in via the water tanks that separated them from the ship's sides. Once emptied of water and allowed to dry out they proved to be amazingly complete. Cleaning such awkward spaces was not easy, but making them accessible for display purposes will be far more difficult. Having been built as small secure working spaces for a few men they will perhaps be best left for special inspection. The long-lost forward magazine lies directly in the path of the public access to the boiler room. It might therefore prove possible to build a replica around the steps leading down, making the ammunition supply comprehensible to all at a glance. This access requirement has also prevented the cupola used to prepare the molten iron for Martin's shells from being replaced where it stood, between the two foremost boilers on the centre line. The paying public will be walking right underneath the site.

Replication of *Warrior*'s substantial outfit of small arms has been much simpler than that of her main armament. The short sea service Enfield rifle and the Colt Navy revolver were both widely used in the American Civil War and have been reproduced for the enormous number of black powder shooting enthusiasts across the Atlantic. The rifle is made in England by Parker Hale of Birmingham. However demand is so great and outside suppliers so problematic that in late 1985 the *Warrior* team were quoted two years delivery on the final batch. Several cutlasses, and both yataghan- and cutlass-bladed bayonets have been bought or lent by the Tower of London Armouries. Further cutlass have been obtained, new, from India. Only the tomahawks, or boarding axes, have had to be reproduced; they were made by a Hartlepool blacksmith and finished by the CCCUP. Associated with the small arms are the racks they were stored in. The rifles were kept on the main and lower deck in special racks. These were reproduced by the project joiners from information in later photographs and period drawings. The pistols were kept in individual racks, one over each gun bay and in a large wheel arrangement on the after deck. Both have been made again by the CCCUP, the former from an original found still in place, the latter from available information.

The exact location of the main armament, the light guns, small arms and even the war rockets was a matter of the profoundest concern. None of the basic texts concerning *Warrior* gave any reliable information. Fortunately during her first commission one of *Warrior*'s midshipmen, Henry Murray, prepared sketch plans of her decks showing the location of all these items, along with many others. These plans, of which two copies were eventually located, proved an invaluable aid to restoration. Without them much would have had to be left to conjecture, which as the earlier works on *Warrior* demonstrate, cannot be accurate, and often ignores awkward questions.

CHAPTER SIX
Machinery

The marine steam engine was the first of the great products of the Industrial Revolution that changed the nature of seapower. At first the the only method of using steam, the paddle wheel, had precluded the introduction of steam into the largest classes. Battleships and heavy frigates, primarily intended for combat, could not afford to sacrifice large areas of their broadsides to paddle wheels. The successful introduction of the screw propellor by Francis Petit Smith, aboard the aptly-named *Archimedes*, promised to solve this problem. Firstly, the screw did not take up any space on the broadside. Secondly, it allowed the entire propulsion system to be placed below the waterline. This provided a large measure of safety from the effects of gunfire. Even where the engines and boilers of a well-designed paddle steamer, such as Captain Sir Charles Napier's *Sidon* of 1846, were below the waterline, the paddle wheels and their propelling shaft were still dangerously exposed to gunfire. With a modicum of good design, no part of a screw ship's machinery needed to be so exposed.

Early marine steam engines were arranged in the same upright form as their land-based predecessors. As a result they were tall and had vertical connecting rods acting directly on the paddle shaft. For a screw steamer the whole structure had to be turned on its side and made more compact, so as to fit in the lower portion of the hull. This would allow the crankshaft to transmit power directly to the propeller shaft. The first attempt at such engines, basically simple conversions of paddle wheel machinery, were not very effective. However by 1851 the work of John Penn & Sons and Maudslay, Son & Field, both based on the Thames, had made the marine steam engine sufficiently powerful and reliable for universal naval service. The age of the sailing warship ended just before the Russian War could prove the point. The success of machinery built by the two London companies during the Russian War ensured that while Walker remained in office no large new ships were fitted with engines by any other firm. The war had emphasised that steam would be essential in all future naval conflicts.

The French had been the pioneers in this area. In the mid-1840s the Prince de Joinville had argued that a steam navy would allow France to challenge Britain, by rendering obsolete her superior reserves of sailing ships and seamen. Furthermore and French view of naval war was dominated by the demands of the Western Mediterranean and English Channel, where long range was unimportant. In consequence they made the shift to steam warships, leaving Britain to follow suit. From 1850 all French warships were designed with sails only as an auxilliary to steam. Britain, with her world-wide commitments, could not follow this bold step. Walker's policy was to shift the emphasis gradually from steam as an auxilliary to sail to something approaching equality. This process was complete by the late 1850s, reflecting a combination of technical development and seagoing experience. *Warrior* was among the first, if not *the* first, ship to give steam the dominant role, even though sail remained a vital element in the design.

As *Warrior* was intended to select the range at which she fought, rather than being tied to the line of battle, the engines were vital to the success of the concept. *Warrior* was a fast frigate, with armour. The requirement for 13.5 knots, in view of the limited power available from contemporary machinery, forced the adoption of a very long and fine hull. It also called for the largest set of engines yet built. Having taken those major steps forward the cautious conservatism of the Surveyor's Department took over.

Walker specified the unheard-of speed of 13.5kt for two clear reasons. Firstly, *Warrior* was a frigate and had to avoid being brought to action by a fleet of wooden ships. Secondly, in the long term speed would keep her in front line service. Having ordered a very expensive ship he was determined that she would not be rendered rapidly obsolete. If future ships were much faster *Warrior* would be relegated to harbour duties. Both objects were achieved. They form another facet in the design limitations that help to explain why *Warrior* was built in the form finally adopted.

The engines selected were the twin cylinder horizontal single expansion trunk engines designed and

A model of the trunk engines fitted to the *Northumberland*. In a trunk engine the connecting rod is attached directly to the piston, as in an internal combustion engine. This saves the space otherwise taken up by a piston rod. The single trunk engine was patented by James Watt in 1784, but the double trunk type, which equalised pressure on either side of the piston, and thus allowed for horizontal working, were patented by John Penn in 1845. This design was used extensively for screw propulsion up to the early 1870s.

The *Northumberland* engines represented were generally identical to those of *Warrior*, although slightly larger internally, and worked with steam at up to 25lbs per square inch, unlike the *Warrior*'s which used only 20. *SCIENCE MUSEUM*

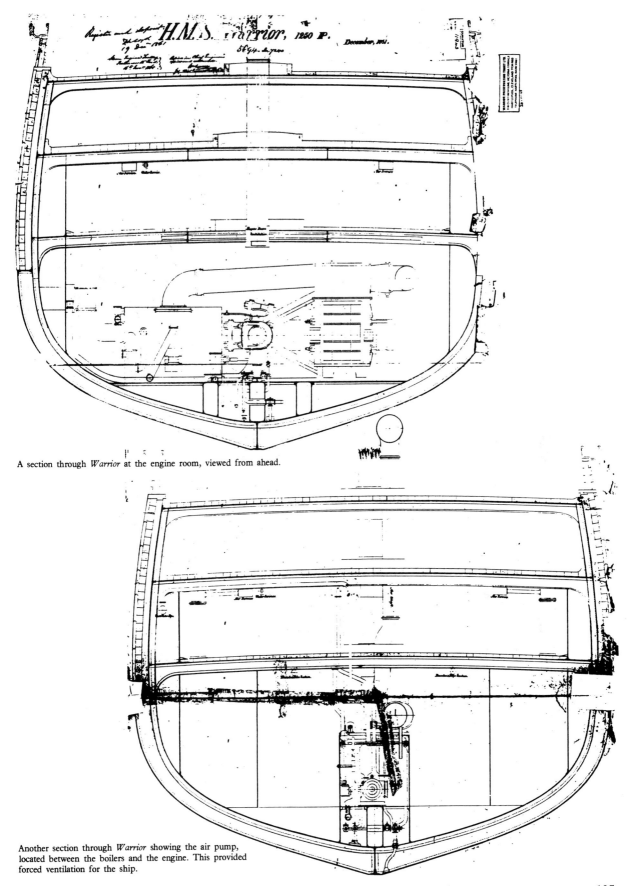

A section through *Warrior* at the engine room, viewed from ahead.

Another section through *Warrior* showing the air pump, located between the boilers and the engine. This provided forced ventilation for the ship.

A model of the boiler room aboard HMS *Thunderer*, showing the damage caused by an explosion while running trials, in July 1876. The boilers of this ship were generally similar to those of *Warrior*, especially after she had been reboilered in 1871. The accident aboard *Thunderer* was caused by a faulty safety valve. This view shows the internal layout of the boiler, a multi-tubular box type.

built by Penn's. During the previous fifteen years the machinery Penn fitted to such ships as the frigate *Arrogant* and the pioneer steam battleship *Agamemnon* had built the firm an unequalled reputation for sound design, quality workmanship, reliability and performance. The 1859 Committee on Marine Steam Engines declared that Penn's Trunk engine was the best type for high power installations, despite their higher cost. This opinion was no more than a reflection of the Surveyor's view. Prior to constructing the engines for *Warrior* the largest installations yet built had been the 1000 nominal horse power (nhp, a measure of power based on the bore and stroke of the engine; by 1859 this was only $\frac{1}{4}$ the shaft horse power) engines for the frigate *Orlando* and the three-decker *Howe*. Both used eight boilers to generate steam at 20–22lb per square inch, working the engines at 50–56 rpm. *Warrior*'s engines were merely

an enlarged version of these engines, which themselves were not technically different from those built ten years before. The new engines were rated at 1250nhp. Two more boilers were added, primarily to provide 11kt cruising speed from the six boilers in the after boiler room. Bunker capacity was fixed at 850 tons, exactly the same as *Orlando*, reflecting the frigate emphasis in the design.

The specification called for a speed of 13½ knots under steam alone. A combination of good lines and efficient engines allowed *Warrior* to exceed this figure. Her sister, *Black Prince*, was never as fast, either under steam or sail. In reaching 14.3kts, after her funnels had been raised by 6ft in 1863, to improve the draught to the boilers, *Warrior* set the standard for all future ironclads. It was not significantly surpassed for nearly fifteen years, when new machinery designs entered service. The era of the single expansion engines lasted until 1870, and Penn's received two-thirds of all machinery contracts for the large ironclads. *Warrior's* success must have played a large part in the new Controller deciding to follow Walker's policy.

Warrior's steam plant worked on the same lines as all its predecessors. The ten rectangular hearth box boilers generated steam. This worked the cylinders, driving the crankshaft. After leaving the cylinders the steam was passed through the jet condenser and then returned, as water, to the boilers. To avoid undue wear on the trunks the engine was worked left-handed. This directed the push and pull of the pistons onto the upper surfaces of the cylinder, away from the lower bearing area. Expansion gear was fitted, to allow the inflow of steam to be cut off at any point, usually $\frac{5}{8}$ of the stroke. While this offered a measure of economy the gear was not satisfactory in early trials, and was removed.

The weak point of the system was the boiler design. They were started up with fresh feed water, but the jet condenser cooled the steam leaving the cylinders with a spray of seawater before returning it to the boilers. The excess water that built up as a result was regularly pumped overboard. However the salt levels rose during sustained steaming, rapidly scaling up the boilers. This reduced their efficiency and occasionally fouled the safety valve. This occurred aboard the *Thunderer* in 1876, with fatal results. Damage to the fire tubes, caused by salt water, ensured that reboilering was a regular and expensive task for the Dockyards. Several of *Warrior's* wooden hulled contemporaries were laid up with defective boilers and left to rot because the Admiralty would not spend the necessary money on them. Most had served only one, three year, commission. In an attempt to mitigate the dangers the salinity of the boilers was regularly checked with a hydrometer. The Bowden steam pressure gauges were backed up the more primitive alternative of a 3ft long 1½in diameter U-tube filled with mercury. However the concern was more that the boilers might collapse when blown down, rather than burst. The reinforcement was designed accordingly.

Despite Penn's reputation for excellence the engines of the period were by no means perfect. Penn built the best engines, but they were not inherently reliable. Both *Warrior* and *Black Prince* suffered from cracked cylinder covers. Maintenance was a regular chore, and when steaming the engineers were kept busy attempting to lubricate as many of the bearing surfaces as possible. Breakdowns were not infrequent. With only one propeller there was always the potential for the ship to be completely disabled. As a result this imperfect and uneconomic system was not trusted to propel *Warrior* at all times. A full sailing rig was fitted,

The stern aperture of *Warrior*, showing the ladder that would have been used by the man sent down to lock the propellor in the upright position before it could be hoisted up into the ship. *DAVE MORRELL*

One of the original coal trolleys found in the port side bunker. Note the open side, which would have been fitted with a door. This saved the stokers the extra labour of shovelling the coal out of the trolley. *AUTHOR'S COLLECTION*

and the propeller was, like that on all her wooden predecessors, arranged for lifting. As the bronze two bladed 10 ton screw was mounted between double stern posts in a special banjo frame it could be disconnected and hauled out of the water. This was no easy task. Once the engines had been locked in place the screw would be wedged into the lifting position and the connecting tongue that fixed it to the propeller shaft removed. A pair of sheers had to be rigged over the circular lifting well that ran right up the quarter deck, and some 600 men then hauled on two 8in ropes to lift the screw into the ship or onto the quarter deck. As a safety precaution the banjo frame clicked past a series of ratchets as it came up. The whole structure of frame and screw weighed 35 tons. Little wonder that the

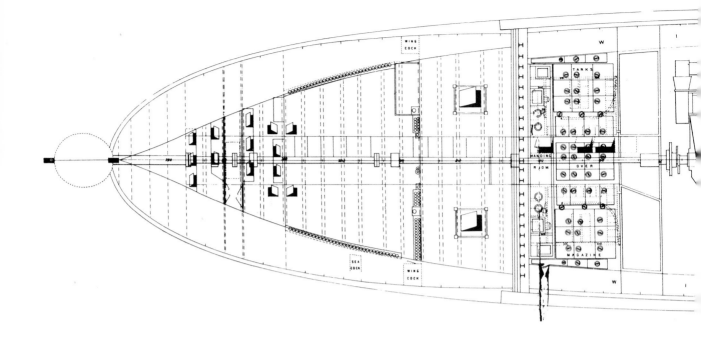

operation was only carried out at anchor or hove to. If the screw were badly damaged there was a replacement blade which could be fitted by the ships' company without dockyard help.

Hoisting the propeller clear of the sea had a marked effect on the ship's performance under sail. The drag of a 24ft diameter propeller would spoil the performance of any ship, even with as fine a model as *Warrior*. The sluggish sailing of the fixed propeller *Minotaur*s, which were even finer than *Warrior*, was clear proof of this point. However there were drawbacks. If the engines were reversed the thrust was placed on the weak rudder post. Should the screw be kept up for too long the cheese head connection would become fouled with marine growths and refuse to reconnect with propeller. Some of the wooden hulled ironclads sent out to the Pacific suffered this affliction. Finally the hoisting arrangement added to the cost of the ship. It did not survive long in the ironclad fleet. *Warrior* rarely hoisted her screw. Being a squadron ship she required steam for safe manoeuvring. It was simpler to keep the propeller turning under easy steam while relying on sail for propulsion. As a result it was only hoisted for sailing trials, which gave her an unfair advantage over late ships not so fitted. While smaller cruising ships kept this feature for another twenty years only a handful of ironclads were to follow *Warrior*. Despite the opinion of Parkes to the contrary *Black Prince* had a hoisting screw, along with *Achilles*, *Defence* and *Resistance*, the seven ex-wooden two deckers, the curiosity *Penelope* and the later overseas flagships *Triumph* and *Swiftsure*.

As the steam engine came of age such contrivances made little sense, especially for ships that spent their careers in the Channel or Mediterranean Fleets. The French never adopted the hoisting screw for battleships. Their pioneer steam battleship *Le Napoleon* did not have one, and neither did *Gloire*. Steam was paramount in the French service, where range was less important.

To parallel the hoisting screw *Warrior*'s two funnels were telescopic. They would be lowered when the propeller was raised, to reduce wind resistance, and keep them out of the way of the sails. They were of little use and passed into oblivion with their underwater counterpart. The expression 'Down Funnel – Up Screw' remained as an exaggerated symbol of the conservatism of the age.

THE MACHINERY

Cylinders

Number: 2
Diameter: 112⅛in. Minus trunk = 104⅝in effective diameter.
Stroke: 48in
Maximum revolutions per minute: 56 (Average 51–4)
Piston speed: 434ft per minute
Indicated horse power (ihp): 5269
Nominal horse power (nhp): 1250

Auxiliary engine

Steam-driven air pump for the ventilation system, also

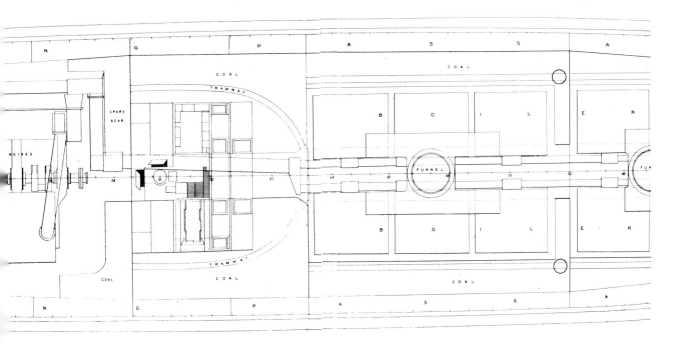

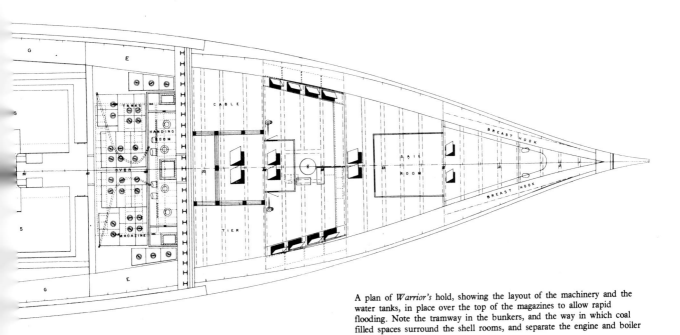

A plan of *Warrior's* hold, showing the layout of the machinery and the water tanks, in place over the top of the magazines to allow rapid flooding. Note the tramway in the bunkers, and the way in which coal filled spaces surround the shell rooms, and separate the engine and boiler rooms.

driving two boiler feed pumps, ash hoists and bilge pumps. All other machinery on board was hand-powered.

Boilers

Heating surface: 22,469sq ft
Pressure: 20–21psi
Vacuum: 25–26½ mxHg average, depending on ambient temperature

Weights

Machinery and boilers with water at working height: 898 tons
Engines, main and auxiliary: 422 Main 226
Boilers, water at working height: 477 tons
Water in each boiler: 17.114 tons

Indicated Horse Power per ton

Engines: 23.3 main engine

Boilers: 11.0
Water in boilers: 30.8

Temperature
Engine room: 104 max, 85–92 average
Stokehold: 126 max, 98–113 average

Propeller
Diameter: 24ft 6in
Pitch: 27ft 8⅜in
Blades: 2
Length: 5ft 6in

The pitch of the propeller blades could be adjusted between 25ft and 32ft, when the propeller was lifted. This was a manual task, unlike the modern controllable pitch propeller.

Propeller efficiency has been calculated using modern techniques to be in the region of 80%.

At full power *Warrior* would have burnt between 3¾ and 5lb of coal an hour for each indicated horse power, that is, up to 25,000lb per hour.

The safety valves on the boilers were of the simple 'deadweight' type, set at 22 psi. The boilers were the box tubular type, the furnaces and tube plates were required by contract to be built of iron from the Low Moor or Bowling companies. The 440 firetubes were brass, and it was specified that every part of the boiler was to be in contact with the water or steam. The total fire grate area was 900sq ft.

The contract further specified that the piston packing rings were to be metal, and that no hemp or similar material should be required. This is an important indication of the improving engineering tolerances that could be achieved. Only a decade before such a stipulation would have been unthinkable. The engines were built of cast and wrought iron, gunmetal (a mixture of nine or ten parts of bronze with one of brass) and Muntz and white metal for smaller parts and bearings. The cylinders were insulated with a wooden jacket to cut down the power loss caused by the large surface areas of the trunks, which reduced the steam temperature, and therefore the pressure. The most significant trials were those carried out on the Stoke's Bay measured mile off Portsmouth. The depth of water, some 100ft, would be perfectly adequate for a ship of *Warrior*'s size and speed, needing no depth correction. All the trials were carried out within days of leaving drydock, which ensured that the hull would be clean. In the 1861 series a fresh coat of Hay's Anti-Fouling paint had been applied. Even though this was of little value, only slime could develop inside a week.

Warrior was always a faster ship than *Black Prince*, despite their engines built by the same firm, and to the same specification. In the era of hand-finished engineering this was not surprising. While the hulls would have been marginally different, explaining why *Warrior* was also faster under sail, the main difference lay in the engines. The set fitted to *Black Prince* must

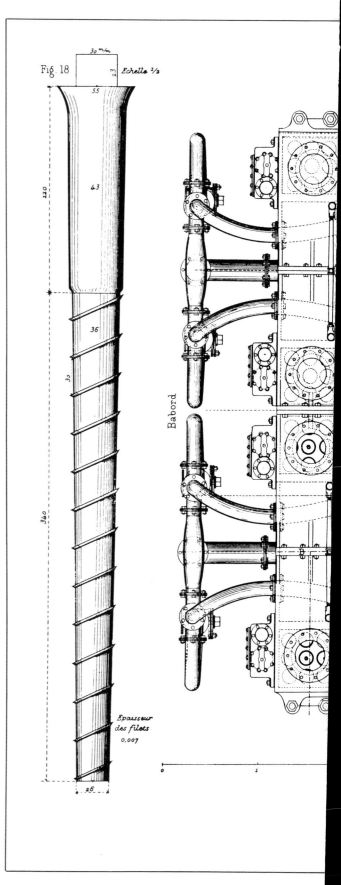

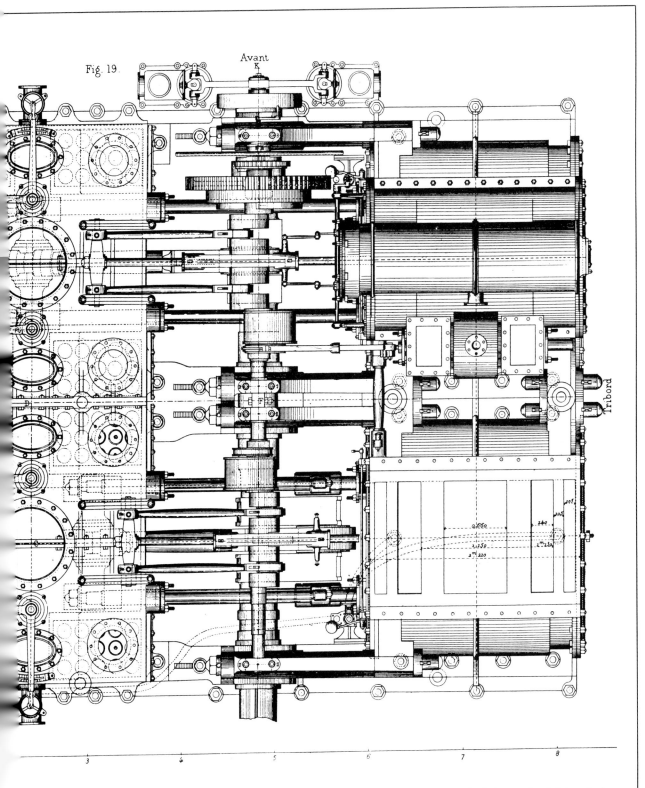

Fig. 19.

Avant
K

Tribord

The engines of *Gloire*, from overhead; the propeller shaft is at the lower edge. These engines were of the horizontal return connecting rod type (HRCR) similar to those of Penn's great rival, Maudslay, Son & Field. Also included is a detail of the French system of collapsible funnel, which was quite unlike that used by the Royal Navy. *PARIS*

Results of Trials

When tried	19.09.1861	17.10.1861	25.10.1861	25.10.1861
Where tried	Stoke's Bay	Stoke's Bay	Stoke's Bay	Stoke's Bay
Nominal horse power	1250	1250	1250	1250
Maker's name	Penn	Penn	Penn	Penn
Draught of water:				
Forward	25ft 11½in	25ft 6in	25ft 6in	25ft 6in
Aft	26ft 1½in	26ft 5in	26ft 5in	26.5in
Load on safety valve	20lbs	22lbs about	22lbs	22lbs supposed to be
Pressure of steam in boilers	12–15lb	22lb about	18½ to 21lb	20–21lb
Vacuum in condensors:				
Forward	26in	25in	26–27in	28in
Aft	26in	25in	25–26½in	27in
No of revolutions of Engines:				
Maximum	49	55	45	38
Mean	46	54½	44½	38
Mean pressure in cylinders	22.11	24.37lb	15.575lb	12.65lb
Indicated horse power	4389.4	5471.4	2868.40	1988.80
Speed of vessel	not taken	14.354kt	12.17kt	11.04kt
Weather barometer	30.25	30.35in	30.210in	30.210
Winds:				
Force	3 to 6	no 2	Calm	Calm
Direction	Off the bow	On port bow running up		
State of the sea	smooth at starting	smooth	smooth	smooth
State of masts, yards etc	complete	rigged	rigged	rigged
Quantity of coal on board	830 tons	760 tons about stored for sea	700 tons about stored for sea	700 tons about stored for sea
Quantity of stores	complete			
Propeller:				
Description	Griffiths	Griffiths	Griffiths	Griffiths
Diameter	24ft 6in	24ft 6in	24ft 6in	24ft 6in
Pitch	30.0	30.0	30.0	30.0
Length	5ft 6in	5ft 6in	5ft 6in	5ft 6in
Immersion of Upper Edge	6	11	11	11
Temperature:				
When taken	12pm/12am	1st run/6th run	1st run/4th run	2nd run
On deck	67° 64°	56° 56°	64° 63°	62°
In engine rm	78° 100°	82° 86°	85° 90°	92°
Stokehold:				
Forepart	102° 101°	76° 70°	—	—
Middle	114° 113°	101° 100°	—	—
After	100° 103°	102° 110°	—	—
In After Stokehold:				
Fore part	100° 102°	97° 100°	98° 98°	86°
Middle	115° 118°	105° 125°	102° 108°	90°
After part	99° 100°	93° 129°	108° 113°	108°
Remarks as to performance of vessel, engines, boilers etc	Engines performed well, steam could not be maintained owing inexperienced stokers.	Engines worked satisfactorily, boilers generated an ample supply of steam.	Engines and boilers worked satisfactorily, but expansion gear not satisfactory. This trial was made with 6 boilers.	Engines and boilers worked satisfactorily.

have been hampered by a combination of inferior balance or greater internal friction. The trunk engine had large rubbing surfaces, and they absorbed a considerable part of the absolute power of the engine. If, as is likely, *Black Prince*'s engines were inferior in this respect that fact alone would go a long way towards explaining why the ship was slower. Similarly it was then impossible to achieve a perfect balance with such large engines. Only static balancing of components was possible. In an engine with the cranks set at 5°, like the trunk type, good rotating balance was a matter of luck. The trunk engines fitted to the *Lord Clyde* were so ill balanced that they destroyed the wooden fabric of the ship, and wrecked themselves inside three years. They were, it must be noted, copies of Penn's engine, of inferior construction. Clearly there was a great deal of scope for power loss.

By contrast to the *Black Prince* engines the next set of 1250nhp Penn machinery, installed in *Achilles* proved to be in every way as successful as that in *Warrior*. Those built for *Minotaur* and *Northumberland* were also very satisfactory. For all that the single expansion engines remained inefficient and a great consumer of coal.

In service *Warrior* proved to be a relatively economic steamer. On early trials with the wooden two-decker *Revenge* she consumed only two-thirds of the coal used by the smaller ship. With her greater ultimate speed, and fine hull lines, this was hardly surprising. *Warrior*'s radius of action under steam, cruising at 11kts was 2100 miles. This was a frigate feature. Only the *Mersey*s which had the same bunker capacity, could better these figures. By contrast *Duncan*, among the best of the battleships could only manage 1260 miles, at a lower speed. Only the acceptance of the triple expansion engine removed the need to carry sails, if only for cruising. From the mid-1870s the cruising range of new British capital ships, which had hitherto not equalled that of *Warrior*, began to rise.

Throughout her career *Warrior* remained a fast ship, justifying Walker's decision to build such a long model. Her combination of speed, endurance and number of heavy guns was unequalled. Of the later ships only her half sister, *Achilles*, was significantly better. All the rest, despite their theoretical increase in fighting power, were deficient in at least one of the areas in which *Warrior* excelled.

After the 1864–7 refit *Warrior* rejoined the Channel Fleet, under Admiral Sir Frederick Warden in time for a steam trial on 26 November. Only *Achilles* and the new *Lord Warden* finished ahead of *Warrior*. On the 26 November 1867 the weather being favorable a full speed trial under steam was made from 8am to 4pm. The patent log of the *Minotaur* the sternmost ship but one, showed 90 miles and that of the *Helicon* which was the headmost ship, showed 104 miles, and the following was the result:

Achilles gained on	Lord Clyde	13½ miles
	Bellerophon	10¼ miles
	Minotaur	10 miles
	Pallas	8¾ miles
	Prince Consort	8¼ miles
	Warrior	6¾ miles
	Lord Warden	4¾ miles
Achilles lost on	Helicon	1½ miles

Here again the *Achilles*, one of the first ironclad ships built after the *Warrior* and *Black Prince*, distances in a run of 100 miles occupying 8 hours, some of the latest constructed ships in a very remarkable manner.

The results of the trial, while they confused Admiral Warden, were easy enough to interpret. The later ships were much more closely aligned with the concept of the battleships, in which speed was subordinate to fighting power. *Warrior* and *Achilles* were heavy frigates, in which the two qualities were much more nearly in balance. *Lord Warden*'s performance reflected an excellent and very powerful set of engines by Maudslay's. The lowly position of her sister, *Lord Clyde*, says far more about the hull form.

As a gun platform *Warrior* was a considerable advance over the wooden ships, largely on account of her bilge keels. There were two ½in deep bulb plates attached to the hull by double angle brackets, the upper 89ft, the lower 136ft long. With better weight of

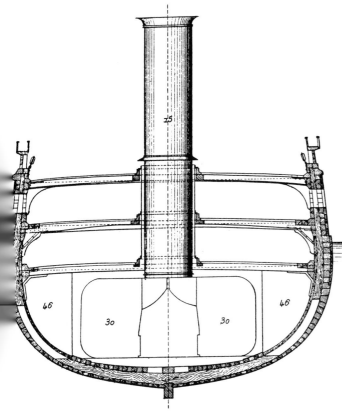

A section through *Gloire* in the centre of the boiler room. Note the coal bunkers along both sides. Aboard *Warrior* this space was also used for the watertight wing passages. *PARIS*

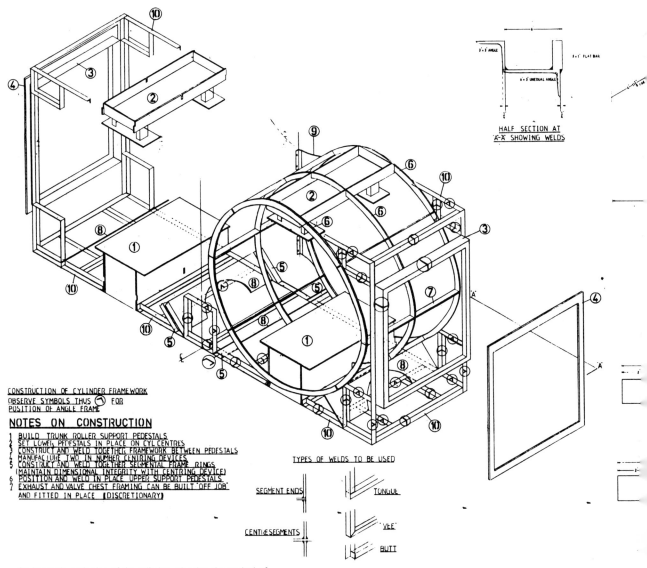

HALF SECTION AT
'A'-'A' SHOWING WELDS

CONSTRUCTION OF CYLINDER FRAMEWORK
OBSERVE SYMBOLS THUS ⊕ FOR
POSITION OF ANGLE FRAME

NOTES ON CONSTRUCTION

1. BUILD TRUNK ROLLER SUPPORT PEDESTALS
2. SET LOWER PEDESTALS IN PLACE ON CYL CENTRES
3. CONSTRUCT AND WELD TOGETHER FRAMEWORK BETWEEN PEDESTALS
4. MANUFACTURE TWO IN NUMBER CENTRING DEVICES
5. CONSTRUCT AND WELD TOGETHER SEGMENTAL FRAME RINGS
   (MAINTAIN DIMENSIONAL INTEGRITY WITH CENTRING DEVICE)
6. POSITION AND WELD IN PLACE UPPER SUPPORT PEDESTALS
7. EXHAUST AND VALVE CHEST FRAMING CAN BE BUILT 'OFF JOB'
   AND FITTED IN PLACE (DISCRETIONARY)

TYPES OF WELDS TO BE USED

SEGMENT ENDS — TONGUE

CENTRE SEGMENTS — VEE

BUTT

An isometric projection of the cylinders, showing the method of
construction. *WPT*

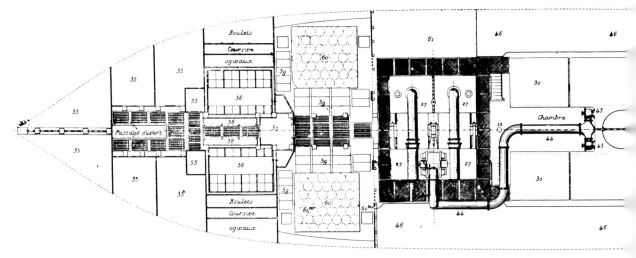

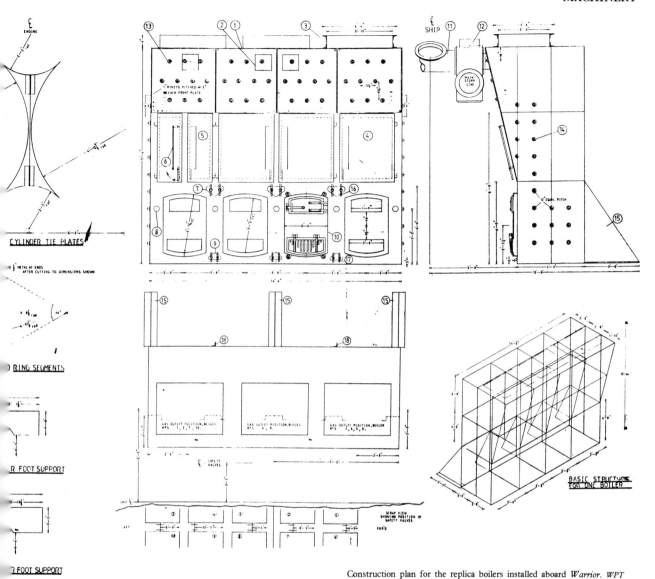

Construction plan for the replica boilers installed aboard *Warrior*. WPT

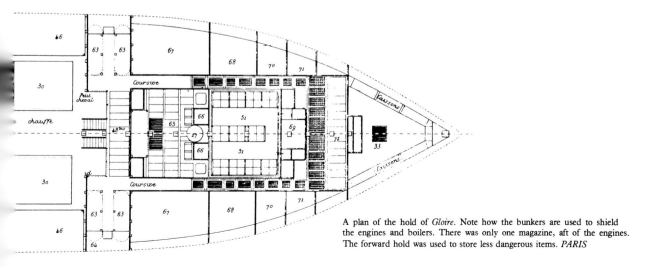

A plan of the hold of *Gloire*. Note how the bunkers are used to shield the engines and boilers. There was only one magazine, aft of the engines. The forward hold was used to store less dangerous items. *PARIS*

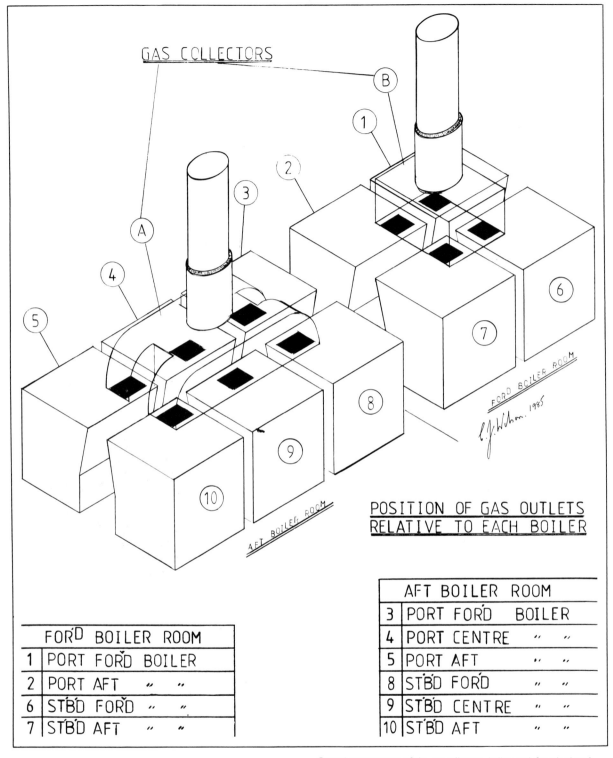

GAS COLLECTORS

POSITION OF GAS OUTLETS
RELATIVE TO EACH BOILER

FORD BOILER ROOM
1985

AFT BOILER ROOM

FORD BOILER ROOM	
1	PORT FORD BOILER
2	PORT AFT ʺ ʺ
6	STBD FORD ʺ ʺ
7	STBD AFT ʺ ʺ

AFT BOILER ROOM		
3	PORT FORD BOILER	
4	PORT CENTRE	ʺ ʺ
5	PORT AFT	ʺ ʺ
8	STBD FORD	ʺ ʺ
9	STBD CENTRE	ʺ ʺ
10	STBD AFT	ʺ ʺ

distribution *Achilles* and the *Minotaur*s were even steadier, being the finest gun platforms of the age. *Warrior* was occasionally reported on as a bad roller, but this problem was not consistent and rarely troublesome.

The helm response of *Warrior* and all her type was poor, for reasons that will be elaborated on in the next

General arrangements of the gas collectors, boilers and funnels aboard *Warrior*. WPT

chapter. This gave them a very large turning circle. *Warrior* required some 1500yds for a full 360° turn, whereas *Bellerophon* needed only 559yds at the same speed. This problem was alleviated by steam steering gear, but never solved.

In retrospect it must be concluded that *Warrior* matched the expectations placed in her as a steam warship by her projectors. Only hard-earned experience with *Warrior*, mainly at the drawing board, allowed Watts to improve his original and create *Achilles*, one of the finest ships of the ironclad era. By contrast Dupuy de Lôme did little to improve his basic model; *Gloire* had two sisters and ten marginally improved derivatives. Only the unusual two-deckers *Magenta* and *Solferino* were good seaboats, and none of the French ships made any speed at sea.

REPLICATION OF THE MACHINERY

Before taking up her career with HMS *Vernon*, *Warrior*'s machinery was scrapped. The large open space that resulted was then put into service as the ships' theatre, and served as such for some twenty years. When she reached Hartlepool nothing remained of the original machinery. Some later pattern Belleville water-tube boilers had been installed to produce

The construction of the boilers, viewed from the funnel uptakes directly overhead. This aspect emphasises the simplified construction methods shown in the drawing. *Author*

A view through the cylinders from aft on the port side, taken at an early stage in construction. The graffiti proclaims that only second class citizens work in the boiler room! *AUTHOR'S COLLECTION*

electricity for the two wooden ships that housed the crew of the *Vernon* establishment. One of these was removed from the forward boiler room in October 1982 and presented to the Science Museum. From the date of removing this item it can be seen that the engine and boiler rooms were not cleared out and cleaned until two years had passed. Because the project had to start with the upper deck the large areas below the waterline, which were in the filthiest condition, had to be left until everything above had been prepared. The major issue of constructing replica engines and boilers was falling behind the rest of the ship because of the large financial commitment it would represent. The prevalent idea seems to have been that an outside contractor would be found to take on the daunting task, and discussions were entered into to this end.

In 1982 an outside contractor was approached to estimate for the work. The figure for the main engine alone was alarming and this put back the decision to start work even further. In 1984 the brave, but ultimately right, decision was taken that the task should be carried out within the project organisation, using skilled labour on the MSC scheme. This, it was hoped, would save a great deal of money.

Jim Wilson was appointed as Project Engineer in early December. Through a long career in engineering, afloat and ashore, Jim had been greatly interested in the history and development of large Marine engines. Before joining the project he had been researching the P & O steamship *Himalaya* of 1853, another Penn-engined ship built by the Thames Ironworks, while it was trading as C J Mare.

Before any work on the reconstruction could begin it was necessary to understand what had to be reproduced. Hitherto research had concentrated on material directly attributed to *Warrior*. The existing engine drawings for the ship were inadequate. The Penn Trunk engines and standard box boilers of *Warrior* were reproduced in several other ships of the period with very little variation. Indeed the trunk engines only ever varied in their dimensions and fine detail. The engines of *Black Prince, Achilles, Minotaur* and *Northumberland* were researched. A very detailed set for the *Black Prince* were then uncovered at the National Maritime Museum. These may reflect the greater distance from London at which *Black Prince*'s engines were installed, along with Robert Napier's great experience of constructing steamships. Models of *Northumberland*'s and *Minotaur*'s engines are on display at the Science Museum.

With this information it was possible to outline the work that would be required. Sketch general arrangements were drawn up in February. Major elements in the engine room were then redrawn for reproduction during March and April 1985. At the end of April a

The forward boiler room, viewed from ahead. *AUTHOR'S COLLECTION*

trainee Technical Clerk was taken on to assist the work.

However the object was not to reproduce the engines as built. As with the guns the expense of reconstruction using the original materials and methods would have been prohibitive. Cast and wrought iron, and gunmetal were too costly, casing the cylinders and condenser, too complex. However the decision was taken not to use non-metal elements. This eventually forced Jim to return to cast iron in several areas. Instead modern ferrous materials would have to be used to produce a replica that would turn, albeit not under steam. This called for new engineering drawings, based on new methods of assembly.

The essential design considerations were: to use stock sizes of steel wherever possible, to manufacture the lightest structure consistent with strength and minimal deformation during the welding process, and finally to be cost-effective. The boiler structures were designed to make use of the jig construction method – in all fifty frames, five per boiler, were constructed on one jig. An

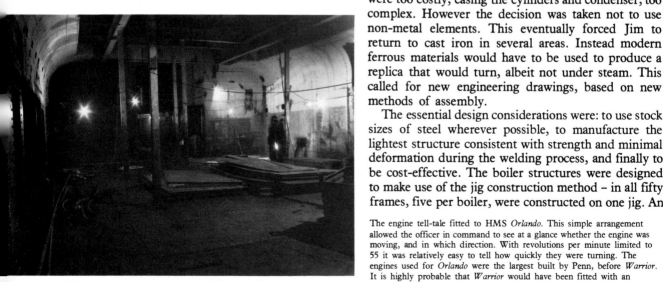

The boiler room looking aft, April 1985, just before the erection of the first frames. Note the bunkers on either side of the central passage through to the engine room. *WPT*

The engine tell-tale fitted to HMS *Orlando*. This simple arrangement allowed the officer in command to see at a glance whether the engine was moving, and in which direction. With revolutions per minute limited to 55 it was relatively easy to tell how quickly they were turning. The engines used for *Orlando* were the largest built by Penn, before *Warrior*. It is highly probable that *Warrior* would have been fitted with an identical arrangement. The idea is similar to the old method of recording rpm with internal combustion engines, a mechanical device working directly off the crankshaft. *WPT*

Tell Tale from Engine Room to Upper Deck. H.M.S. "Orlando"

Scale one inch = one foot

Upper deck

Main deck

Lower deck

for Shaft

The Science Museum model of the *Minotaur/Northumberland* engines, viewed from aft. This model gives an excellent impression of the compact spaces available, and the limitations this imposed on the designs. *WPT*

ability to visualise the end result was a major factor in explaining the success of the work, and an isometric view of each large item was provided with the engineering drawings. As Jim Wilson explained, 'One picture conveys more than a thousand words'. He also kept a close, daily, liaison with the workforce, to ensure that the plans were translated into the correct shapes. Simulation techniques, using steel plate, instead of heavy cast items, reduced weight by more than one third, while preserving strength and appearance.

The first item redrawn for fabrication was the jet condenser, which occupies the starboard side of the engine room. This is, in outline, no more than a large box and was designed to be built from steel plate around an angle iron frame. At this stage the first workmen were taken on. The engine room gang of seven men started building the condensers in May. A draughtsman was also brought in to reinforce the drawing office team, as once fabrication had begun there was a requirement for on-site supervision. In June another seven-man squad was taken on to start work on the ten box boilers. A healthy rivalry quickly built up between the two squads.

One major factor that controlled the design and construction of the replica engines was the limited space available for bringing material into the boiler and engine rooms. Although the normal pattern of installation was followed everything had to be built up from sections that could be lowered down the funnel casings into the boiler rooms. This placed an outside limit of 11ft × 14ft with 18ft available across the diagonal. The bulkhead between the boiler and engine rooms precluded the use of pieces even this size for the engines. The maximum available there was the size of the engine room gratings, 50in × 44in. As the drawings of the cylinders reproduced here show, the solution was to build them out of sections of sheet steel.

The decision to produce an all-metal replica created several problems; some items were not suitable or even practical for sheet steel fabrication. First off were the large, pipe bends on top of the condensers. These have an acute angle. Nothing commercially available could fit the bill, while the cost of building up items in sheet would have been negated by the impossibility of achieving the effect of the original. Therefore the original method, using cast iron, was adopted. This ensured

The trunk engine in close-up. The crankshaft is on the right, the cylinders on the left. The trunk itself is the tube which encloses the piston rod, similar in function to the correcting rod of an internal combustion engine. *WPT*

that the large diameter bends with tight radius were achieved. The fire doors of the ten boilers were also cast, that being the most effective method of including all the detail work on these identical fittings.

As with other aspects of the *Warrior* project, outside assistance played a part in the machinery fabrication. The local firm of Specialist Welding and Fabrication, only recently set up, took on several complex tasks. Notable among these were the safety valves, the main steam separator, 9in Downton pumps and a working replica of the galley stove. Subcontracting out these awkward detail jobs allowed the Engineering Department to concentrate on the already delayed major task of restoring the engine and boiler rooms.

As the work of the Engineering Department progressed the most noticeable feature for the non-specialist observer was the sudden, and rapid, filling-up of the one capacious spaces. Eventually the engine and boiler rooms became the cramped, awkward spaces they had once been. This had the effect of pointing out just how difficult maintenance and running repairs had been; it also allowed the more imaginative to consider the effect of working in the stokehold, sandwiched between two rows of furnaces, in temperatures up to 126°. Little wonder the engine room crew were awarded extra money when serving in the tropics.

Visitors will be led down the stokehold through the engine room and up the engine room ladder. With the view from above, through the gratings, this should provide a good impression of the scale and form of the machinery. Once again the demands of a warship both for the most effective use of space and to keep the machinery below the waterline militated against a more open display.

When *Warrior* reaches Portsmouth the major elements of the machinery will be in place. However a few of the details that are vital to the success of the reconstruction might not be aboard. To enable the work to continue the MSC community scheme had to be extended beyond its one year term, after April and June 1985 respectively. This was another example of the local flexibility in the scheme that has often benefitted the project. The future of the engineering aspects of the project is, as yet, uncertain.

One aspect of the project has been the entirely separate nature of the work of the engineers. With a single task uninterrupted by the weather, or the demands of other jobs, they have been able to make startling progress deep inside the ship. After the late start to the work, this development has helped to create a separate identity for the small workforce within the team at Hartlepool, and their own *esprit de corps*.

The floor of the engine room in April 1985. The bolt holes are a reminder of the original set of engines, and form a link with the engineers of John Penn & Sons who installed them. *WPT*

CHAPTER SEVEN
Rig

After the experience of the Russian War the Royal Navy and its French rival were both quite certain that warships would never again go into action under sail. The French had been leading the way toward this major shift in design emphasis from the mid-1840s, with the British reluctantly forced to follow suit. The Royal Navy had abandoned the construction of pure sailing warships in 1851, but this decision has passed almost unnoticed. What happened in the war only confirmed the wisdom of Walker's advice.

While steam offered enormous tactical advantages the single expansion machinery working at no more than 20psi was so uneconomic that even *Warrior*'s massive bunker capacity of 850 tons was inadequate for oceanic voyages. Furthermore the reliability of the machinery, depending on a single engine with only one propeller, was poor. For these reasons British warships

Warrior at Portsmouth after her 1871-5 refit. Note the long bowsprit, modified bow bulwarks and the new funnels. Another significant change, painting the hammock netting covers buff instead of black, has had the effect of lightening the overall appearance of the ship. *IWM*

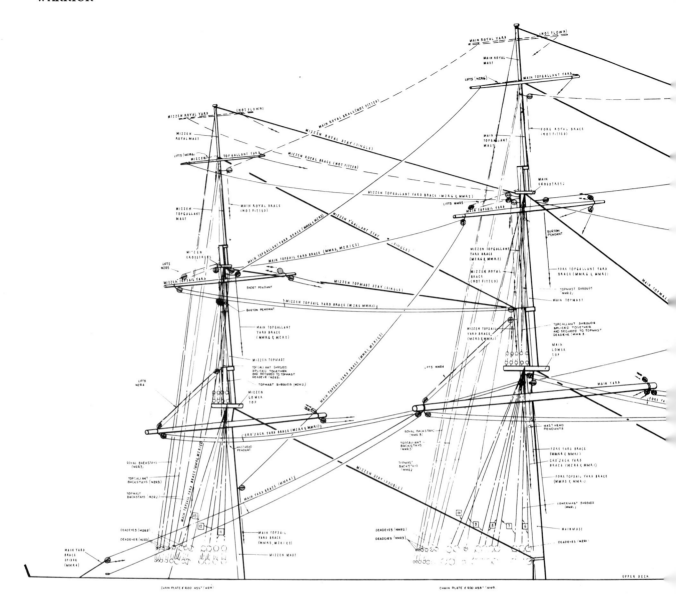

of the later 1850s, culminating in *Warrior*, were designed with a shifting emphasis towards steam as the predominant power. Even *Warrior* was to carry a full rig for ocean cruising. This could also be used in action, should the machinery be disabled. There was never any question of building her without sails. Even the coast defence ships were equipped with pole masts, so that they could spread some canvas in the event of an accident. *Gloire* was originally completed with a light barque rig, but the French had gone ahead of the technology of the age, and they tacitly admitted this by refitting her with a much more substantial full outfit of sails.

While steam had taken over as the tactical motive power, sail still had a major role to play in providing strategic mobility. Several of *Warrior*'s wooden hulled ironclad contemporaries made long voyages under sail,

notably *Ocean*, *Repulse* and *Zealous*. Even in the late 1880s the flagships on the Pacific station, *Triumph* and *Swiftsure*, spent most of their time under canvas, to save the cost of shipping coal out to South America or the west coast of Canada. In the early 1860s such problems were more widespread. Quality steam coal, from South Wales, was only available to Admiralty order. Even the process of coaling ship was time consuming, the competitive coaling of the late nineteenth century being unknown.

Warrior's reduced derivatives, *Defence* and *Resistance*, *Hector* and *Valiant*, were all masted on the scale for coast defence and Channel service; even so, they carried a full complement of square rigged masts. Being smaller than *Warrior* the first pair saw service in the Mediterranean fleet, at a time when the long ironclads were held in reserve in the Channel, for lack of a suitable

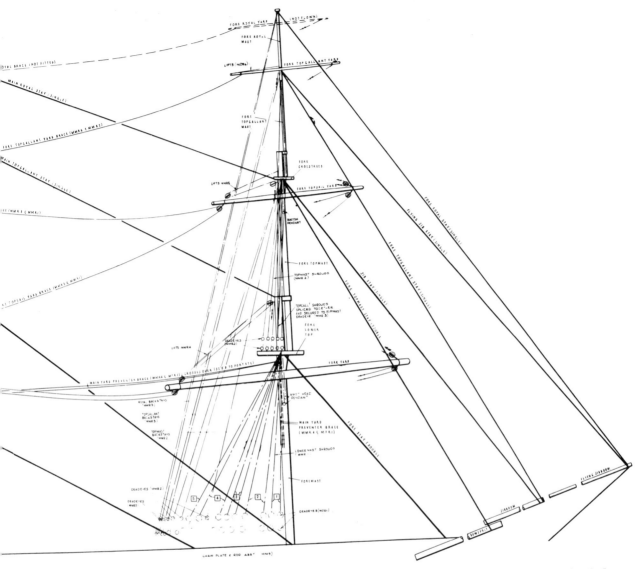

The standing rigging of *Warrior*. This supports the masts and yards. It also provide the rope work for the men to use when ascending to work the sails. *WPT*

dock outside the British Isles.

The rig selected for *Warrior* has always been referred to as that of an 80-gun ship. These vessels were the small Second Rate two-deckers designed by Sir William Symonds. While the same masts and yards were used by these short, beamy ships their selection for *Warrior* was based on their use in the *Mersey* class heavy frigates. They were the largest masts yet carried by a single decked fighting ship, and *Warrior* being a direct descendant of *Mersey* the use of the same rig was logical. Walker had been concerned that three masts would appear inadequate. He wanted to step four or five iron masts. However the difficulties of stepping so many masts in the crowded machinery spaces, although resolved, pointed up other problems. The original rig was retained, for *Warrior* and *Black Prince* at least, yet another example of the conservative detailed design. It

was left for *Achilles* to step four masts on the *Warrior* hull, and the *Minotaurs* to attempt five on a slightly lengthened hull. Neither arrangement affected any improvement. *Achilles* soon returned to the *Warrior* sail plan, and while the *Minotaur, Agincourt* and *Northumberland* retained their distinctive rig they were among the most sluggish of all the ironclads under sail, largely on account of a fixed propeller and a reduced sail area.

In one respect *Warrior* and *Black Prince* were unique. They were the only ironclads to be fitted with wooden lower masts, like all their wooden hulled precursors. All subsequent ironclads, even those converted from two deckers, were fitted with iron masts. These provided much improved ventilation on the orlop and lower decks, by cutting special slots in the mast head

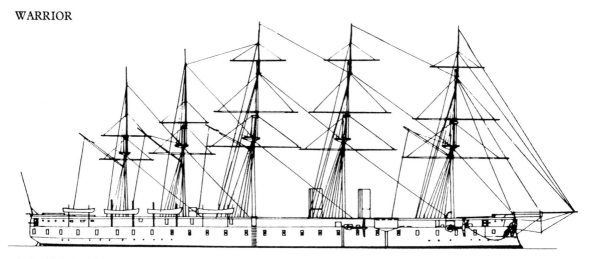

A simplified view of the standing rigging of *Minotaur*. Although she carried five masts this ship actually spread less canvas than *Warrior*; note how the chains have been moved inside the bulwark, because the lighter masts require less width for their support.

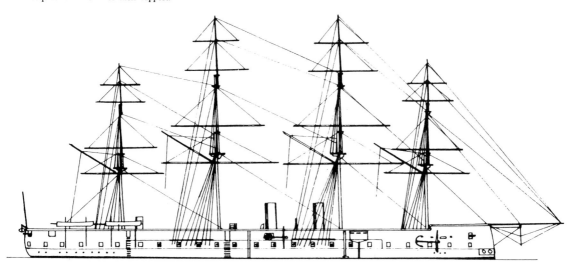

The original standing rigging of *Achilles*. No warship ever spread more canvas. She was remasted along the lines of *Warrior* after problems with this massive tophamper.

Below: *Warrior*; with the exception of her bowsprit, she retained this original plan throughout her career.

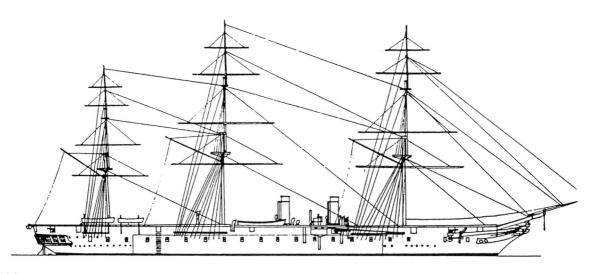

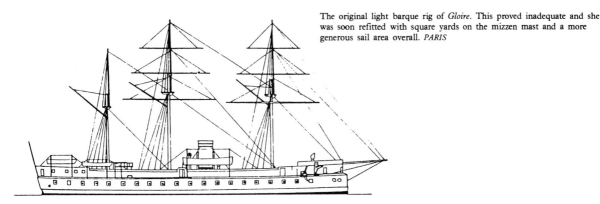

The original light barque rig of *Gloire*. This proved inadequate and she was soon refitted with square yards on the mizzen mast and a more generous sail area overall. *PARIS*

The mainmast fife rails in position, with the brass plate, blocks and one belaying pin. The fore yard and main yard are to the left and right of the picture, while the mizzen stays are being tensioned. *AUTHOR'S COLLECTION*

and scuttles in the mast below deck a constant and powerful updraught could be achieved. This effect can be observed aboard *Warrior* today. The lack of this extra ventilation was often reported on during *Warrior*'s two full commissions, and was blamed for her sick list, which was consistently higher than that of the other ironclads. *Black Prince* was remasted with the iron lower masts of the wooden hulled *Ocean* in 1875. Plans have been found for remasting *Warrior* with new iron masts in 1876, but it is doubtful that this work was ever carried out, although it appears that she was given an iron bowsprit, either after the 1868 collison or when the longer item was stepped during her second refit. However the iron mast plans have been used for the reconstruction. The cost of wooden lower masts to the scale required for *Warrior* would have been astronomical, and wood does not have the durability of steel.

The need to combine steam and sail had been a major problem for naval architects long before *Warrior* was designed. In basic terms there was a clash of requirements, calling for a balance of priorities. To fight her guns while steaming, as it was assumed would be the case, the ship needed to be steady, and not prone to rolling. This called for a high centre of gravity. To use her sails in strong winds, for oceanic cruising, the ship needed stability, which in turn called for a low centre of gravity. All the masted ironclads were attempts to reach a compromise. *Warrior* rolled, although not as badly as

The foretopmast, emphasising the amount of cutting, shaping and welding required to build up this complex shape. *WPT*

her wooden predecessors, but stood up well to a press of canvas. Her half sister, *Achilles*, was given a higher centre of gravity and proved to be a superb gun platform, and very steady under canvas.

> Observations of Rear Admiral Warden on a Memo of the Controller of the navy respecting the proceedings of Channel Squadron in 1867.
>
> The ships stand in the following order of merit as to the capacity for fighting their guns;
> 1st   *Minotaur* & *Achilles* – equal
> 2nd *Lord Warden* & *Warrior* – equal
> 3rd   *Bellerophon*
> 4th   *Royal Oak* & *Prince Consort* – equal
> 5th   *Lord Clyde*

Report on Cruise of Channel Squadron 11 July 1868

> The *Minotaur*, *Achilles* and *Warrior* are three very noble ships. The last named however I look upon as the least valuable of the three, her unarmoured ends, exposure of steering wheel, her rolling propensities (as compared with the other two) are defects which are not compensated for by any good qualities superior to theirs.

Warrior, with her bilge keels and greater design emphasis on steadiness under steam, was stiffer under canvas than her wooden precursors. Along with wire rigging, this allowed her to hold onto her sails far longer than earlier ships, providing a remarkable performance. Using all plain sail and stunsails on the fore and mizzen masts, *Warrior* reached 13kt with the screw raised. With steam and sail combined she managed 17.5kt

Ship Manager Stan Morrell overseeing the construction of the main yard. *WPT*

larger rudder could not have been worked by hand.

A similar combination of problems ensured that all the long ironclads were slow to answer the helm. Steam steering gear did affect a marked improvement, notably in the *Minotaurs*. This sluggish manoeuvring, especially under sail, was responsible for *Warrior*'s collision with *Royal Oak* at 10.55pm on 14 August 1868. The Channel fleet was sailing in line ahead off the Scilly Isles at night. *Royal Oak* was leading *Warrior* when some of her rigging parted and she lost speed. *Warrior*, unable to clear her, overran and crashed along her lee quarters, losing her figurehead and destroying her consort's boats, main and mizzen chains.

The fore mast being lifted...

while running between Portsmouth and Plymouth in November 1861. These remarkable figures reflected her fine lines and hollow bow profile. On the other hand the hull form was also responsible for her dangerously poor manoeuvrability. Equipped with a small hand-turned rudder *Warrior* was very slow to answer to helm, which made her unreliable when wearing and staying, and a positive menace while sailing in squadron formation. The comparisons made with the two deckers *Revenge* and *Edgar* were all to the detriment of *Warrior*. Senior Officers all commented on the poor handling of the ship. Rear Admiral Sir Sidney Dacres, as Commander-in-Chief of the Channel Fleet during the round Britain cruise, went so far as to prefer *Defence* as a fighting ship, solely on account of her superior handiness under sail and steam. Matters were improved by steam-powered steering gear in 1879. Until then the high geared steering, which allowed only three and on half turns of the wheel to put the helm hard over often required up to 40 men on relieving tackles to operate at any speed, and took up 90 seconds to shift. Three turns at the wheel was a hangover from sailing ships, in which the rudder had a much simpler task. With all the friction of the multiplicity of tackles this was too high a ratio when the rudder was being forced to the centre by the thrust of the propeller. Even when hard over no more than 33° of helm were available, while the rudder area, 160sq ft, was less than half that of a modern vessel of *Warrior*'s size. However a

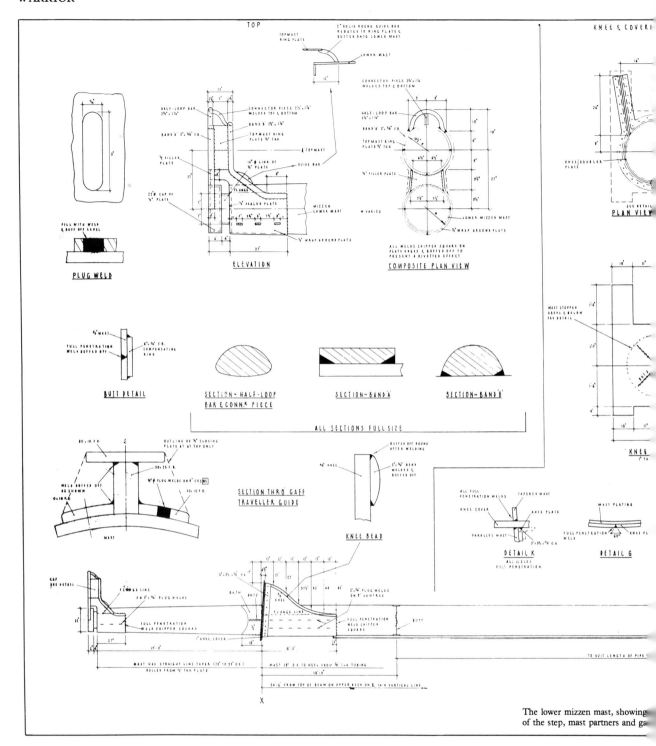

The lower mizzen mast, showing
of the step, mast partners and ga

This unhandiness under sail and the fact that *Warrior* spent her active career in the Channel Fleet ensured that she generally proceeded under sail and easy steam. The shorter ironclads, and the converted wooden two deckers, all handled far better. So curiously enough did the 330ft long *Mersey* class frigates from which *Warrior* was descended. Without twin screws and balanced rudders ships of *Warrior*'s length must always be slow to answer the helm. Some thought was given to enlarging the rudder, but by the late 1860s the long ships were accepted with their faults. No more were ordered after Walker retired in early 1862. The length of the *Minotaurs* was not to be exceeded until the turn of the century, by which time the problems of controlling such ships had been largely solved.

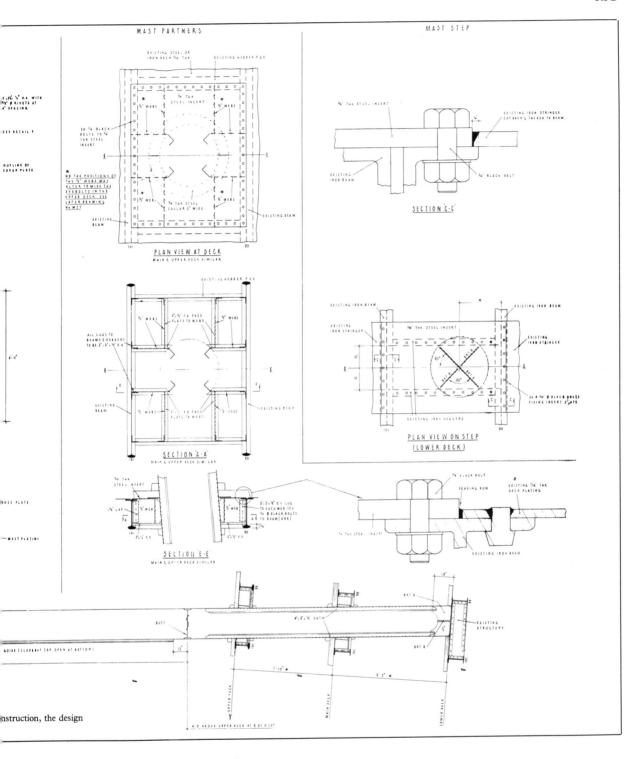

THE SAILING PERFORMANCE OF THE IRONCLADS

In 1861 the performance of a warship under sail was still considered the true test of a good design. The wooden steam battlefleets were regularly exercised under sail, their steam speed and ability to fight their guns being relegated to the second rank of importance.

The explanation for this lay in the long history of the sailing battlefleet, when such matters were a vital part of naval warfare, and the long post-1815 peace. During prolonged periods of peace all fighting services gradually lose touch with the central and grim reality of their business. Other essentially non-military aspects of the service assume a greater significance, to the detriment of preparations for war. In the Royal Navy

...being jibbed out over the ship...

...and lowered home. *WPT*.

between 1815 and 1860 skill in sailing became the measure of an officers' merit. It is worth noting that the single greatest naval controversy of the era concerned the sailing qualities of the large ships designed by the Surveyor, 1832–47, Captain Sir William Symonds. These vessels were effectively large yachts, extremely fast in ideal conditions, when skillfully handled and well set up, but otherwise slow and prone to a chronic rolling that ruined them as gun platforms.

Captains who had learnt their profession in this period naturally looked to show their skill in command of the ironclads. They were to be disappointed. Only the small and converted ships were ever reliable squadron sailing ships. *Warrior, Black Prince* and *Achilles* were all fast on a wind, with such fine hulls and hoisting propellers they had to be, but they never handled well. The explanation for this was simple. Being masted on the scale of 80-gun ships they had only half the sail area per ton of the wooden ships: 6.15sq ft of sail to the ton, compared with 13.9 for the wooden ships. Therefore to generate the same power under sail as the wooden ships, *Warrior* would have needed to double her sail area. As a later Chief Constructor, Sir Nathaniel Barnaby, pointed out, this would have required a broader ship, and therefore reduced speed under steam. It would also have created an over-stiff platform, ruining gunnery much as Symonds' ships had done only 20 years before.

Clearly in designing *Warrior* performance under sail was given second place behind steam. This was logical, and perfectly in tune with the tactical doctrine of the age. However Government and Admiralty parsimony with coal meant that all the ironclads spent much of their time economising on coal by using sail whenever possible. The quick and precise handling of masts and yards remained the ultimate test of seamanship and smartness well into the 1880s. As such it did serve a purpose. Exercise aloft was dangerous. It called for a high degree of co-ordination and training. This was a substitute for combat training, instilling into the men the qualities required by the late Victorian Navy. When the Fleets were at anchor shifting topmasts and yards was *the* competitive drill, long before coaling and accurate gunnery. The Channel Fleet flagships *Minotaur* and *Agincourt* were always noted for their speed and precision in these competitions; having five masts served to emphasise these qualities.

That such matters remained high on the Naval Officers' list of priorities indicated a stubborn reluctance to change. This reached a fitting climax with the *Captain* disaster. An unstable turret ship was equipped with masts on the scale of *Warrior*, to meet the prejudices of the service and the whim of an amateur designer. Caught in a gale off Cape Finisterre she was forced beyond her pathetically small angle of safety, 15–16°, and capsized. The 472 men lost with her, more than were killed at Trafalgar, were victims of a misguided attempt to combine the sails of the wooden period with the turrets and low freeboard of the 1870s. Even before *Captain* went down, the first mastless battleship, *Devastation*, had been designed. The broadside ironclads, being professionally designed, had far greater stability. In a gale similar to the one that destroyed *Captain*, *Achilles* heeled only 10°, despite snapping two topgallant masts and splitting her topsails.

Dimensions of Masts, Yards, Tops & Gaff

MIZZEN MASTS

Lower Mast:	28in OD × ⅞ thick steel tube. 67ft 6in from upper deck to cap. The heel is on the lower deck (17ft 0in below upper deck).
Topmast:	16in square at heel to 11in dia at cap. Length 50ft 6in
Topgallant & royal mast (in one piece):	Topgallant 9in square at heel, 7in dia at top. Length 23ft 6in. Royal 5½in diameter at stop. 3½in diameter at truck. Length 16ft 0in

YARDS

Crossjack yard:	71ft 0in long, 17in diameter tapering to 7¼in.
Topsail yard:	51ft 6ins long, 11½in diameter tapering to 5in.
Topgallant yard:	33ft 6in long, 7in diameter tapering to 3½in.
Royal yard:	24ft 6in long, 5in diameter tapering to 2¼in.

TOPS

Lower top:	11ft 0in long × 19ft 0in wide.
Crosstrees:	5ft 0in long × 15ft 0in wide.

GAFF
49ft 0in long, 5½in diameter at end, 11in diameter at centre, 9in diameter at end.

MAIN MASTS

Lower mast:	42in OD × ¾in thick steel tube. 86ft 3in from upper deck to cap. The heel is on the tank top. (33ft 8in from upper deck).
Topmast:	22in square at heel to 15in diameter at cap. Length 65ft 0in.
Topgallant & royal mast (in one piece):	Topgallant 12½in square at heel, 9½in diameter at stop. Length 31ft 6in. Royal 8in diameter at stop, 6in diameter at truck. Length 21ft 0in.

YARDS

Lower yard:	105ft 0in long, 33in diameter tapering to 10½in.
Topsail yard:	74ft 0in long, 16in diameter tapering to 7in.
Topgallant yard:	46ft 0in long, 11in diameter tapering to 5in.
Royal yard:	32ft 6in long, 8½in diameter tapering to 2¾in.

Tops

Lower top:	15ft 6in long × 24ft 0in wide.
Cross trees:	74ft 0in long × 17ft 6in wide.

Gaff 41ft 0in long, 5½in diameter at end, 11in at centre, 9in diameter at end.

NB: Fore masts, yards, tops & gaff are the same dimensions as the main except for the lower mast:

Fore lower mast:	40in OD × ¾in thick steel tube. 79ft 3in from upper deck to cap. The heel is on the tank top. (38ft 0in from upper deck)

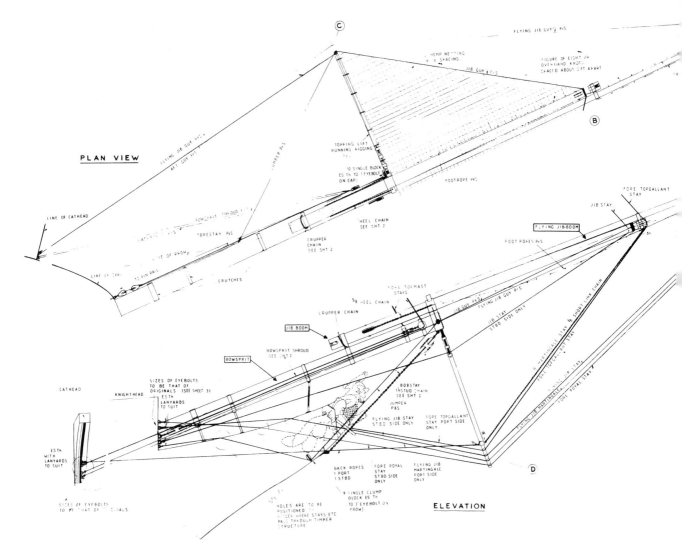

PLAN VIEW

ELEVATION

Dimensions of bowsprit, jibboom, flying jibboom martingale and spreaders.

Bowsprit: 40in /D × ⅜in thick steel tube. 49ft 0in from bow. Total length 70ft.

Jibboom: 42ft 0in long: 15½in diameter tapering to 10½in diamater.

Flying jibboom: 44ft 9in long: 6⅜in diameter tapering to 5⅝in diamter.

Martingale: 17ft 0in long: 6in diameter.

Spreaders: 17ft 0in long: 6in diameter.

NB The main and mizzen yards carried no stunsail booms. Earlier experience with steamships indicated that these would be rarely used, and would only suffer from smoke and heat-induced rot. The Royal Navy at this time had accepted iron lower masts, but rejected iron yards on account of the difficulty experienced attempting to mend them. Wooden yards were easy to mend, but suffered from all manner of damage due to water, smoke and heat.

All plain sail (excluding royals):	28,809sq ft (1861),
including royals and gaffs:	37,546sq ft (1875)
Total	48,400sq ft

RESTORING THE RIG

Of *Warrior*'s original rig little remained when she reached Hartlepool, save a few mizzen chain plates and the wooden step for the bowsprit. In aesthetic terms this was the greatest single loss the ship had suffered during her career. Like all her contemporaries *Warrior* was somehow less than half the ship when shorn of her tophamper. Until the masts were replaced she would remain a hulk and make only a limited impression on the layman. This was not surprising. *Warrior* was conceived as a masted ship, intended to sail just as all her predecessors had done. The masts were an essential part of the ship.

In restoring the rig there were a few major decisions to be taken. The only definite change in the rig during her active career was the reduction of the bowsprit between March and June 1862, to counteract a bow trim, and its restoration to the original length although not the diameter during the 1872–5 refit when a counterbalancing poop was fitted. Although Parkes claims she was remasted in iron, there is no proof of

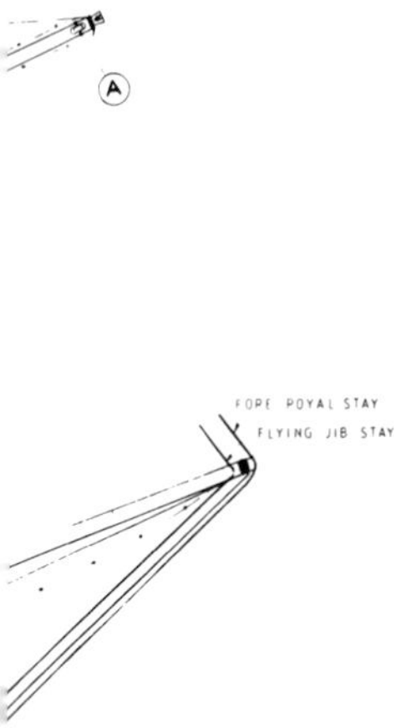

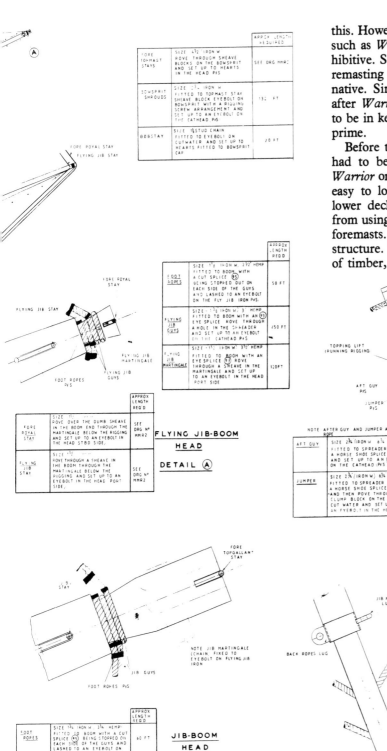

		APPROX LENGTH REQUIRED
FORE TOPMAST STAYS	SIZE 4½" IRON W ROVE THROUGH SHEAVE BLOCKS ON THE BOWSPRIT AND SET UP TO HEARTS IN THE HEAD P/S	SEE DRG MMR2
BOWSPRIT SHROUDS	SIZE 2¾ IRON W FITTED TO TOPMAST STAY SHEAVE BLOCK EYEBOLT ON BOWSPRIT WITH A RIGGING SCREW ARRANGEMENT AND SET UP TO AN EYEBOLT ON THE CATHEAD P/S	132 FT
BOBSTAY	SIZE 1⅝ STUD CHAIN FITTED TO EYEBOLT ON CUTWATER AND SET UP TO HEARTS FITTED TO BOWSPRIT CAP	20 FT

this. However the cost of built-up wooden lower masts, such as *Warrior* had originally, would have been prohibitive. Steel masts, built to the plans of the proposed remasting of 1876 were an economic and durable alternative. Similarly the short bowsprit, installed shortly after *Warrior* effectively entered service was adopted, to be in keeping with the appearance of the ship in her prime.

Before the masts could be replaced the lower decks had to be opened up and cleaned. Unlike *Achilles*, *Warrior* only had one rig, hence her mast steps were all easy to locate. The mizzenmast was stepped on the lower deck, because the propeller shaft prevented it from using the floor of the tank deck, like the main- and foremasts. All three were stepped straight into the iron structure. The bowsprit was stepped into a large block of timber, just as all previous ships had stepped their

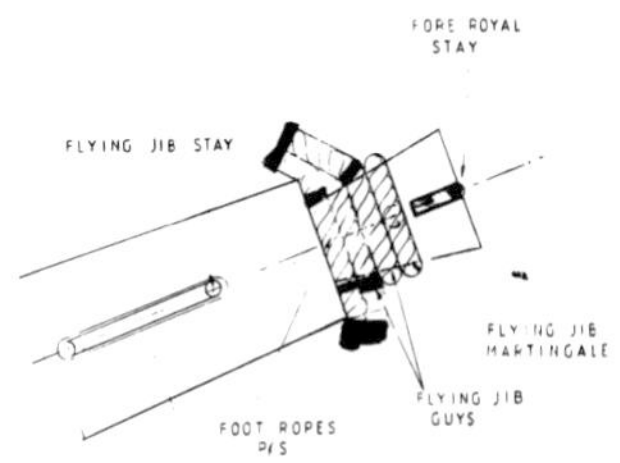

		APPROX LENGTH REQ'D
FOOT ROPES	SIZE 1⅛ IRON W, 2½" HEMP FITTED TO BOOM WITH A CUT SPLICE (95) BEING STOPPED OUT ON EACH SIDE OF THE GUYS AND LASHED TO AN EYEBOLT ON THE FLY JIB IRON P/S.	50 FT
FLYING JIB GUYS	SIZE 1⅜ IRON W) 3" HEMP FITTED TO BOOM WITH AN (93) EYE SPLICE ROVE THROUGH A HOLE IN THE SPREADER AND SET UP TO AN EYEBOLT ON THE CATHEAD P/S	250 FT
FLYING JIB MARTINGALE	SIZE 1½ IRON W) 3½" HEMP FITTED TO BOOM WITH AN EYE SPLICE (93) ROVE THROUGH A SHEAVE IN THE MARTINGALE AND SET UP TO AN EYEBOLT IN THE HEAD PORT SIDE	120FT

		APPROX LENGTH REQ'D
FORE ROYAL STAY	SIZE 1½ ROVE OVER THE DUMB SHEAVE IN THE BOOM END THROUGH THE MARTINGALE BELOW THE RIGGING AND SET UP TO AN EYEBOLT IN THE HEAD STBD SIDE)	SEE DRG Nº MMR2
FLYING JIB STAY	SIZE 1½ ROVE THROUGH A SHEAVE IN THE BOOM THROUGH THE MARTINGALE BELOW THE RIGGING AND SET UP TO AN EYEBOLT IN THE HEAD PORT SIDE)	SEE DRG Nº MMR2

FLYING JIB-BOOM HEAD

DETAIL (A)

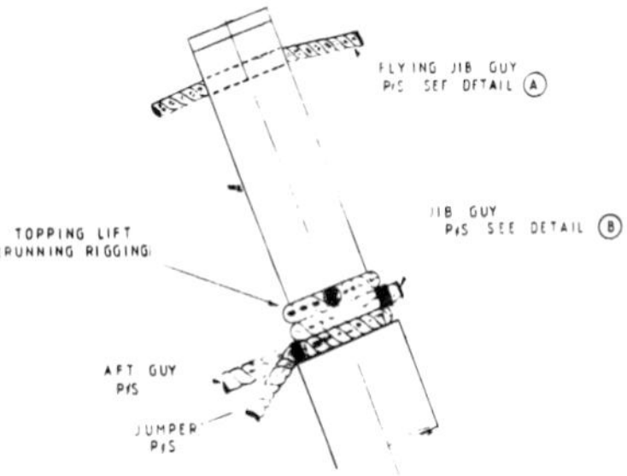

NOTE AFTER GUY AND JUMPER ARE ONE ROPE

		APPROX LENGTH REQ'D
AFT GUY	SIZE 2¾ (IRON W 6¼ HEMP) FITTED TO SPREADER WITH A HORSE SHOE SPLICE (97) AND SET UP TO AN EYEBOLT ON THE CATHEAD (P/S)	270 FT
JUMPER	SIZE 2¾ (IRON W) 6¼ (HEMP) FITTED TO SPREADER WITH A HORSE SHOE SPLICE (97) AND THEN ROVE THROUGH A CLUMP BLOCK ON THE CUT WATER AND SET UP TO AN EYEBOLT IN THE HEAD P/S)	

		APPROX LENGTH REQ'D
TOPPING LIFT (RUNNING RIGGING)	SIZE 2½ HEMP FITTED WITH AN EYE SPLICE (93) ROUND THE SPREADER ROVE THROUGH A BLOCK ON THE BOWSPRIT CAP AND SET UP WITH A PURCHASE ON THE KNIGHTHEAD NOTE SOMETIMES FITTED ON FIRST TO STEADY THE SPREADERS)	120 FT

SPREADER HEAD

DETAIL (C)

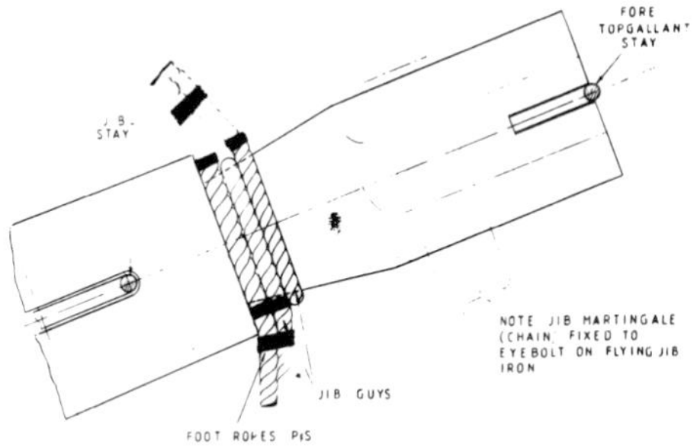

		APPROX LENGTH REQ'D
FOOT ROPES	SIZE 1¾ IRON W, 3¾ HEMP) FITTED TO BOOM WITH A CUT SPLICE (95) BEING STOPPED ON EACH SIDE OF THE GUYS AND LASHED TO AN EYEBOLT ON THE BOWSPRIT CAP (P/S)	60 FT
JIB GUYS	SIZE 2¾ (IRON W) 6¼ HEMP FITTED TO BOOM AND SPREADER WITH AN EYE SPLICE (93) IN EACH END P/S	140 FT
JIB MARTINGALE	SIZE ⅞ SHORT LINK CHAIN FITTED TO BOOM IRON EYEBOLT AND MARTINGALE HOOP	36 FT

		APPROX LENGTH REQ'D
FORE TOPGALLANT STAY	SIZE 2¼" IRON W) ROVE OVER A DUMB SHEAVE IN THE BOOM THROUGH THE MARTINGALE BELOW THE RIGGING AND SET UP TO AN EYEBOLT IN THE HEAD PORT SIDE)	SEE DRG Nº MMR2
JIB STAY	SIZE 2¾" IRON W) ROVE THROUGH SHEAVES IN THE BOOM AND MARTINGALE AND SET UP TO AN EYEBOLT IN THE HEAD STBD SIDE	SEE DRG Nº MMR2

JIB-BOOM HEAD

DETAIL (B)

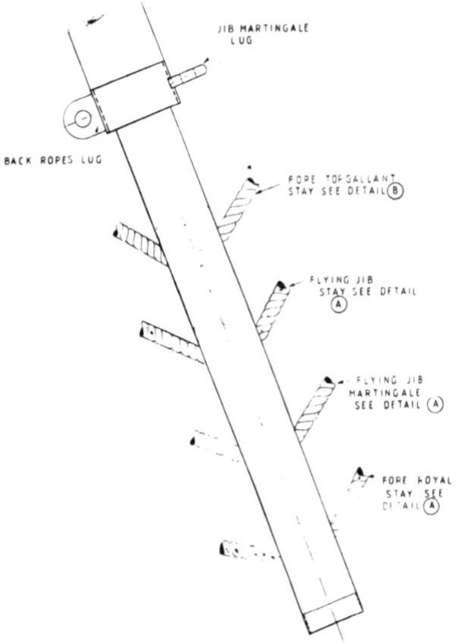

		APPROX LENGTH REQ'D
BACKROPES	SIZE 2½" (IRON W) 5½" (HEMP) FITTED WITH A THIMBLE IN THE BIGHT TO AN EYEBOLT ON THE MARTINGALE HOOP AND THE AFTER ENDS SET UP TO EYEBOLTS ON THE CATHEAD P/S	140 FT

MARTINGALE HEAD

DETAIL (D)

The bowsprit originally installed. This was replaced in early 1986 by a larger and longer item. *WPT*

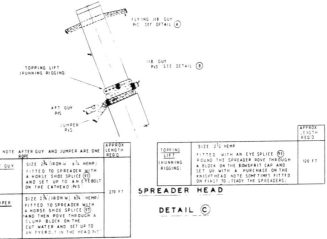

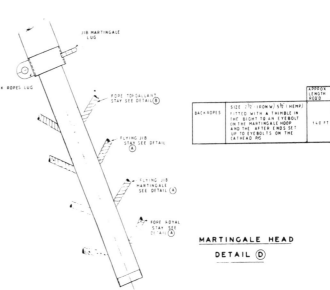

The special beam showing the reduced bowsprit in place, emphasising the extra width of the full size 40in diameter item originally fitted. *WPT*

The bowsprit being lifted aboard. *WPT*

bowsprits. This baulk of timber had unfortunately rotted at the base, presenting the project with another large bill for wood.

Construction of the lower masts began in early 1984. The material used was steel pipe prepared for the North Sea Oil industry. This was cut and welded into the required lengths, and shaped according to the 1876 drawings. A glance at the production drawing of the lower mast will show the complex shapes and the multitude of fittings that had to be installed, accurately, before the job was complete. The step for the topmast had to be made very precisely if the topmast was to work up and down. The lower platform also had to be redesigned to mount on the iron mast. A ladder was installed inside each mast to facilitate reaching the platform in safety. The complex shapes of the iron topmasts were contracted out to local training colleges. The whole structure was then zinc sprayed, painted and assembled on the dockside. The topmast was tested in the extended position before being secured housed for the difficult task of stepping. The topmast would have been housed alongside the lower mast before the ship went into action – she was intended to fight under steam. The mizzenmast, with the top and topmast, was hoisted aboard *Warrior* and guided into place on 25 September 1984, under the direction of Shipwright Supervisor Arthur White who had been responsible for the construction of the mast. To provide the lift a 300-

Detail of the foreyard, including the bracket for the stunsails. *AUTHOR*

The main chain plates in place ready for the riggers. These are new items copied from the small number of originals that had survived. Note the platform welded onto the hull to allow easy access and a safety rail. The bulwarks have not yet been painted. *AUTHOR*

The standing rigging of the mainmast in place. When complete much of this detailing, especially the deadeyes used to tension the ropes, will be obscured by the hammock nettings. *AUTHOR*

ton mobile crane was hired. Although the mast itself weighed less than 20 tons the height it had to be lifted, and the distance the crane would have to jib out over the ship, meant that only the largest crane could attempt the work.

This event was of considerable significance. Aside from the impact on the project team it attracted television coverage from both local channels, and provided a new, and highly visible feature on the local skyline. As a result of the excellent preparation the job went ahead without a hitch. Ship Manager Stan Morrell's journal entry for that day included the laconic observation 'Erected mizzenmast. Went very well.' With the previously prepared collar of wooden chocks put into place the mast was secured with the proper $4\frac{1}{2}°$ rake. In the sailing navy the masts were often altered by rechocking in an attempt to improve the ships' sailing. This was unlikely to have been attempted with *Warrior*.

The next mast to be attempted was the heavier and longer mainmast. This weighed 33 tons, complete with topmast and top. It was to have been hoisted aboard during the second week of November. However the weight had been undercalculated at only 27 tons. The 300-ton crane was unable to lift the mast over the ship, and the first attempt had to be aborted. The ship was then unmoored and hauled along the dockside by the entire workforce to give the crane a better lift. Once this

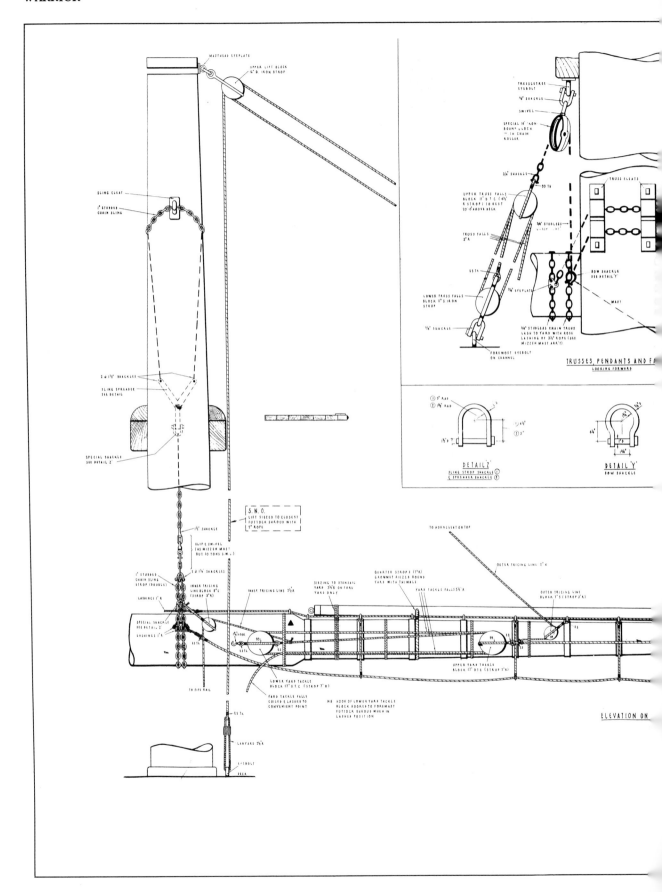

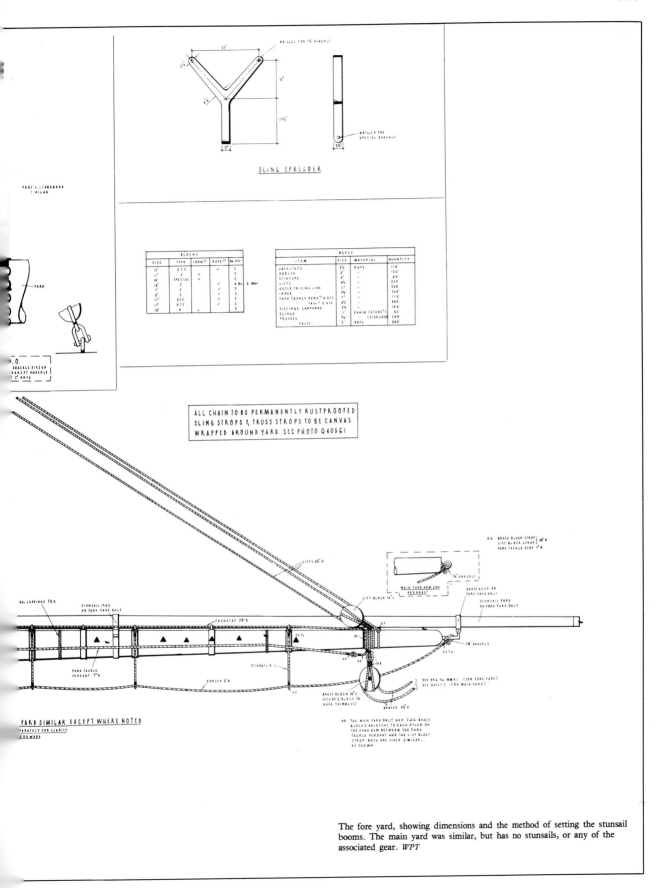

SLING SPREADER

ALL CHAIN TO BE PERMANENTLY RUSTPROOFED
SLING STROPS & TRUSS STROPS TO BE CANVAS
WRAPPED AROUND YARD. SEE PHOTO Q40561

The fore yard, showing dimensions and the method of setting the stunsail booms. The main yard was similar, but has no stunsails, or any of the associated gear. *WPT*

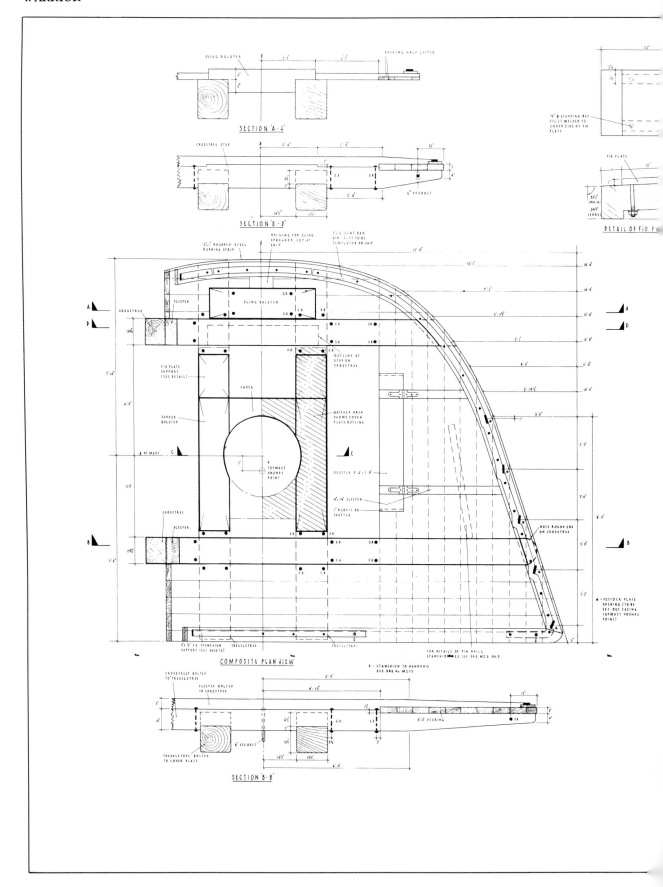

SECTION 'A-A'

SECTION 'D-D'

DETAIL OF FID P

COMPOSITE PLAN VIEW

SECTION 'B-B'

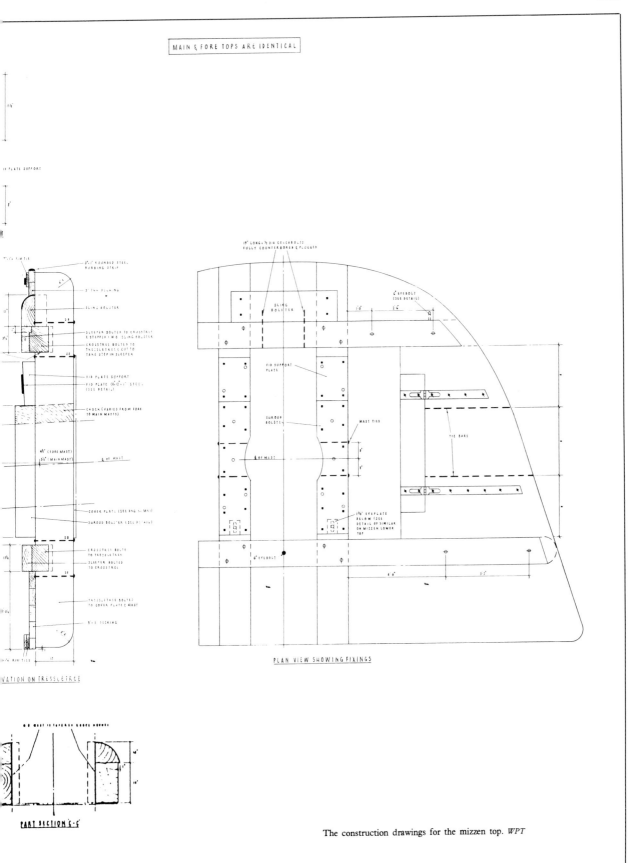

The construction drawings for the mizzen top. *WPT*

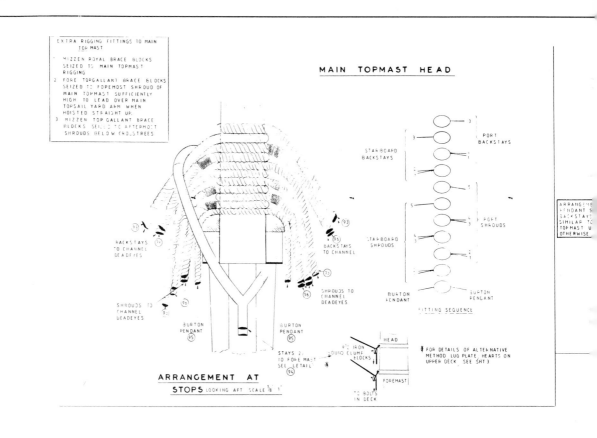

EXTRA RIGGING FITTINGS TO MAIN
TOP MAST

1 MIZZEN ROYAL BRACE BLOCKS
   SEIZED TO MAIN TOPMAST
   RIGGING
2 FORE TOPGALLANT BRACE BLOCKS
   SEIZED TO FOREMOST SHROUD OF
   MAIN TOPMAST SUFFICIENTLY
   HIGH TO LEAD OVER MAIN
   TOPSAIL YARD ARM WHEN
   HOISTED STRAIGHT UP.
3 MIZZEN TOP GALLANT BRACE
   BLOCKS SEIZED TO AFTERMOST
   SHROUDS BELOW CROSSTREES

MAIN TOPMAST HEAD

STARBOARD
BACKSTAYS

PORT
BACKSTAYS

STARBOARD
SHROUDS

PORT
SHROUDS

BURTON
PENDANT

BURTON
PENDANT

FITTING SEQUENCE

ARRANGEMENT
PENDANT S
BACKSTAYS
SIMILAR TO
TOPMAST U
OTHERWISE

BACKSTAYS
TO CHANNEL
DEADEYES

BACKSTAYS
TO CHANNEL

SHROUDS TO
CHANNEL
DEADEYES

SHROUDS TO
CHANNEL
DEADEYES

BURTON
PENDANT

BURTON
PENDANT

STAYS 2.
TO FORE MAST
SEE DETAIL

R'D IRON
ROUND CLUMP
BLOCKS

HEAD

FOREMAST

TO BOLTS
IN DECK

* FOR DETAILS OF ALTERNATIVE
METHOD LUG PLATE, HEARTS ON
UPPER DECK SEE SHT 3

ARRANGEMENT AT
STOPS LOOKING AFT SCALE ⅛"1'

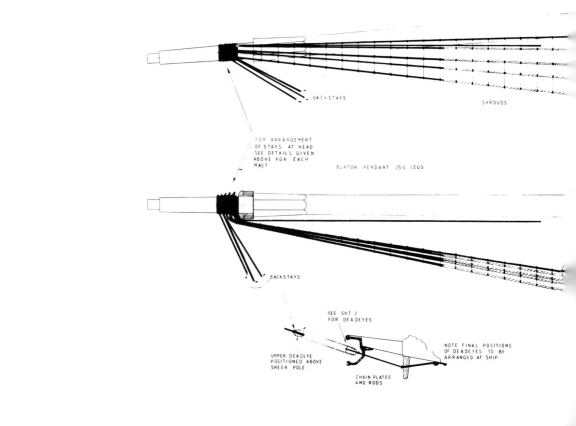

BACKSTAYS

SHROUDS

FOR ARRANGEMENT
OF STAYS AT HEAD
SEE DETAILS GIVEN
ABOVE FOR EACH
MAST

BURTON PENDANT 25.0 LEGS

BACKSTAYS

SEE SHT 2
FOR DEADEYES

NOTE FINAL POSITIONS
OF DEADEYES TO BE
ARRANGED AT SHIP

UPPER DEADEYE
POSITIONED ABOVE
SHEER POLE

CHAIN PLATES
AND RODS

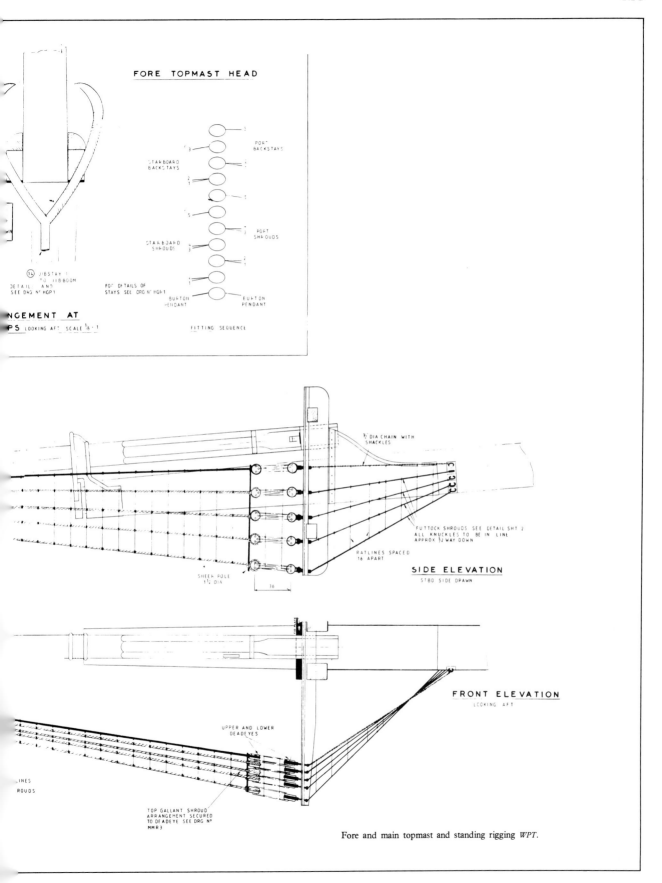

FORE TOPMAST HEAD

PORT
BACKSTAYS

STARBOARD
BACKSTAYS

PORT
SHROUDS

STARBOARD
SHROUDS

FOR DETAILS OF
STAYS SEE DRG Nº HGR1

BURTON
PENDANT

BURTON
PENDANT

JIBSTAY 1
TO JIBBOOM
DETAIL AND
SEE DRG Nº HGR1

FITTING SEQUENCE

NGEMENT AT
PS LOOKING AFT SCALE ⅛ = 1

½ DIA CHAIN WITH
SHACKLES

FUTTOCK SHROUDS SEE DETAIL SHT 2
ALL KNUCKLES TO BE IN LINE
APPROX ½ WAY DOWN

RATLINES SPACED
16 APART

SHEER POLE
1½ DIA

36

SIDE ELEVATION
STBD SIDE DRAWN

FRONT ELEVATION
LOOKING AFT

UPPER AND LOWER
DEADEYES

INES
ROUDS

TOP GALLANT SHROUD
ARRANGEMENT SECURED
TO DEADEYE SEE DRG Nº
MMR3

Fore and main topmast and standing rigging *WPT*.

The mizzen top under construction, March 1984. *WPT*

The main mast standing rigging going up, November 1985. Note the cover over the port side chains, to protect the riggers from a wind temperature well under zero. *AUTHOR*

had been done, at the cost of a considerable disruption in the other work aboard the ship, the mainmast was lifted aboard without further problems on 19 November.

During the spring of 1985 the Warrior Association, the Portsmouth-based society, launched an appeal among members to raise the £750 needed to pay for the mast. Over £2000 was raised, paying for the entire mast! At the same time the justly famous figurehead was brought up to Hartlepool after a period in the Dockyard at Portsmouth, advertising the ship. On 6 February the spirit of *Warrior* came aboard the ship. This was followed by the foremast on the morning of 23 February, and the bowsprit in the afternoon of the same day.

With that accomplished the first, and most obvious stage of the rigging process was complete. However there was still much to be done before *Warrior* assumed the appearance of 1862. The entire standing and running rigging had to be set up, with all the attendant miles of rope, chains, blocks and sails; not to mention the topgallants and royals. The impact on the public was nonetheless greatly increased.

During 1985 the yards were constructed on the dockside, and after painting were placed on the upper deck. Once again these complex shapes were reproduced in steel, whereas the Navy had preferred wooden yards. Before these could be hoisted into place the ships' riggers had to set up the standing rigging, the ropework that holds the masts in place. This would be made up from steel rope, wrapped with hemp and then pre-stretched using a frame set up on the port side of the main deck. Once ready these rope shrouds would be lifted over the mast head and secured to the chain plates. The chain plates were the wrought iron bars bolted to the outside of the bulwarks and angled out from the ship. This had the double benefit of keeping the upper deck free from cordage and increasing the base for the triangulation of the rigging. The chain plates were remade, using the few that remained aboard as patterns. Between the chains and the rope a system of deadeyes with lanyards was used to haul the rigging

taught. The whole system had been perfected over the preceding four hundred years; it was the neatest and most effective solution, combining strength with a facility for adjustment. The topmast and topgallant were each rigged in the same way, although on a much reduced scale. The principal function of the top and crosstrees was to act as spreaders for the standing rigging of the smaller masts. Of the running rigging, the ropes used to control the sails, only the upper deck fittings were set up in 1985. These comprised the fife rails at the foot of each mast – another large job for shipwrights with a good eye and a sharp adze.

Once the full complement of masts were in place the short 24in diameter bowsprit tube appeared inadequate. It was decided to replace it with the longer 40in tube and the full collection of boom and flying jib-boom, as originally fitted. In aesthetic terms this will make some improvement. The steering system, especially the crosshead tiller and the wheels were also necessary parts of the reconstruction. The tiller yoke was fabricated in sheet steel by apprentices at Hartlepool College of Further Education on the Engineering Industries Training Board Course during 1982. The solid wrought iron original had long ago disappeared; the modern replacement is of such quality that it passes unnoticed. The three sets of four quadruple 6ft diameter wheels, with spares were remade by Kelseys of South Shields, in the traditional manner; teak with brass ribs and bindings.

CHAPTER EIGHT
Detail

When she was completed *Warrior* was the most complex machine yet built. Her fitting-out entailed far more than just adding guns, machinery and masts to the bare hull. In order to present the ship as she was it was necessary to consider an enormous number of points of detail. A book of this length cannot hope to touch on all the areas brought up by the reconstruction process. Instead it will have to attempt an appraisal of a cross-section.

The first thing that has to be stressed is the sheer scale of the task. The fine details that made *Warrior* a working warship were the first to be lost when she became a hulk. However, this process was entirely random; some items survived *in situ* while others were removed or broken.

All these details were representative of the era when *Warrior* was built, few were novel, and fewer still unique to the ship. Most passed into and out of naval

HMS *Narcissus*, a 3535-ton 51-gun wooden screw frigate, completed at Devonport in December 1860. Seen here with her yards down across the hammock nettings, possibly during fitting out from the amount of clutter on the upper deck. Her 40pdr Armstrong guns are under white canvas covers. *CPL*

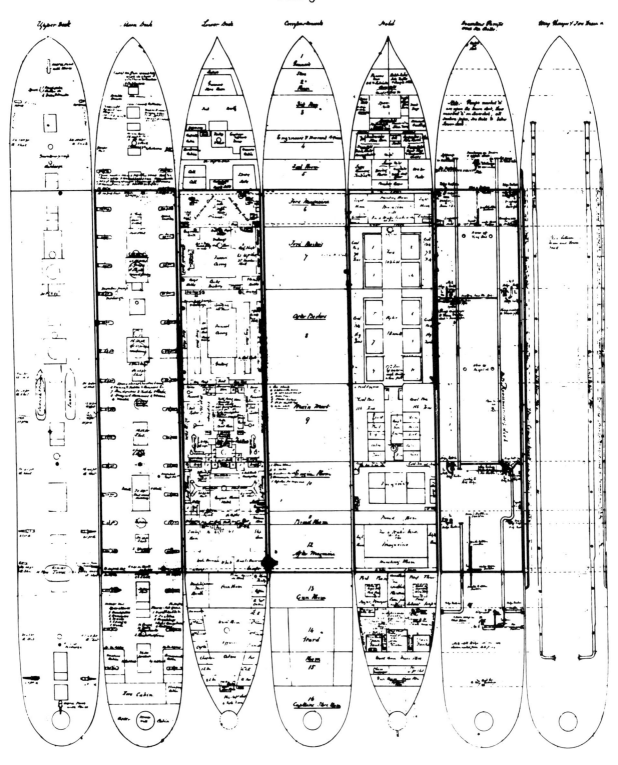

Midshipman Murray's plan. The detail in this sketch proved invaluable during reconstruction. *WPT*

Officers aboard *Narcissus* with her yards still down. *CPL*

service without comment, leaving little *exact* information of the kind required to refabricate. Unless examples could be found, primarily aboard *Warrior*, a host of minor items would have to be researched and redrawn in just the same way as the major elements. This re-emphasised the value of research aboard the ship, and in the archives. *Warrior* was full of useful information on the size, shape and location of many lost fixtures. Bolt holes and slots in the deck became just as significant as period drawings. Only if the two sources matched up could the item be refabricated. For this task to be carried out thoroughly a combination of skills was required. The Research and Drawing Office collaborated in producing a concensus based on inspecting all the evidence and airing all the possibilities.

ARTIFACTS

Essential to the restoration has been the collection of numerous artifacts and equipment, ranging from a six pounder gun, a stream anchor for the upper deck to the ship's bell and mess table utensils. Almost all have

Another view aboard *Narcissus*, looking aft showing the funnel and steam pipe in the raised position. A canvas awning has been rigged overhead. A similar feature will be required aboard *Warrior* when she is opened for display. *CPL*

147

Officers in the quarter deck watching seamen preparing ropes. Note that *Warrior* did not have a poop deck like this until after her 1871–5 refit. *CPL*

resulted from the searches and the naval connections of Captain John Wells. More recently this has included contributions from the Warrior Association in Portsmouth, now chaired by John Wells, which includes ditty boxes, hammocks and Victorian knick-knacks.

One thing that the reconstruction did reveal was a surprising lack of concrete knowledge of the mid-Victorian Navy. Existing books were soon revealed as inadequate, yet for a generation they had been regarded as a substitute for new research. Only when the team at Hartlepool began to ask awkward questions and require solid information did the poverty of existing sources become apparent. As a result the research for the *Warrior* project involved a large amount of primary materials, the basic archival sources for the history of the Navy in the period. In this respect the *Warrior* project has already made significant steps toward improving our knowledge of the fabric of seapower. The

archive collected will hopefully form the basis for further work on the structure of the Navy, its ships, dockyards, ship and engine builders, officers and men. The period 1815–1880 has long been recognised as one of the least well documented and studied epochs of the navy's history.

A major element in the presentation of *Warrior* as a meaningful exhibit lay in the ability of the project to achieve the highest standards of accuracy. With major items this was relatively simple; but for small, or move-able items there was little guidance as to their location and relationship to other fixtures. The growing dif-ficulties of the team at Hartlepool were solved by the discovery in the Royal Naval Museum archive of a mid-shipman's logbook containing a sketch plan of the decks. Henry Murray joined *Warrior* when she was

Wash day aboard *Narcissus*. The curious device in the foreground is almost certainly an early steam powered fire engine. *CPL.*

first placed in commission, and served aboard until 1863. He had only joined the Navy in the previous year, at the tender age of thirteen. Midshipmen and Sub-Lieutenants were then expected to keep a logbook and illustrate it with drawings of equipment aboard the ship and scenes viewed from the upper deck. Murray was ordered to make a plan of the decks and his effort was considered worthy of preservation. It clearly shows the arrangements along with the moveable fittings and stores. Whatever his reasons Murray prepared a major guide to the layout of the ship. Clearly it had some contemporary value, as a copy was found in Captain Cochrane's Letter Book. Dating from 1862, these plans have saved the team countless hours, offering simple answers to complex questions.

THE UPPER DECK

The only two upper deck photographs credited to *Warrior* were not very helpful for the reconstruction.

They had been taken in the late 1860s by photographers who were concerned to include all the officers, who managed to obscure much useful detailing. However *Narcissus*, a 3535-ton wooden screw frigate completed for service in late 1860, was photographed on two occasions during fitting out. As a frigate her fittings and detailing would have been generally similar to those of *Warrior*, and they are clearly shown in a sequence of shots. Among the major items shown are the capstan, an item the team at Hartlepool were convinced they would not find, along with the binnacle, wheels, hammock nettings, 40pdr Armstrong gun, canvas awnings, fife rails and masts.

Some features of *Warrior*'s upper deck were novel. One, the bulletproof conning tower, had been copied from the French. On the floating batteries that were used at Kinburn, the French had constructed an armoured pilot house. A much larger structure of 4in plate was placed abaft the mainmast on *Gloire*. The object in both cases was to provide the captain of the ship with a position from which he could control the ship without having to expose himself to gunfire, splinters and musketry. While the British were quite happy to copy the structure they did not fully grasp its significance. They failed to provide the 3in armoured oval tower with the necessary facilities for controlling the ship. Behind the armour and the heavy wooden backing the tower had a raised platform, to allow the occupants to see over the bulwarks, a view denied to anyone standing on the upper deck. It was open topped, to ensure that the captain could see the set of the sails at a glance. Entry into the tower was from below, via a hatch just to the rear of the citadel. Orders for the wheel were passed down into the citadel by voice pipe. Over the top ran the light navigating bridge, which would have been used to control the ship.

It has been suggested that the purpose of the tower was to provide a vantage point from which boarders could be shot down by the ships' Marines. A brief

Seamen at cutlass drill, wearing an early naval uniform. When the capstan was in use the companionway rails were lowered and gratings placed over the ladders and skylights. The men could then run around the deck unimpeded, pushing on the bars. *CPL*

Officers aboard *Narcissus*. Note the rainwater chutes, rigged to fill the boiler feed water tanks with fresh water. Also in the picture is one of the ship's pets. *CPL*

period spent inside will demonstrate the folly of this notion. It is completely unsuitable for such a purpose, the ports are too small and the whole structure too cramped for effective rifle fire. Instead this was the first conning tower fitted to a British warship, and the ancestor of the massive structures of the Dreadnought age. Some of the later ironclads, starting with *Northumberland*, were fitted with a larger tower which held the binnacle and fire control equipment along with the all-important wheel. This paved the way for the 12in thick armoured steel structure aboard HMS *Hood*, which weighed over 600 tons and carried a 30ft long range finder. This was a descendant of the *Gloire*'s conning tower, protected against the heaviest shells. The *Warrior* idea of bulletproof plating was reintroduced during the Second World War as a protection against strafing aircraft.

The capstan, evidently new from the crisp edges to the squares left for the bars. Behind are the port side bulwarks, hammock nettings and a 40pdr Armstrong on a rear truck carriage, identical to those fitted to *Warrior*. *CPL*

FIGUREHEAD AND DECORATIVE CARVING

Warrior and *Black Prince* were almost the last British front rank ships to carry a figurehead. Only the battleship *Rodney* of 1888 was to mount such an archaic throwback. The origins of this crowning decorative glory of the wooden warship go back beyond the carved stem posts of the Vikings. During the fifteenth century the changing shape of ships provided a logical position for the head. In the form seen aboard *Warrior*, the head was influenced by the shift in bow design instituted by Sir Robert Seppings in the years after Trafalgar. Where *Victory* carried her figure upright *Warrior*'s was fixed almost horizontally. This was the style of the wooden steam warship, and like much else about the ship reflected the earlier *Mersey* class.

As the form of the *Warrior*'s bow was a direct copy of that of *Mersey* a figurehead was inevitable. There appears to have been no thought of abandoning the head; in aesthetic terms a knee bow without the crowning element did not work. The resultant three-quarters figure double life-size carvings of the two ironclads were, both in scale and artistic quality, among the finest ever executed. They were designed and carved by the Hellyer family of Portsmouth, for many years the leading decorative carvers for the Royal Navy. The original design was for the figure to be armed with a scimitar. However before it was fitted the more correct Roman *gladius* was substituted. Despite this the model in the Science Museum, and the plans published by Rankine both show the curved sword.

Before any more ironclads were designed, in the period of confusion resulting from the return of

The upper deck wheels, clearly marked with the ship's name. Unlike *Warrior* the smaller and more manoeuvrable *Narcissus* only had a double set of wheels; *Warrior* had a quadruple set on all three decks, although the individual wheels were identical. Note the steps up to the binnacle and the curious noticeboard on which it is mounted. The ropes around the fife rails are rather more untidy than they would be when the ship was at sea.

Palmerston, the figurehead lost its place. When *Defence* and *Resistance* were conceived ramming had become a significant warlike feature. The resultant sloping bow gave no logical position for a figurehead. It was replaced by a small bow scroll. The original draft for the *Achilles* was of a full sister to *Warrior*, complete with knee bow and figurehead. However Reeds' damning criticism of the unarmoured bow and stern of Watts' design led to the more functional form of the new ship and the end of figurehead. The next class of large ironclads, the *Minotaur*s, adopted a much more elaborate bow scroll. This had the effect of not projecting beyond the ram bow, where the old figurehead acted as a shock absorber in the event of a collision. This was the case in the *Warrior/Royal Oak* collision of 1868.

The figureheads of *Warrior* and *Black Prince* made them unique in the Black Battlefleet. Smaller ships, corvettes and gunboats, persisted with them into the twentieth century. However these figures only served to make the ships look ridiculous. They had all the grace of last minute afterthoughts and were decidedly incongruous. Aboard the first pair or ironclads the figurehead was the focal point of the ship, a fitting culmination to an overall aesthetic layout, that arose naturally out of the form of the hull. Without it *Warrior* was incomplete. In this respect the fitting of the new figurehead had an enormous impact on the project, especially as it greeted all who visited the ship.

Warrior's figurehead in the 1870s, showing details of the bowsprit cap, the canvas screen set up to give the men a measure of protection from the elements. *CPL*

Warrior's figurehead ashore in the early years of the twentieth century. It remained in the Portsmouth Dockyard for many years. The new head spent much of 1984 in almost the same spot. *CPL*

The figurehead of *Black Prince* was in every respect the equal of her sister's fitting. She is seen here late in her career, while serving as a training ship. Note the more substantial screen around the heads. *CPL*

The original carving was dismounted during the collision with *Royal Oak*. Tradition has it that *Royal Oak*'s officers carried it below as a trophy, and that it was never recovered. Certainly there are significant variations between the figure on either side of the collision. The second head, or perhaps the repaired original, was detached from the ship before her *Vernon* period and displayed ashore at Portsmouth. Parkes reports that it was repaired in the 1930s, after the shield and sword arm had fallen off through dry rot. Later it was taken to the Fleet Headquarters at Northolt, and appears to have collapsed in the late 1960s, weakened by further ravages of dry rot. The principal result of this recent loss was to make the task of replacing the head at once more complex and more satisfying.

The awesome task was entrusted to Jack Whitehead and Norman Gaches, based at Wootton on the Isle of Wight. Assisted by a liberal supply of photographs of the very photogenic figures they began work in 1981. This was one of the first significant tasks undertaken off the ship. Before the carving could begin a 3-ton block of Canadian Yellow Pine was glued together to meet

the outline of the head. A full size painting of the design was also made as a guide to the work. The carving, when almost complete, formed the centrepiece of a display at the London International Boat Show in January 1983. The area around the stand, generously provided by the Daily Express, was dominated by the figure, now a third lighter but decidedly more handsome. As a result *Warrior* was the most talked about feature of the show. Staff from the SPT were on the stand throughout to answer queries and accept numerous donations towards the cost of the work. The two craftsmen also carried on carving during the show. The show success led to an appearance on the BBC's 'Blue Peter' television programme. The benefits to the project brought about as a direct result of these two public outings were enormous. *Warrior*, or at least her figurehead, was now a national celebrity; the project had achieved an identity. The 12ft high Graeco-Roman Warrior projected an unforgettable image of power, just as the original had done 120 years before.

The head was completed in mid-1983, and then painted in the white and gold colour scheme of the era.

The figurehead on display at the 1983 London Boat Show. Norman Gaches and Jack Whitehead can be seen at work surrounded by a large and appreciative audience. *WPT*.

Warrior with her figurehead aboard for the first time in a century; the steel supporting arms are being welded onto the beak while the crane carries the weight. *WPT*

It was displayed at Portsmouth for much of 1984, just inside the Main Gate of the Dockyard. Once again the figure served to give advanced notice of the arrival of the ship. Head and ship were finally united on 6 February 1985. The visual impact of the ship was doubled by this single act – there was now a logical culmination to the lines of the hull. The figurehead also proved an irresistable lure for the camera, in a way that the long unrelieved darkness of the hull could never be. Ask anyone not connected with the project what they remember most about the ship, and the figurehead will be at the top of most lists.

One unusual feature of the *Warrior*'s bow was the heavy teak cladding over the narrow iron beak. It carried the trailboards behind the figurehead, and the hawse pipes and scupper pipes for the seamen's heads. An iron structure could have been devised to do the same job, at a fraction of the weight. However this feature had to be replaced, the wood having rotted, and one of the hawse pipes had been ripped off in the 1976 collision.

During the summer of 1985 the port side fairing was replaced. This was another heavy job involving large baulks of timber, cut to shape by hand and bolted into place. Once complete, this structure was used to mount the hawse pipes and the trailboards. The former were still in place when the ship reached Hartlepool, apart from the one that had been recovered from the sea. The trailboards were carved by Richard Barnet from Torrington, Devon. Once painted they blended in perfectly with the figurehead.

At the stern *Warrior* was almost as original as she

was at the bow. Her wooden style frigate stern with its projecting galleries and windows was retained in *Defence* and *Resistance*, but abolished in *Achilles* with the advent of the complete waterline belt. Although the stern galleries made a brief reappearance aboard later ironclads they had no place in armoured warships. For all the embellishment of the frigate sterns in the first four ironclads they were in fact little more than box rooms. The intrusion of the hoisting propeller well and the massive curved tiller yoke ruined the space. As a result the Captain's day and sleeping cabins were forward of the stern cabin. This was reduced to service as a store room and passage to the Captain's heads, located in the overhanging quarter galleries. Most of the windows were dummies, only the three across the stern opened. Furthermore there was no provision for arming the stern, on the main deck level, that function being left to the upper deck stern pivot gun. The whole stern structure was built of wood, bolted to the iron hull. Consequently it had rotted away over the years, leaving little more than the bolts along the quarters and the windows across the stern to indicate its former glory.

The quarter galleries were reconstructed in steel, late in 1985, being bolted onto the hull. Once fitted with timber cladding inside and out they would be indistinguishable from the wooden originals. The structure itself was quite a straightforward replication. However the decorative carving between the dummy windows of the quarters proved to be a mystery. Even blowing up the existing photographs produced only a messy blur, for no pictures existed which provided any details of the stern of *Warrior* or *Black Prince*. As a result further research on other frigates of the period had to be undertaken.

THE HEADS

Aboard *Warrior*'s wooden predecessors the heads for the seamen were situated over the knee bow, on either side of the bowsprit. The 'seats of ease' and urine dales discharged directly into the sea, being located above the flare of the bow. When at sea the men were expected to use the facilities on the lee side, to ensure that the effluent did not foul the side of the ship. The floor of this area was normally a grating, allowing the sea to enter and assist the cleaning process, although hardly conducive to the comfort of the occupants.

This pattern was repeated aboard *Warrior* and *Black Prince* as a normal part of the bow structure. Soon after completion both ships were fitted with additional heads just outside the bulwarks on the both sides, abreast the fore funnel. These facilities discharged by way of a scupper pipe at sea level. While additional facilities

The *Rodney* of 1890, displaying positively the last figurehead to be carried by a British capital ship. No satisfactory explanation has yet been found for the appearance of this absurd anachronism. The 13.5in guns were mounted on barbettes to keep them clear of spray. Unlike the *Devastation* type turrets this arrangement allowed the guns to be fought in a seaway. Later ships retained the barbettes, and added increased freeboard. Note that the ship is riding some five feet high. *CPL*

Stern of *Warrior*, compare with that on page 48. The bulwarks are being clad. Note the surviving stern gallery detail, the real and false windows. Below the aperture for the hoisting screw and its banjo frame can be seen. *AUTHOR*

were welcome they were not entirely satisfactory. In certain states of the wind they created a 'nuisance'. When *Bellerophon* was built the old position was resumed, to the general satisfaction of all.

The Captain's toilets were located in the quarter galleries, where they had been for generations. *Warrior*'s only claim to novelty here was that one of them was flushed by a Downton pump. The other officers had their facilities on the main deck just abaft of the citadel.

When the team at Hartlepool came to examine the heads in detail, preparing for replication, they made a curious discovery. The ten 'seats of ease' shown on the original plans were, when redrawn for reconstruction, quite impossible. There was only one inch between each of the holes. As a result the whole structure would have been impossible to use and far too weak to bear the weight of a man. The reconstructed heads will show a more realistic number of seats. This surprising discovery helps to demonstrate the wide latitude given to the Dockyards when fitting out a warship. Unimportant details, such as the number of seats in the heads, would be left to the Master Shipwright of the responsible yard to fill in according to the accepted fashion of the service. Each Dockyard would have had its own designs and methods. *Warrior*, fitted at Sheerness, would have been different to *Black Prince* which was fitted out at Devonport. The quarter galleries that housed the Captain's facilities were also replaced, albeit in steel, and fitted accordingly. The officers' toilets on the main deck were the simplest to construct, being

little more than partitioned spaces. The heads required the reconstruction of the whole platform that carried them, a wide area overhanging the bow and built entirely of wood. This work was commenced in late 1985 and brought to completion by mid-1986. One additional feature to be considered was the canvas screen erected around the heads to offer some shelter to the men from the elements, and to preserve decency while in harbour. These can be seen in the two photographs of the figureheads in the preceeding section.

Unlike the original ventilation system, the heads will not be returned to service when the ship is opened to the public.

BOATS

The boat outfit of *Warrior* was determined by the size of her crew. In a submission of 6 May 1861 the Controller gave the following outfit:

2 pinnace launches	42ft long.
1 pinnace	32ft
1 galley	32ft
2 cutters	30ft
1 gig	30ft
1 jolly boat	18ft
1 dinghy	14ft
9 boats in all	

Two months later, November 1985, the bulwarks have made some progress and the starboard quarter gallery frame is being bolted aboard the ship. The original galleries would have been wooden, but only the bolts remain. The pontoon, while vital to the work, is hardly the most comfortable place to work in rough weather. *AUTHOR*

However with the crew increased from 550 men, as first proposed, to 707 additional boats would have been shipped. Early in her first commission Captain Cochrane called for the replacement of some boats by larger models.

3 April 1862

Sir,

I have the honor to bring to your notice the establishment of boats of this ship, and to request that you will be pleased to allow of the following changes to be made, vizt. the substitution of 2 cutters pulling 12 oars, 2 Cutters pulling 12 Oars, 1 26 Foot Gig, 1 28 Foot Cutter, for the Boats we have at present vizt. 2 Cutters pulling 10 Oars, 1 20 Foot Gig, 1 18 Foot Jolly Boat.

I beg to add that our present Cutters are the same length and weight as the Cutters pulling 12 Oars without their advantages – that the 20 foot Gig only pulls 4 oars and is very heavy to pull – and that the Jolly Boat of 18 feet is so small as to be unable even to bring the fresh beef off in ordinary weather.

Vice Admiral Sir Houston Steward K C B

I have signed A A Cochrane Captain

The trail boards, carved by Richard Barnett, mounted on the bow cladding on the port side. Note the thickness of the cladding, and the shape, another hand finished item. *WPT*

During her second commission *Warrior* received at least one steam launch. However the boats have not been made a major item of the reconstruction, from the ease with which they can be added later. Consequently *Warrior* will arrive at Portsmouth without a full complement. Work has been put in hand on the 30ft cutters.

In the Victorian Navy ships' boats served a variety of functions, some of which are outlined in Cochrane's

The stove that provided heat for the drying room alongside, as found. Cleaning spaces like this provided an enormous amount of very unpleasant work during the reconstruction. *WPT*

letter, namely bringing aboard stores. While at sea, or anywhere except alongside a quay every single item that went aboard or left the ship did so by boat. Provisions, including huge water casks and barrels of salted meat were accompanied by ammunition, spare parts and even coal. In the first two commissions all these movements would have involved extensive use of human musclepower.

In time of war the boats came into their own as small war vessels, able to operate in waters too shallow for ocean-going ships like *Warrior* and as landing craft for marines and armed seamen. For these functions they carried small guns and war rockets. During the Russian War the boats of the Fleets in the Baltic and Black Sea

The upper deck of *Warrior* during her second commission. Contrary to received opinion the man leaning on the binnacle is not Lord 'Jackie' Fisher. He was only aboard as Gunnery Lieutenant towards the end of the first commission, and furthermore there is no physical resemblance **whatsoever**. *WPT*

had been used extensively for landings, raids, rocket bombardments and, most spectacularly, the disembarkation of the Allied armies in the Crimea. In truth the boats were just as much an extension of the ships' war capacity as the modern day helicopter.

Another function of the boats was to act as ceremonial transport for Senior Officers. Captains always had a gig set aside for their use, and if an Admiral was embarked he also had his barge. Every boat had its own crew. Captains and Admirals often carried their personal boats' crews from ship to ship.

Finally boats had a training function. Even the mundane and routine work of embarking stores gave junior officers a taste of command. They also offered a grounding in seamanship. Through the routine of boat drill officers and men achieved a degree of familiarity with one another that was vital if they were to act together effectively in wartime.

VENTILATION

The need to provide a supply of fresh air aboard warships had been a problem for centuries before *Warrior* was built. When a two- or three-decker line of battleship was forced to close her gunports by the weather the air below decks quickly became stale and sour. The reason for this was simple. Up to 1000 men lived

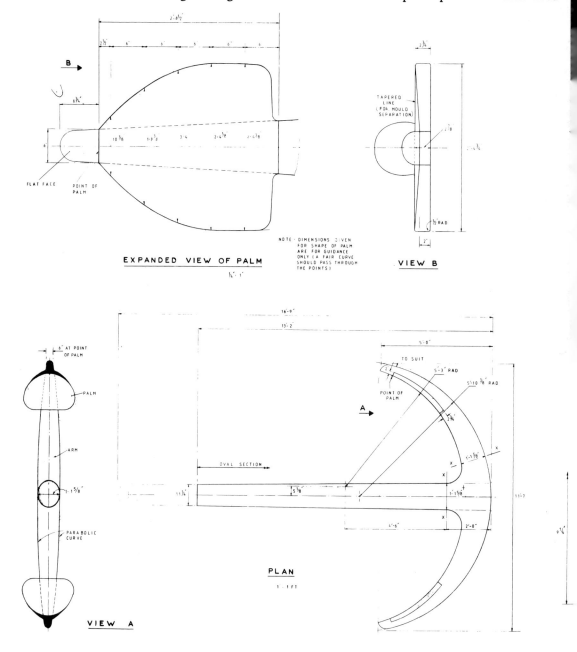

The bower anchor. *WPT*

The stern anchor as completed, before the welds were polished and painted over. This view emphases the built-up sheet steel method used to build these items. The saving in weight is immense. *WPT*

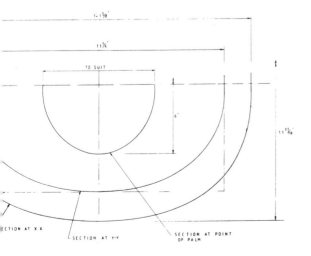

FULL SIZE SECTIONS

aboard comparatively small ships in cramped and unhygenic conditions. Furthermore wooden ships were never watertight. Their bilges always contained some stale water. In a hot climate this helped to provide an atmosphere in which diseases like cholera and typhoid could thrive. Early attempts to channel air into the ships, using canvas windtraps, were largely futile.

The adoption of steam power only added heat and damp to an already unpleasant environment. Aboard the 120-gun *Marlborough*, Flagship of the Mediterranean Fleet 1860–1865, the problem was exacerbated by overcrowding. The result was an unhealthy and inefficient crew with an over-large sick list. For *Warrior* an attempt was made to solve the problem. One set of published plans, based on early drawings, show a large number of ventilating cowls on the upper deck, clustered around the funnels. However these were soon almost entirely removed. Instead *Warrior* relied on a pioneering system of mechanical ventilation. A large fan, powered by a donkey engine between the boilers and the main engines, drew air into the ship and then forced it up through a system of trunking on the lower deck. Here there were no ports that could be opened while at sea, only the small plug scuttles for harbour use.

This arrangement also provided for the fresh air to be directed into the main deck citadel during combat. The pressure of air would then help to clear away the thick clouds of black powder smoke that built up during sustained gunfire. The system provided for positive air pressure inside the citadel which would force the smoke out through the gunports. The original ventilation system has been restored, and, using new electric pumps, will continue to operate.

THE DRYING ROOM

Another attempt to improve the lot of the seamen came through the fitting of a drying room. Aboard wooden ships the fear of fire, the greatest of all dangers at sea, had ensured that only a galley, and later steam engines, were fitted. *Warrior*, being built of iron, was much less susceptible to the danger, both in war and peace, a fact quickly recognised even by the cautious Admiralty.

Soon after *Warrior* was commissioned Captain Cochrane was approached by a Mr Williamson of High Holborn. Williamson wanted to install a heating system in the ship, specifically to dry clothes and hammocks. The age-old method of hanging them out in the lower rigging was not very satisfactory. Improved facilities would also encourage the seamen to keep their clothes, and perhaps even themselves, clean. On 9 October 1861 Cochrane formally applied to the Admiralty for permission to have the apparatus installed, in the position it still occupies. Permission was granted, and the work was carried out at Devonport in early 1862. The stove was kept separate from the drying room, passing hot air through it by a system of pipes and ducts. All this was located on the port side of the bow on the orlop deck, underneath the sail lockers. It was suspended away

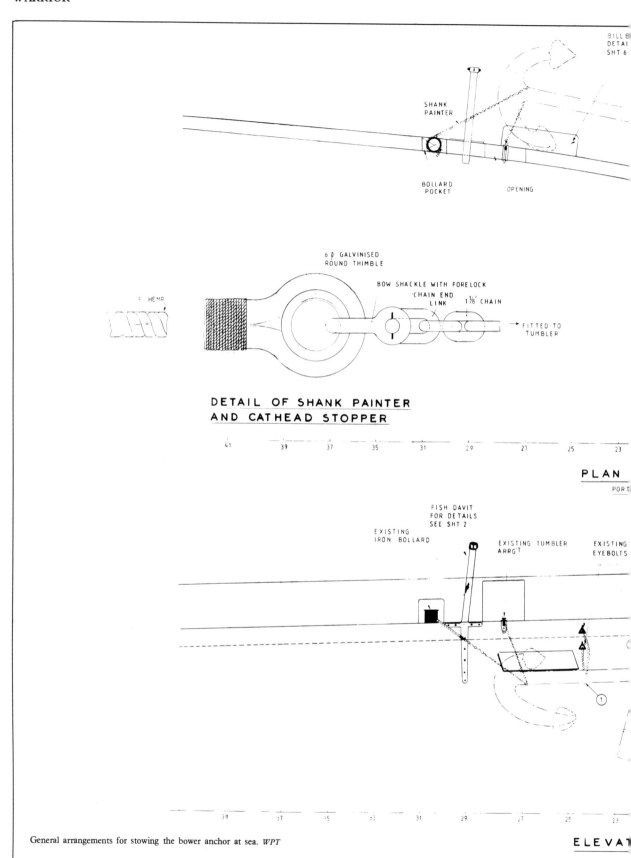

BILL B
DETAI
SHT 6

SHANK
PAINTER

BOLLARD
POCKET

OPENING

6 Ø GALVINISED
ROUND THIMBLE

BOW SHACKLE WITH FORELOCK

CHAIN END
LINK

1⅛" CHAIN

9 HEMP

FITTED TO
TUMBLER

DETAIL OF SHANK PAINTER
AND CATHEAD STOPPER

41   39   37   35   31   29   27   25   23

PLAN

PORT

FISH DAVIT
FOR DETAILS
SEE SHT 2

EXISTING
IRON BOLLARD

EXISTING TUMBLER
ARRG'T

EXISTING
EYEBOLTS

39   27   25   23   31   29   27   25   23

General arrangements for stowing the bower anchor at sea. *WPT*

ELEVA

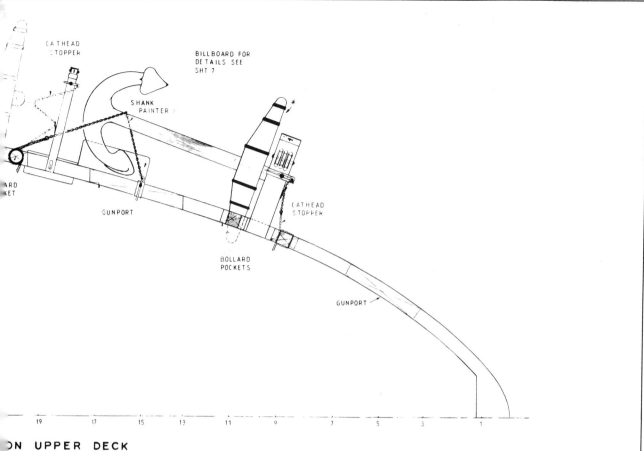

CATHEAD
STOPPER

BILLBOARD FOR
DETAILS SEE
SHT 7

SHANK
PAINTER

ARD
KET

GUNPORT

CATHEAD
STOPPER

BOLLARD
POCKETS

GUNPORT

19   17   15   13   11   9   7   5   3   1

ON UPPER DECK

STBD SIDE SIMILAR

IRON CATHEAD
FOR DETAILS
SEE SHT 3

CATHEAD FOR
DETAILS SEE
SHT 4

EXISTING
EYEBOLTS

BOLLARDS FOR
DETAILS SEE SHT 5

TING
RD

EXISTING
TUMBLER ARRGT

①

①

① LASHINGS SHOWN ON ELEVATION ONLY,
9" HEMP

19   17   15   13   11   9   7   5   3   1

SIDE DRAWN STBD SIDE SIMILAR

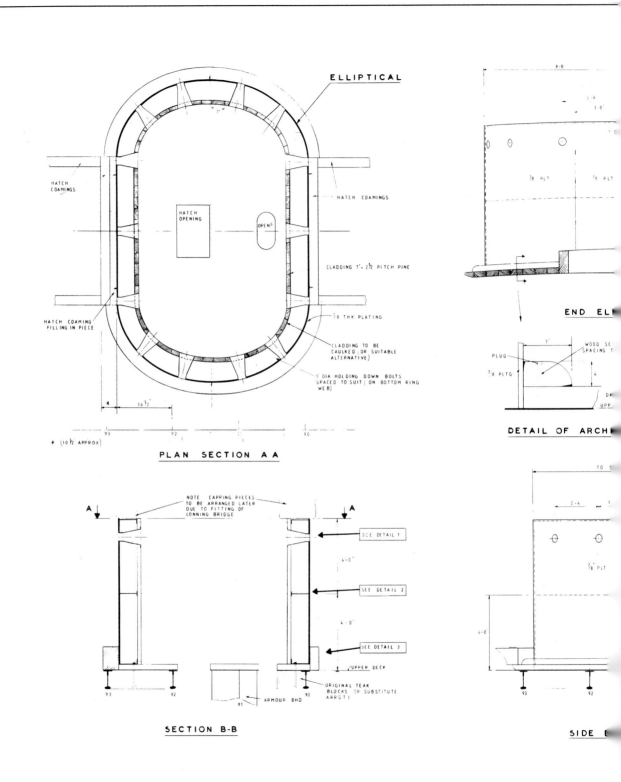

ELLIPTICAL

HATCH
COAMINGS

HATCH COAMINGS

HATCH
OPENING

OPEN^G

CLADDING 7'. 2½ PITCH PINE

⅞ THK PLATING

HATCH COAMING
FILLING IN PIECE

(CLADDING TO BE
CAULKED (OR SUITABLE
ALTERNATIVE)

1' DIA HOLDING DOWN BOLTS
SPACED TO SUIT (ON BOTTOM RING
WEB)

36 ½"

93   92   90

* (10 ½ APPROX)

PLAN SECTION A A

8-0

2-8

3-0

⅞ PLT   ⅞ PLT

END EL

7'

WOOD SC
SPACING T

PLUG

⅞ PLTG

4

DK

UPP

DETAIL OF ARCH

NOTE CAPPING PIECES
TO BE ARRANGED LATER
DUE TO FITTING OF
CONNING BRIDGE

A   A

SEE DETAIL 1

4-0'

SEE DETAIL 2

4-0'

SEE DETAIL 3

UPPER DECK

ORIGINAL TEAK
BLOCKS OR SUBSTITUTE
ARRGT)

93   92

91   90   ARMOUR BHD

SECTION B-B

TO S

2-4

⅞ PLT

4-0

93   92

SIDE

General arrangement of the conning tower, emphasising the pitch of the deck.
The light navigating bridge will be erected above the tower, hence the flat top.
WPT

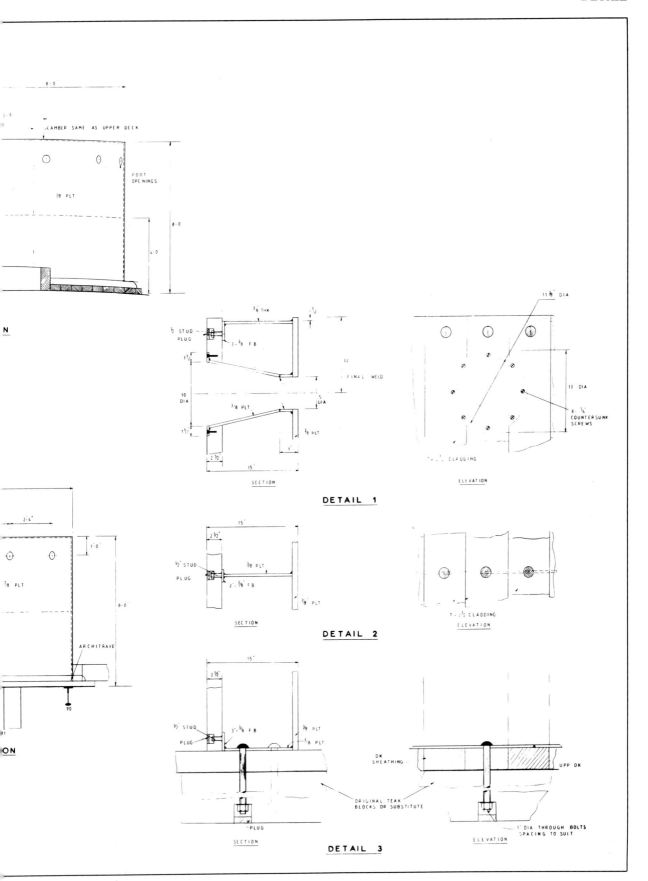

8-0

CAMBER SAME AS UPPER DECK

PORT OPENINGS

7/8 PLT

8-0

4-0

N

3/8 THK

1/2 STUD
PLUG

3-3/8 F B

FINAL WELD

10 DIA

3/8 PLT

7/8 PLT

2 1/2

15

SECTION

11 7/8 DIA

13 DIA

8-1/4
COUNTERSUNK
SCREWS

CLADDING

ELEVATION

DETAIL 1

2-4

1-0

7/8 PLT

8-0

ARCHITRAVE

90

ON

15

2 1/2

1/2 STUD

PLUG

2-3/8 F B

3/8 PLT

7/8 PLT

SECTION

7-2 1/2 CLADDING

ELEVATION

DETAIL 2

15

2 1/2

1/2 STUD

PLUG

3-3/8 F B

7/8 PLT

3/8 PLT

DK SHEATHING

UPP DK

ORIGINAL TEAK
BLOCKS OR SUBSTITUTE

1 DIA THROUGH BOLTS
SPACING TO SUIT

PLUG

SECTION

ELEVATION

DETAIL 3

167

from the ships' side. The funnel passed up through the four decks above to the upper deck. The drying room was officially tried out in June 1862. Cochrane reported that it was a complete success. It took only five hours to dry 120 hammocks, or 320 items of clothing, using only 80lb of coal.

Like the after magazine, the drying room and its stove survived aboard *Warrior* because they were small spaces located so low in the ship, and in such a difficult place to reach, that no-one bothered to take them out. After cleaning and painting, which was no easy matter, they provide another example of a prototype fixture,

The beak as arrived at Hartlepool, showing the damage from her collision. *Warrior* was moored with the starboard side inshore at Milford Haven also, hence the warning painting on the bow. *DAVE MORRELL*

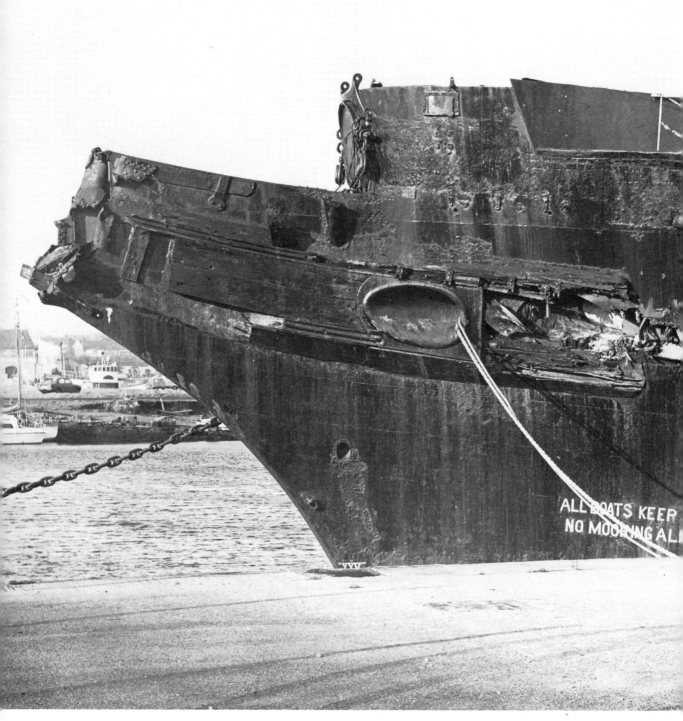

first used aboard *Warrior*, that set the pattern for later ships.

The problem of personal hygiene aboard ship was an old one. With the introduction of steam engines the Admiralty had made an effort to provide washing facilities for the engine room crew and the stokers. However the seamen were considered, largely as a result of long

Inside one of the ship's prisons, before cleaning. These unlit cubicles were located low in the bow. They must have had a considerable deterrent effect on men used to the open air. The bull's eye glasses allowed the sentry to illuminate the cell, but no permanent lighting was installed. *WPT*

experience, to be incorrigibly dirty. The main result of this was to postpone the fitting of washrooms aboard a British capital ship until the mid-1860s, *Penelope* being the first. Before that the Admiralty ordered that every man should wash one of his two hammocks once a fortnight, along with most of his clothes. Such cleanliness by order did not extend to personal bathing. Although a sail was often rigged on the upper deck for this purpose it was understandably not very popular in the cool climate of the Channel.

LIFE ABOARD SHIP

The environment aboard *Warrior* was not greatly changed from that to be experienced on her wooden predecessors. The deckhead was noticeably higher, allowing tall men to stand upright. This was in marked contrast to some of the smaller ships of the preceeding generation. One tall Captain used to shave standing in his cabin, with the mirror on the quarter deck above and his head out of the skylight.

There was also more space. The seamen were berthed on the main deck, with their mess tables between the guns. In comparison to earlier ships there were less guns, and therefore less men. This ensured that only the junior officers were accommodated on the lower deck. While *Warrior*'s iron hull and subdivision made cleaning out the bilges a simpler task it also promoted condensation. In the absence of the ventilating hollow masts *Warrior* and *Black Prince* were damp ships, with proportionately higher rates of sickness, especially for respiratory and rheumatic complaints.

As with so many other aspects of the ship *Warrior* demonstrated the potential improvements in the seaman's environment that could be achieved, but did not make the greatest use of them. She was the inspiration, not the realisation.

PUMPS

Warrior was a very labour-intensive ship. There were no auxilliary machines aboard the ship, no steam capstan, no steam bilge pumps. Instead the ship had twelve 9 and 12in bore Downton pumps, almost all on the lower deck. They were used for draining the bilges, not a common task aboard *Warrior*, ventilating the magazines, flushing the Captain's heads and fire-fighting. They could be operated by one man, turning a large iron wheel. For a more determined usage they were connected up to a spindle on the main deck which allowed up to 48 men to work them.

ANCHORS

Warrior's original outfit of anchors comprised the following. Their location and design can be seen on the plan on p40–1.

2 bower	112cwt	mounted forward
2 sheet	112cwt	mounted just aft of the bower
2 stern	50cwt	
1 stream	28cwt	
1 kedge	16cwt	
1 kedge	8cwt	

The two stern anchors were copied in sheet steel by the Billingham Industrial Training Centre during 1983. Being hollow replicas they weigh only 5cwt. The design was unusual, being a type of Rodger's anchor with the palms facing out from the stock, the reverse of the common type.

Suitable kedge anchors were found in a local scrapyard, and have been restored, along with a stream anchor from Portland. The largest anchors have not yet been reproduced.

CHAPTER NINE
Conclusions

Warrior marked the greatest single development in the history of warship design. She opened up the unlimited possibilities inherent in the use of iron and steel as structural materials for shipbuilding. With the end of the art of wooden ship construction the industrial technology of iron took over. The pace of scientific advance has not slackened. *Warrior*, as befits a ship conceived and designed by men familiar with wooden practice, had very little direct influence on the future designs, her type being abandoned only four years later. However, her very existence stimulated the Victorian engineers, already confidant of the inevitable and desirable nature of progress, to renewed efforts. Every aspect of her conservative design was challenged, and after a decade only the iron hull remained; masts, single expansion engines, hull form and smooth bore artillery were all obsolete.

The path from *Warrior* to the *Devastation* of 1872 and the *Dreadnought* of 1906 has been examined many times and in much detail. *Warrior*'s importance remains unquestioned, but the assumption of previous generations that every stage in the process was both necessary and an improvement must be open to doubt.

No foreign Navy attempted anything so large as *Warrior* in the ironclad era. With her five near-relations she formed a unique squadron that played a vital deterrent role in avoiding a conflict with France, and possibly the United States.

Warrior was designed to fill a role in the wooden fleet of the 1850s, taking her place as a specific counter to the French ironclad *Gloire*. Yet, while *Gloire* was a battleship that had sacrificed a gundeck in return for armour, *Warrior* was a frigate. *Gloire* was intended to take her place in the line of battle that *Warrior* was specifically designed to avoid.

Although *Warrior* war originally intended to act outside the line of battle, as a heavy frigate, the rapid build-up of the French ironclad fleet and the even more precipitous decline of their wooden two-deckers made *Warrior* and her type the only capital ships worthy of the rank long before the rational men of the age had anticipated. Within five years a new type of ironclad, Edward Reed's centre battery ships, reflected a new conception of seapower. Ships like *Bellerophon*, *Hercules* and *Monarch* were true battleships. They maximised protection and artillery power at the expense of speed, strategic endurance and volume of fire. *Warrior* was to them what the battlecruiser was to the *Dreadnought*. By 1870 she would have been most accurately termed an armoured cruiser, were it not for her great size.

The ironclad era brought many changes to warship design. Not all of them were improvements. Armour offered ships a relative invulnerability at the cost of firepower. However, it so increased the size and cost of the ships that carried it that they were no longer expendable. This in turn prompted large scale work to find new methods of destroying the ever more costly vessels. Battleships were no longer warships to be used everyday. They had become scare resources. Effectively irreplaceable in wartime, they had to be carefully husbanded against disaster for the decisive battle. Explosive shells, mines and torpedoes were all perfected because the sinking of one capital ship could now alter the balance of power at sea in a way that Nelson and his contemporaries would not have understood.

Heavy guns, developed to defeat armour on the proving ground quickly became divorced from the reality of war at sea. The early turret ships could not have dealt with a small vessel with the ease of a wooden three-decker. Specialisation dramatically altered the way in which ships operated. Within three decades of *Warrior*'s completion no battlefleet would proceed without an escort. Wooden battleships were never escorted.

The central failing of the ironclad revolution was that it did not reflect relevant war experience. The Russian War had re-emphasised old lessons about ships and forts and proved the value of steam. It did not demonstrate anything about the combat between ships at sea that could explain or justify the development of the ironclad between 1858 and 1868. The armoured floating battery was a solution to the ships and forts question, but *Warrior* and *Gloire* were not designed for such duties.

While Sir Baldwin Walker remained in office the practical efficiency of the ironclad as a fighting machine was kept in the forefront. Both *Achilles* and the *Minotaur*s were attempts to increase the number of guns mounted behind armour, guns that would survive during battle. They were modified *Warrior*s, with more emphasis placed on fighting at the expense of speed and endurance. After the departure of Walker the ability of the Controller's Department to make the best use of the admittedly ever increasing amount of technical information declined. Similarly the ability of the new Controller to exercise any influence over his political masters was reduced. With the increased intervention of amateur designers and publicists, technological determinists and politicians dominated by the need for economy it was little wonder that the battlefleet turned into a collection of ill-matched experiments, lacking the homogenity that would be provided by a single guiding intelligence. Little wonder *Achilles* remained one of the best ships afloat for fifteen years.

Later, smaller and more 'battleworthy' first class ships like *Bellerophon* and *Hercules* were a reaction to the cost, size and unhandiness of the *Warrior* type; in that order of significance. Edward Reed made a brilliant career out of them, so did Spencer Robinson. Their popularity was largely a political matter. They were the cheapest ships that could be sold to the electorate as first class units. The frequent attempts of the Governments of the day to make do with second rate, or even ludicrous, coast defence ships demonstrate where their priorities lay. Reed also hoped that by keeping his ships small he could stave off the challenge from the turret ships of the brilliant amateur Cowper Coles. At every stage of this process the number of heavy guns mounted, which determined the ability of the ship to hit a moving target, was reduced. *Warrior* had 36, *Bellerophon* 15, *Devastation* 4 and the ill-fated *Victoria* of 1890 only 2.

With the inaccurate and slow-firing guns of the era

Sans Pareil, 1891, sister of the ill-fated *Victoria* of 1890. With only two, slow firing 16.25in guns in a single turret, this class must have been poor fighting ships. *CPL*

after *Warrior* such concentrated armaments were absurd. The effective range anticipated for naval battles did not increase beyond 1500yds, common long before *Warrior*, until the turn of the twentieth century. Fire control was equally crude. With so few guns

The *Dreadnought* of 1906, marked a major shift in design. She made every other battleship obsolescent. Fisher's inspired concept marked a return to the idea of a large battery of heavy guns, 10 12in aboard this ship with a broadside of 8. He hoped to secure a large number of hits from heavy guns, as the decisive requirement for naval combat. *CPL*

Agincourt as completed. This class was conceived as a modified *Warrior* with fifty guns behind armour. They were a direct counter to the French *Solferino* type (see p39) which also had fifty protected guns, albeit on two decks. *CPL*

Devastation and *Victoria* would have been hard pressed to hit anything outside 1000yds.

The underlying cause of this nonsense was the lack of real combat to test the new weapons and ideas. Ships were designed to meet the latest achievements of the gunfounders and plate makers, who carried on a private war on the prooving grounds. The opinion of experienced men like Walker in favour of a large number of guns was at first ignored and then forgotten. As a result design became divorced from function. When

Lord Fisher sketched out the *Dreadnought* of 1906 his purpose was to secure a large number of hits from heavy guns. This had not been a primary consideration since Walker proposed the *Minotaur* as a 50-gun version of *Warrior*.

In conclusion it is possible to see *Warrior* as a triumph of technological potential over functional requirement. She was an aberration that followed the *Mersey* in sacrificing combat potential for speed. In a ship of such size and cost more guns could have been mounted, and a more effective fighting machine produced. The speed of *Warrior* was bought at too high a price. Yet after Walker's term of office ended later ships took the reduced armament to its crowning folly. The essential failing of *Warrior* was not a question of design. She achieved exactly what her designers were instructed to achieve. The failing was conceptual, and the blame lies with Walker. That he realised this is clear from the development of the type before his departure. Even Walker was not infallible, he had comprehensively misunderstood the design function of *Gloire*, attaching too much significance to her single gun deck, and not enough to the cessation of wooden battleship construction in France. Even so the speed he secured for *Warrior* was to give the Royal Navy a decisive edge over the French, and was considered worth keeping by his successors. The continued popularity of *Achilles* demonstrated that he was more closely in touch with the opinion of practical naval officers. Only the test of war could have settled the argument.

Now that the *Warrior* project is reaching its conclusion, it is only natural to hope that further work will be found for the Hartlepool workforce. The Corporation has plans for establishing Hartlepool as a centre for ship restoration and, to this end, has purchased the 1934 Humber paddle steamer *Wingfield Castle*. An-

other scheme has been for the establishment of a new local shipyard, specialising in the luxury market. One thing is sure – with *Warrior* an advertisement for their skills and dedication, their future should be secure.

The project itself has been a 'one-off'. There are no more *Warriors* to be saved, no surviving ships from the era of such size. The great fleets of the nineteenth and twentieth centuries have all gone. Not a single British battleship remains afloat, and only a few still exist as wrecks.

Only time will tell if *Warrior* was of sufficient interest to generate the vital public interest needed to keep her afloat. Wisely the WPT have only committed themselves to the Portsmouth location so long as the funds are adequate. Her size and aesthetic appeal will help. However it would be a very brave man indeed who attempted anything else on this scale.

The project, from inception to completion, has been a learning process. The team overcame all the problems that arose, took on new roles and tasks not originally anticipated and created a code of practice that will stand as an example to all future ship restorations. The more obvious elements, starting off the project, control and management, labour and outside help should not exclude the less direct contribution of administrators, fund raisers, researchers and support services. Many names have been mentioned in this account, more will be found in Appendix I. *Warrior* is their ship.

APPENDIX I: LIST OF WORKFORCE ENGAGED BOTH DIRECTLY AND VIA THE MSC. WITH SKILLS AND PERIOD OF SERVICE.

PAINTERS

Name	Start	Finish	Job Description
G.S. Conroy	14.3.84		Painter Labourer (part-time)
S.J. Layton	14.3.84	5.3.85	Painter Labourer (part-time)
L.C. Maddison	14.3.84	4.9.84	Painter Labourer (part-time)
D.J. Robinson	14.3.84	5.3.85	Painter Labourer (part-time)
M. Trotter	14.3.84	14.8.85	Painter Labourer (part-time)
P.J. Wilkins	14.3.84	5.3.85	Painter Labourer (part-time)
K. Graham	14.3.84		Painter Labourer (part-time) to Painter Labourer (full-time)
G.H. Baker	20.3.84	10.1.85	Painter Labourer (part-time)
B. Hodgson	20.3.84		Painter Labourer (part-time)
I.P. Pounder	20.3.84	23.10.84	Painter Labourer (part-time)
L. Raw	20.3.84	12.3.85	Painter Labourer (part-time)
L. Atkinson	3.4.84	26.3.85	Painter Labourer (part-time)
F.J. Boarder	10.4.84	2.4.85	Painter Labourer (part-time)
G. Crosby	10.4.84	17.1.85	Painter Labourer (part-time)
A. Dodsworth	10.4.84	28.3.85	Painter Labourer (part-time)
D.J. Green	3.7.84		Painter Labourer (part-time) to Painter Labourer (full-time)
K. Guffick	14.5.84	7.6.84	Painter Labourer (part-time)
A.E. Harrison	3.4.84		Painter Labourer (part-time) to Painter Labourer (full-time)
P. Hegarty	10.4.84	1.5.84	Painter Labourer (part-time)
P.E. Ingledew	21.8.84	26.3.85	Painter Labourer (part-time)
A. Johnson	14.8.84	28.3.85	Painter Labourer (part-time)
R. Kidson	2.11.84	26.3.85	Painter Labourer (part-time)
M. Kinsella	3.4.84		Painter Labourer (part-time) to Painter Labourer (full-time)
C. Merchant	3.4.84	26.3.85	Painter Labourer (part-time)
M.H. Maunder	10.4.84	2.4.85	Painter Labourer (part-time)
D.A. Muspratt	11.9.84	28.3.85	Painter Labourer (part-time)
L.F. Raper	10.4.84	26.6.84	Painter Labourer (part-time)
W. Robinson	8.6.84	7.8.84	Painter Labourer (part-time)
T. Robson	3.4.84	26.3.85	Painter Labourer (part-time)
B. Short	10.4.84	2.4.85	Painter Labourer (part-time)
M.R. Smallwood	3.4.84	26.3.85	Painter Labourer (part-time)
W.H. Swanson	11.5.84	15.5.84	Painter Labourer (part-time)
D.T. Usher	3.4.84	26.3.85	Painter Labourer (part-time)
M. Wilkins	3.4.84	15.8.84	Painter Labourer (part-time)
P.A. Wilkinson	15.6.84	28.3.85	Painter Labourer (part-time)
W. Wright	3.4.84	26.3.85	Painter Labourer (part-time)
G. Wall	7.3.83		Supervisor (full-time)
M. McCoy	15.4.85		Charge Hand to Painter Supervisor (full-time)
R. Chapple	13.1.81		Painter (full-time)
H. Rutterford	2.4.84		Painter Supervisor (full-time)

LABOURERS (FULL-TIME)

Name	Start	Finish	Job Description
L. Kay	22.10.79		Labourer (full-time)
R.W. Foster	21.1.80		Labourer (full-time)
D. Simpson	28.4.80		Labourer (full-time)
A. Sotheran	15.10.79		Labourer (full-time)
E. Docharty	20.3.81		Labourer (full-time)
M. Balderson	16.2.81		Driver (full-time)
D. Morfitt	22.10.79	29.9.80	Labourer (full-time)
A.W. Walton	22.10.79	30.6.80	Labourer (full-time)
J.W. Reynolds	22.10.79	22.5.80	Labourer (full-time)
G.E. Edmenson	16.4.82		Labourer (full-time)
R. McQue	30.4.82	14.4.83	Labourer (full-time)
F.W.M. Hutton	2.4.84	10.5.84	Labourer (full-time)
E. Murphie	11.5.84	28.3.85	Labourers (full-time)
S. Boagey	4.1.82		Labourer (full-time)
J.W. Austin	18.4.83	15.9.83	Labourer (full-time)
K. Graham	14.3.85		Labourer (full-time)
B. Hodgson	15.3.85		Labourer (full-time)
A.E. Harrison	3.4.85		Labourer (full-time)
M. Kinsella	3.4.85		Labourer (full-time)
D.J. Green	3.7.85		Labourer (full-time)

LABOURERS (PART-TIME)

Name	Start	Finish	Job Description
N. Brown	16.3.83	15.3.84	Labourer (part-time)
A. Cotson	16.3.83	24.11.83	Labourer (part-time)

Name	Start	Finish	Job Description
D. Goldsmith	16.3.83	15.3.84	Labourer (part-time)
D.A.W. Goodings	14.3.83	13.3.84	Labourer (part-time)
T. Graham	16.3.83	2.12.83	Labourer (part-time)
J.R. Humphrey	16.3.83	15.3.84	Labourer (part-time)
A. Keenan	14.3.83	13.3.84	Labourer (part-time)
W. Leighton	16.3.83	15.3.84	Labourer (part-time)
M. Pennick	14.3.83	13.3.84	Labourer (part-time)
G.J. Priest	14.3.83	22.6.83	Labourer (part-time)
S. Ross	14.3.83	13.3.84	Labourer (part-time)
B. Smith	14.3.83	13.3.84	Labourer (part-time)
P. Corbett	6.4.83	6.4.83	Labourer (part-time)
C. Corbett	13.4.83	2.6.83	Labourer (part-time)
A.G. Pounder	22.6.83	6.10.83	Labourer (part-time)
J.A. Cannon	12.10.83	30.3.84	Labourer (part-time)
M. Wilkins	29.6.83	30.3.84	Labourer (part-time)
B. Spowart	21.4.83	30.3.84	Labourer (part-time)
G.S. Conroy	14.3.84	5.3.85	Labourer (part-time)
J. Crompton	3.4.84	18.5.85	Labourer (part-time)
S. Colby	14.1.85		Labourer (part-time)
A. Coulson	9.1.85	15.8.85	Labourer (part-time)
G. Coward	2.4.84	26.3.85	Compound Labourer
N. Dobson	2.4.84	8.5.84	Compound Labourer
C. Faulkmer	12.9.84	28.3.85	Compound Labourer
J. Hurrell	6.6.84	18.12.84	Compound Labourer
C. Iddon	4.4.84	28.3.85	Compound Labourer
J. McIntosh	2.4.84	26.3.85	Compound Labourer
B. Middleton	4.4.84	5.9.84	Compound Labourer
J.S. Ross	2.4.84	8.1.85	Compound Labourer
I. Simons	7.11.84	28.3.85	Compound Labourer
R.W. Smart	14.5.84	7.5.85	Compound Labourer
D. Walker	4.4.84	23.3.85	Compound Labourer
K. Williams	4.4.84	1.11.84	Compound Labourer
M. Williams	2.4.84	26.3.85	Compound Labourer
H.R. Wrighley	4.4.84	26.3.85	Compound Labourer
C. Ellis	7.5.85		Labourer (part-time)
M.J. Jefferies	7.5.85		Labourer (part-time)
L. Jemmet	7.5.85		Labourer (part-time)
S. Rose	7.5.85		Labourer (part-time)
A. Bell	15.4.85	23.4.85	Labourer (part-time)
D. Murray	1.4.85	7.5.85	Labourer (part-time)
D. Noble	16.4.85	7.5.85	Labourer (part-time)
D.C. Mordaunt	7.4.85	7.5.85	Labourer (part-time)
I.J. Pounder	1.4.85	7.5.85	Labourer (part-time)
C.E. Alton	3.4.85	6.6.85	Labourer (part-time)
T.B.B. Cambell	3.4.85	29.5.85	Labourer (part-time)
M. Duggan	3.4.85	19.6.85	Labourer (part-time)
R.A. Hooper	3.4.85	19.6.85	Labourer (part-time)
J.P. Lupton	3.4.85	27.6.85	Labourer (part-time)
D. Sumpton	3.6.85	23.7.85	Labourer (part-time)
S. Gaffney	3.4.85	25.7.85	Labourer (part-time)
A. Telfer	1.4.85	23.7.85	Labourer (part-time)
R.A. Lyth	3.4.85	25.7.85	Labourer (part-time)
S. McDonald	3.6.85	27.8.85	Labourer (part-time)
S. Wray	3.4.85	23.8.85	Labourer (part-time)
J.E. Bell	3.4.85	29.8.85	Labourer (part-time)
S. Jenkinson	1.4.85	8.10.85	Labourer (part-time)
J.F. Jackman	1.4.85	29.10.85	Labourer (part-time)
P. Caterdale	15.4.85		Labourer (part-time)
P. Hewitson	1.4.85		Labourer (part-time)
M. Johnson	1.4.85		Labourer (part-time)
T. Lundrigan	1.4.85		Labourer (part-time)
K. Moore	28.1.85		Labourer (part-time)
K. Muir	28.1.85		Labourer (part-time)

Name	Start	Finish	Job Description
A.D. Pape	1.4.85		Labourer (part-time)
J.L. Sanders	1.4.85		Labourer (part-time)
C. James	3.6.85		Labourer (part-time)
I. Taylor	3.6.85		Labourer (part-time)
I.M. Hunter	10.6.85		Labourer (part-time)
M.J. Pollard	12.6.85		Labourer (part-time)
G. Bolton	3.4.85		Labourer (part-time)
G.M. Brown	3.4.85		Labourer (part-time)

SHIPWRIGHTS

Name	Start	Finish	Job Description
S. Relton	22.10.79		Shipwright
A. Robinson	22.10.79		Shipwright
H.F. Boagey	6.5.80		Shipwright
T.I. Boagey	6.5.80		Shipwright
C. Relton	4.1.82	30.3.84	Shipwright
J. Mordey	28.2.83		Shipwright Supervisor
J.R. Wilson	14.4.82	30.3.84	Shipwright
L. Winter	14.4.82	30.3.84	Shipwright
C.M. Wright	28.4.82	30.3.84	Shipwright
K.J. Pickup	23.8.82		Shipwright
T. Ruddy	23.8.82		Shipwright
A. White	13.9.82		Shipwright Promoted to Shipwright 1.1.84
J.A. Cannon	21.2.83		Shipwright
R. Caswell	13.9.82	30.9.82	Shipwright
J. Rooks	17.10.83		Shipwright
J.R. Collinson	19.4.83	30.3.84	Shipwright
A. Mullen	9.4.84		Shipwright
J.T. Newton	2.4.84		Shipwright
D. Pike	2.4.84		Shipwright
A.M. Renwicks	11.6.84		Shipwright
D. Foster	17.10.83		Shipwright
N. Staley	13.7.84		Shipwright Apprentice
R.E. Atchinson	2.4.84		Shipwright
T. Bone	3.5.85		Shipwright
T.W. Calvert	3.5.85		
P. Robinson	23.8.85		Shipwright Apprentice

WELDERS

Name	Start	Finish	Job Description
H.G. Thornhill	6.10.80	3.9.81	Welder
K. Waller	1.9.80		Welder
W. Linton	6.5.80	1.12.83	Welder
J.A. Mitchell	2.3.81	20.7.84	Welder
A. Wilson	10.6.80	21.2.81	Welder
E.J. Percival	6.8.84		Welder
R.T. Waller	2.12.83		Welder
W.E. Wood	10.6.85		Welder
R. Foster	7.5.85		Welder
J. Moulang	3.6.85		Welder
M.R. Trueman	8.6.85		Transferred from Security 1985
J. Cooney	1.4.85		Apprentice Welder

STOREKEEPER

Name	Start	Finish	Job Description
W.T. Robson	23.3.83	22.3.84	Storekeeper
D. Whitelock	30.3.83	29.3.84	Storekeeper
R.C. Tyreman	2.4.84		Stock Controller
A.G. Scully	2.4.84	28.3.85	Storekeeper
G. Skedd	1.4.85		Storekeeper

DRILLERS

Name	Start	Finish	Job Description
E.J. Percival	13.5.80		Driller
A. Salmon	6.9.85		Driller
J. Pounder	13.9.85		Driller

RIGGERS

Name	Start	Finish	Job Description
B. Metcalf	7.8.84		Rigger (Supervisor 1.11.85)
A. Collinson	18.11.85	18.11.85	Rigger
T. Leck	1.4.85		Rigger
J.P. Gamble	13.9.85		Rigger
B.K. Douglas	2.12.85		Rigger

RIGGERS' MATES

Name	Start	Finish	Job Description
G.H. Leighton	29.4.85		Riggers' Mate
D.A. Grieve	13.9.85		Riggers' Mate
J.D. Jefferies	13.9.85		Riggers' Mate
J. Connor	20.9.95		Riggers' Mate
S. Remmer	1.11.85		Riggers' Mate
K. McLane	2.12.85		Riggers' Mate
W. Montgomery	3.12.85		Riggers' Mate

RIVETER (SQUAD SHORT-TERM CONTRACT)

Name	Start	Finish	Job Description
J. Tierney	6.6.83	25.8.83	Riveter
J. Graham	6.6.83	25.8.83	Riveter
G.F. Johnson	6.6.83	25.8.83	Labourer (Riveter)

ELECTRICIAN

Name	Start	Finish	Job Description
A.B. Smith	31.1.83		Electrician to Supervisor 1.11.85
D. Morrell	12.9.83		Electrician Apprentice

PLATERS

Name	Start	Finish	Job Description
T.W. Austin	6.5.80	22.8.83	Plater
J.W. Deer	2.3.81	5.6.84	Plater
J.M. Hewitson	6.7.81		Apprentice to Craftsman 1.7.85
R. Fowdy	11.6.84		Plater
F.W. Foster	30.8.83		Plater
L. Gofton	10.6.85		Plater to Supervisor 1.12.85
R.A. Marwood	7.5.85		Plater to Supervisor 1.12.85
D. Wanley	2.12.85		Plater

BURNERS

Name	Start	Finish	Job Description
G.M. Ainsley	8.9.80		Burner
L.H. Bartlett	13.5.80		Caulker/Burner
T.E. Gibbons	14.5.84		Caulker/Burner
W. Morthey	3.4.84	19.4.84	Caulker/Burner
J.D. Harrington	22.4.85		Caulker/Burner
R.J. Wanley	10.6.85		Burner
J.J. Keers	10.5.85		Caulker/Burner

FITTERS

Name	Start	Finish	Job Description
M. Levoir	7.5.85		Fitter
D. Harrison	12.8.85		Fitter
D.L. Moore	10.6.85	8.7.85	Fitter

JOINERS

Name	Start	Finish	Job Description
T. Humpleby	4.2.80	23.7.82	Joiner
A. Stevenson	6.7.81		Apprentice to Craftsman 1.7.85
J.M. Greenwell	18.1.82		Joiner
N. Breeze	3.3.82		Joiner
B. Harland	9.8.82	8.8.83	Joiner
J. Oswald	3.4.84		Joiner
K. Straughan	30.4.85		Joiner
R. Foster	8.11.85		Joiner

WOOD MACHINIST

Name	Start	Finish	Job Description
G.R. Warnes	8.8.83	6.6.85	Wood Machinist
J.D. Hutchinson	3.6.85		Wood Machinist
D. Hutchinson	6.12.85		Wood Machinist

CLEANERS

Name	Start	Finish	Job Description
J. Docherty	17.11.80		Full-time
J. Scully	2.11.84		Chargehand Cleaner to Supervisor 1.12.85
M. Allison	6.4.84	31.3.85	Part-Time Cleaner
E. Cooper	6.4.84	31.3.85	Part-Time Cleaner
V. Kelly	6.4.84	31.3.85	Part-Time Cleaner
I. Llewellyn	6.4.84	31.3.85	Part-Time Cleaner
S.M. McKenzie	6.4.84	31.10.84	Chargehand Cleaner
J.E. Light	5.4.85	5.5.85	Part-Time Cleaner
J.M. Martin	5.4.85		Part-Time Cleaner
M.A. Sirs	5.4.85		Part-Time Cleaner
L.I. Skedd	5.4.85		Part-Time Cleaner
L. Austwicke	17.5.85		Part-Time Cleaner

SECURITY

Name	Start	Finish	Job Description
P.J. Callagham	22.6.82	21.6.83	Night Watchman (full-time)
S. Jones	25.6.82	24.6.83	Night Watchman (full-time)
G.E. Garnett	23.6.83	10.1.85	Night Watchman (part-time)
H. Cooper	3.9.83		Night Watchman (part-time)
E. O'Connor	27.6.83	2.5.85	Night Watchman (part-time)
K. Lennard	29.6.83	27.6.85	Night Watchman (part-time)
J. Gallagher	18.11.83		Night Watchman (part-time)
J. Smith	20.11.83	16.5.85	Night Watchman (part-time)
C. Saunders	22.11.83		Night Watchman (part-time)
G. Wilson	3.7.83	1.9.83	Night Watchman (part-time)
D. Blake	1.4.84	28.3.85	Night Watchman (part-time)

WARRIOR

Name	Start	Finish	Job Description	Name	Start	Finish	Job Description
E. Eglintine	12.4.84	4.4.85	Night Watchman (part-time)	J. Bartram	3.9.79		PA/Secretary
D. Robinson	12.7.84		Night Watchman (part-time)	J.G. Wells	21.4.81		Researcher Paid by Leverhulme Trust 2 Yrs: City of Portsmouth 2 Yrs.
D. Unthank	8.3.85		Night Watchman (part-time)	A.G. Bridgewater	11.5.81		Fundraiser
H. Vasey	1.4.84	26.10.84	Night Watchman (part-time)	R. Harper	1.9.81	30.8.82	Book-Keeper
G.J. Williams	28.1.85	7.3.85	Night Watchman (part-time)	V.J. Pape	4.1.82		Wages Clerk to Book-keeper 30.8.82
K. Boyd	5.4.85	15.5.85	Night Watchman (part-time)	G. O'Boyle	24.9.82	28.10.83	Clerk/Typist
A. Sanders	1.4.85	31.5.85	Night Watchman (part-time)	I.D. Lester	17.5.82	16.12.82	Technical Clerk
K. Hind	14.6.85	16.8.85	Night Watchman (part-time)	T.A. Chapman	24.1.83	27.6.83	Junior Technical Clerk
W. Thompson	16.10.85	19.11.85	Night Watchman (part-time)	I. Phillips	22.2.83	11.8.83	Accounts Clerk (part-time)
F. Chambers	29.11.85		Night Watchman (part-time)	L.A. O'Connel	25.2.83	9.3.84	Filing Clerk (part-time)
W. Holland	28.6.85		Night Watchman (part-time)	D. Walton	3.5.83		Administrations Officer
G.W. Bell	20.9.85		Night Watchman (part-time)	J. Welsh	16.8.83		Accounts Clerk (part-time)
J. Hunt	26.5.85		Night Watchman (part-time)	C. Holroyd	26.9.83	6.9.84	Clerk/Typist
P.M. Lewis	11.5.85		Night Watchman (part-time)	J. Laws	7.11.83		Research Assistant
J. Storrow	1982/1983		Casual Ships Representative Summer Work	E. Pritchard	28.2.84	14.2.85	Filing Clerk (part-time)
				A.G. Wilson	21.1.85		Trainee Draughtsman
				L. Bird	12.11.84		Research Assistant (part-time)

STAFF

Name	Start	Finish	Job Description	Name	Start	Finish	Job Description
R. Hockey	3.9.79	31.8.83	Project Manager	L.J. Burton	26.3.85	4.10.85	Filing Clerk (part-time)
S. Morrell	22.10.79		Supervisor to Ships Manager Sept 83.	A. Richardson	20.8.84	14.8.85	Wages Clerk (part-time)
J.W. Stevenson	6.10.80		Draughtsman to Project Manager Sept 83.	H. Westhorpe (Bunton)	4.9.84	29.8.85	Clerk Typist (part-time)
K.M. Johnson	3.11.80		Draughtsman	A.J. Welch	14.2.85	22.3.85	Filing Clerk (part-time)
A. Crowe	3.9.79	25.9.81	Wages Clerk	A.C. Gray	9.4.84		Junior Draughtsman
J. Frazer	17.9.79	10.10.80	Receptionist Typist	W. Brownlee	1.9.84		Historian
G. Heslop	25.4.80	17.11.80	Caretaker	C.J. Wilson	19.11.84		Project Engineer
				R.W. Davis	26.11.84		Tourist Guide
				H. Short	5.11.84	7.12.84	Project Engineer
				M. Cookland	20.5.85		Draughtsman
				J. Pouton	28.10.85		Pipework Draughtsman
				J. Standing	22.4.85		Technical Clerk
				A.E. McCreesh	3.6.85		Wages Clerk (part-time)
				C.J. Watson	4.9.85		Clerk Typist (part-time)
				J. Keer	13.9.85		Order Clerk (part-time)
				P.A. Lilley	11.10.85		Filing Clerk (part-time)
				J. West	14.10.85		Managers' Clerk
				E. Wray	9.10.85		Invoice Clerk (part-time)

APPENDIX II: TOTAL EXPENDITURE TO 30 SEPTEMBER 1986

WPT GROSS EXPENDITURE to	30.9.86	4,352,761.37	77.99%
Less Reclaimed VAT to	30.6.86	213,329.86	4.01%
WPT NET EXPENDITURE to	30.9.86	4,139,431.51	
MSC		1,168,533.23	
		5,307,964.74	

FINANCED BY:

Manifold	3,659,000	68.93%
MSC	1,168,533	22.01%
Donations	213,212	4.02%
Admissions	49,092	.93%
Covenants, Rent, etc.	38,454	.73%
Sales, etc. (incl. Souvenirs)	83,385	1.57%
Reclaimed VAT	(213,330)	
VAT due	(25,725)	
Bank Overdraft	96,289	1.81%
	5,307,965	

APPENDIX III: SPECIFICATION FOR AN IRON SCREW STEAM FRIGATE TO BE CASED WITH ARMOUR PLATES.

PRINCIPAL DIMENSIONS.

LENGTH Between the Perpendiculars 380 feet 0 inches

BREADTH Extreme to Outside of Plates 58 feet 0 inches

DEPTH In Hold from Top of Floor to upper side of Lower Deck Beam 21′ 1″

TONNAGE In tons O.M. No. 6038

KEEL to be formed as shown on the Midship Section on the vertical tree plates to be $\frac{3}{4}$ins thick and 40ins deep except the after part, which is to be increased in thickness, and 40 inches deep. The Keel Plates to be worked in two thicknesses, as shown in the margin; the Angle Irons connecting the vertical with the flat Keel Plates are to be 6×6×1 inches, and rivetted to them with 1 inch rivets. All the Plates and Angle Iron are to be wrought in the greatest lengths procurable; the butts are to be well fitted, and properly supported with straps, and shifted to the satisfaction of the Overseer. The vertical Keel Plate is to extend from the Stern Post to the stem, the after end is to be rivetted to the Stern Post, and the foremost end to run up the stem as far as may be directed; the after end of the Plate to be increased in depth as may be required, and the butts of the plates forming the vertical Keel Plate to have double straps, treble rivetted. At the butts of each of the flat Keel Plates and Keel Angle Irons short butt straps of $1\frac{3}{8}$ inch thickness are to be introduced on each side of the Keel Angle Irons; the breadth of the butt straps to be at least ten times the diameter of the rivets, or as broad as the openings will admit; the rivet holes through these Plates and the Keel Angle Irons are either to be drilled or rimed out after being punched so as to remove any burr from the surface, the faying surfaces are also to be carefully scraped and cleaned, and, if required, planed before being worked; the whole of the above work is to be rivetted together with rivets of $1\frac{1}{4}$ inch diameter. At the fore and after extremities of the ship, where the flat Keel Plates are discontinued, a forging is to be introduced, forming the lower part of the stem, agreeably to a sketch that will be furnished.

TOP OF KEEL The Angle Irons on the upper edge of the vertical Keel Plate to be $3\frac{1}{2} \times 3\frac{1}{2} \times \frac{1}{2}$, worked in short lengths.

KEELSON The flat keelson Plate on the throat of the floors to be 3 feet broad and $\frac{1}{4}$ inch thick, worked on long lengths, and to extend as far forward and aft as possible, the butts to be treble rivetted, and to have double butt straps.

The Rudder Post, with eyes, &c. complete, to be forged in one piece; the Body Post, for Propeller Shaft, together with the after piece on Keel for about 11 feet before the aperture are also to be forged in one, the whole to be made of the best hammered iron, in accordance with the Engineer's drawing, or as per sketch that will be furnished.

The general dimensions of the Posts to be as follows:- The Rudder Post to be 10 inches athwartships by 20 inches fore and aft; the Body Post 10 inches athwartships and 18 inches fore and aft.

HOLE FOR THE RECEPTION OF THE ENGINEERS' TUBE The Hole for the Shaft is to be drilled and prepared by the shipbuilder, for the reception of the tube for the Propeller Shaft.

STEM To be forged either in one length or in such lengths as shall be directed; of the best best hammered Scrap Iron; the dimensions, form, and length of Scarphs to be regulated by a Sketch that will be furnished, the lower end to scarph on to the vertical Keel Plate.

All scarphs of the forged keel bars, stem and stern-posts, are to be planed and truly fitted.

LONGITUDINAL FRAMES To have continuous Longitudinal Frames for a length of about 280 feet to 320 feet, formed of plates and angle irons of the following dimensions:-

	Plate	Angle Irons Inner Edge	Angle Irons Outer Edge
The upper Longitudinal Frame, as also the or in breadth as may be req'd Plates forming the fore and after ends of the Recess for the Armour Plates, to be made of a flanged Plate, or to be forged, fitted, and planed as may be directed	$23 \times \frac{7}{8}$	$5 \times 5 \times \frac{5}{8}$	$6 \times 6 \times \frac{3}{4}$ if required
			double
2° Longitudinal Frame	$21 \times \frac{7}{16}$	$3\frac{1}{2} \times 3 \times \frac{1}{2}$	$4 \times 3\frac{1}{2} \times \frac{5}{8}$
3° Do. do.	$27 \times 9/16$	$3\frac{1}{2} \times 3 \times \frac{1}{2}$	$4 \times 3\frac{1}{2} \times \frac{5}{8}$
4° Do. do.	$19 - \frac{7}{16}$	$3\frac{1}{2} \times 3 \times \frac{1}{2}$	$4 \times 3\frac{1}{2} \times \frac{5}{8}$
5° Do. do.	$19 \times \frac{7}{16}$	$3\frac{1}{2} \times 3 \times \frac{1}{2}$	$4 \times 3\frac{1}{2} \times \frac{5}{8}$
6° Do. do.	$27 \times 9/16$	$4 \times 3\frac{1}{2} \times \frac{1}{2}$	$4 \times 3\frac{1}{2} \times \frac{5}{8}$

The Plates and Angle Irons composing the Longitudinal Frames are to be wrought in the greatest lengths procurable, and great care is to be taken that the butts are well fitted. The Angle Irons, if required, are, as well as the Plates, to pass unbroken through the bulk-heads, the surrounding joints being carefully caulked and made water-tight. The butts of the Plates are to be secured by double butt straps of $\frac{1}{2}$-inch Plate, double riveted. The Butts of the Angle Irons are also to be supported by a Strap or covering Angle Irons.

The Longitudinal Frames must be placed in such a direction throughout their length as to clear all the Longitudinal Joints of the outside Plates.

Fillings or liners are to be dispensed with between the Angle Irons on the Longitudinal Frames and the bottom Plates, the Angle Irons are to be bent so as to pass over the Butt Straps, or to be worked as may be directed.

FLOOR AND TRANSVERSE PLATES BETWEEN LONGITUDINAL FRAMES

The Floor Plate on each side of the Vertical Keel Plate to be 9/16 in thick, secured to it, and the sixth Longitudinal Frame by the Frame Angle Irons, which are to be turned up for the purpose, and carefully fitted over the Angle Irons as shown on the Midship Section. The floor plates at the watertight bulkheads to be $\frac{5}{8}$ inch thick.

All the Transverse Plates are to be $\frac{7}{16}$ inch thick, except those at the water-tight bulkheads, which are to be $\frac{5}{8}$-inch thick.

FRAME ANGLE IRONS ON FLOOR AND SHORT TRANSVERSE PLATES

The angle Irons on the outer edge of the Floor Plates are to be 4-inch × $3\frac{1}{2}$ × $\frac{5}{8}$-inch. Those on the other Transverse Plates to be 4 × $3\frac{1}{2}$ × 9/16. All Frame Angle Irons are to be worked double unless otherwise specified, or directions to the contrary be given by the Overseer, and to turn up against and rivet to the vertical keel plate and longitudinal plates as shewn on the midship section.

INTERMEDIATE FLOOR-PLATES, &c.

Intermediate Floor Plates 9/16 inch thick are to be fitted, extending from the vertical Keel Plate to the lowest Longitudinal Frame, or to about 10 feet 6 inches from the middle line. They are to have an Angle Iron 7-inch × $3\frac{1}{2}$ × $\frac{5}{8}$-inch on one side of their upper edge, and an Angle Iron 4 × $3\frac{1}{2}$ × $\frac{5}{8}$ on one side of their lower edge. The upper Angle Irons are to extend in one length right across the Keel. The lower angle requires to be turned up against and rivetted to the vertical keel first, and the longitudinal plates as shewn on the midship section.

CONTINUOUS TRANSVERSE FRAMES

The spacing of the Continuous Transverse Frames to be as follows; viz., 3 feet 8 inches from centre to centre between the Ports as far as the Longitudinal Frames extend. Before and abaft the Longitudinal Frames, or where the Overseer may direct, they are [to] be 22 inches from centre to centre. In wake of the armour plates these Frames are to be formed of $\frac{7}{16}$ inch plates and angle irons; the breadth of the plates to be 10 inches behind the armour plates, tapering to 7 inches below, as shown on the midship section.

The Angle Iron on the inner edge of each frame to be $3\frac{1}{2}$ inch × $3\frac{1}{2}$ inch × $\frac{5}{8}$ inch, and to extend from gunwale to gunwale. The Angle Irons on the outer edge to be double $3\frac{1}{2}$ × $4\frac{1}{2}$ × $\frac{5}{8}$, and to extend from the upper deck down to the third Longitudinal Frame, or as may be directed. The Butts of the Plates and Angle Irons are not to be nearer to the middle line than 6 feet, but to be properly shifted, and supported by Plates and straps; the general arrangement to be previously submitted to the Overseer for his approval. The Angle irons on the inner edges of the continuous transverse frames are to be double between the sections 43 and 84 extending up from the vertical keel plate, to the 3rd longitudinal frame as shewn on the model.

REVERSE FRAMES

A Reverse angle iron is to be fitted to every Frame throughout the Ship.

INTERMEDIATE FRAMES

A short Intermediate Frame is to be worked between each of the regular Frames behind the Armour Plates, and to be of the same Scantlings as the Main Frames, to extend from the Upper Deck to the third longitudinal Frame. Plates similar in all respects to those of the Frames, are to be worked between the two upper longitudinal Frames, to receive their Heels, which are to be secured as the Overseer may direct. The heads of these Frames are to be firmly secured to the under side of the Stringer Plate on Upper Deck by Angle Irons.

TRANSVERSE FRAMES BEFORE AND ABAFT ARMOUR PLATES

For 30 feet next before and abaft the Armour Plates, the continuous Frames are to be formed of Angle Irons 7 × 4 × $\frac{5}{8}$, the reverse Frames to be $3\frac{1}{2}$ × 3 × 9/16 with Plates attached where directed (excepting immediately before and abaft the Armour Plates which will be described by a Sketch). For the next 30 feet before and abaft this, the Frames are to be 6 × 4 × 9/16, the reverse Frames $3\frac{1}{2}$ × 3 × 9/16, and beyond this, the Frames are to be 5 × 4 × 9/16, and the reverse Frames $3\frac{1}{2}$ × 3 × $\frac{1}{2}$. A Floor Plate is to be attached to each of the transverse Frames, with a reverse Angle Iron rivetted to its upper edge is usual. The frames No. 120 and 125 abreast the Propeller shaft are to have double angle irons, on the *outside* extending about eight feet above and below the centre of (the) shaft.

DISPOSITION OF BUTTS OF PLATES, &c.

A Sketch showing the general arrangement of the Butts of all Plates and Angle Irons in the Frame and Keel of this Ship is to be prepared, and submitted to the overseer for approval before the work is commenced, and no deviation therefrom will be allowed, without his consent having been previously obtained.

VERTICAL GIRDERS TO ARMOUR PLATE BULKHEADS

To be formed of $\frac{7}{16}$ in. plate 10ins deep with double Angle Irons $4\frac{1}{2}$ × $3\frac{1}{2}$ × 9/16 on the edge next the wood backing, and one reverse Angle Iron $3\frac{1}{2}$ × $3\frac{1}{2}$ × $\frac{1}{2}$, the whole of the girders to pass through the plating on the main deck, excepting the $\frac{5}{8}$ stringer plates, and to extend from the upper deck to the lower part of the transver Armour Plates, the Angle Irons continuing down the face of the Iron

Bulkheads to the frame of the ship. The iron plating on Girders to be ½ in. thick. Horizontal plates ⅜-in thick, with suitable Angle Irons, are to be fitted between the Girders, as shall be described by a Sketch. Doors are to be fitted in these Bulkheads on the Main Deck for working the Ship as may be directed.

INTERNAL PLATING Plates ½in. thick are to be worked on the throats of the floors between the lower longitudinal frames on each side, extending as far forward and aft as may be required. They are to be attached to the floors and longitudinal frames so as to form water-tight compartments; the whole to be caulked and made perfectly water-tight to the satisfaction of the Overseer. A water-tight man-hold door, is to be fitted to each compartment, or other fittings adopted as may be requisite, for getting into this part of the Ship.

OUTSIDE PLATING To be wrought as shown on the Midship Section, except at the fore and after parts of the topside where both joints and butts are to be worked flush, and as will be described by a Sketch; the Plates are to be in length from 11 to 12 feet, or so as to keep the butts in the middle of the openings, with 3 frames between them, as far as the longitudinal framing extends. Before and abaft this, the same length of Plates is to be maintained; and the butts are to be kept as nearly in the centre of the openings as practicable. The slicer strake and strake next below the Main Deck ports are to be worked in two thicknesses, and in such lengths as to admit of their being properly shifted both with regard to the ports and to the butts of the other Plates. The whole arrangement of the butts, &c. of the outside Plates is to be submitted to the Overseer, and approved by him, before the work is commenced, and no deviation therefrom will be allowed without his consent being first obtained.

The Plates which end in the body post, and those next adjoining them, are to be 1 inch thick, and double rivetted to the post and to each other with great care, the rimer being first passed through all the holes. All butt straps to be cut from plates 1/16 inch thicker than those to which they are attached, having this fibre in the same direction as the plating, to be very carefully fitted, and of a length sufficient to take the edge rivets.

Fillings are to be placed between the frames and plating where required or directed. Fillings are to be solid, and their breadth is to be increased as required at the transverse bulk-heads. All laps, butt straps, and faying surfaces of the plates to be cleaned from rust before being worked. The Plates are to be truly fitted at the joints and butts, as no pieces will be allowed to be put in and caulked over. All Plates requiring such pieces are to be absolutely rejected. The punching and countersinking to be very carefully done, and the rivet holes are to be rimed out, wherever required by the Overseer. All the

The thickness of the outside Plates to be as follows:-

		For a Length of about 250 feet amidships	Forward and Aft
		ins	ins
Middle Line or Keel	Upper	1⅛	1⅛
Strakes	Lower	1¼	1¼
Next two Strakes out on each side		1⅛	1
Next Strake		1	⅞
Thence to 14 feet water-line		⅞	13/16
From 14 feet water-line to port sill, except behind Armour Plates		13/16	12/16
Plating behind Armour Plates, and about 12 feet beyond each end of the recess	Lower Strake	⅝	
	Remainder	9/16 Strake under ports to be double or two of 9/16	
Between the ports, forward and aft			9/16
Sheet Strake to be worked in two thicknesses each		⅛	9/16

N.B.-The plating of the side, at the vertical joints of the recess, is to be rabbetted into the Armour Plates as may be directed.

joints are to be caulked in the most careful manner, and made perfectly watertight, to the satisfaction of the Overseer; and no canvas red lead, or other substance is on any account to be inserted in the seams, but all to be caulked throughout, metal to metal.

DECK BEAMS To be the Patent "Welded Beam" as manufactured by the "Butterley Iron Company," Derbyshire, to be supplied in one length; and of the following dimensions; viz.,

		ins			
Length 50ft and upwards		12½	Deep	Upper	6¼ to 6½
Length from 50ft to 40ft		12	Deep	Deck	12½ to ½
Length under 40 feet		12	Deep	Beams;	3½

		ins			
Length 50 feet and upwards		16	Deep	Main	6¼ to 6½
Length between 50ft and 45ft	15	Deep	Deck	16 to ½
Length between 45ft and 40ft	14	Deep	Beams;	6¼

Length between 40ft and 30ft 13 Deep
Length under 30ft   12 Deep

                                        ins
Length 50 feet and upwards   15 Deep Lower 6¼ to 6½
Length between 50ft and 45ft 14 Deep Deck   15 to ½
Length between 45ft and 40ft 13 Deep Beams; 6¼
Length between 40ft and 30ft 12 Deep
Length under 30ft   11 Deep

N.B. The beams and long carlings for the engine and boiler Hatchways to be ⅝ thick and those on the lower deck to be deeper if required.

Half Beams to be fitted to all the Decks as shown on the plans, and of the forms and dimensions as directed.

Platform Beams to be of the depth shown in the profile, or as directed, and to be either the solid beams as above, or made up by a Bulb Iron with Angle Irons on the top edge as directed. The Flanges to be covered by Mouldings where required.

RIVETTING ON DECK BEAMS The whole surface of the Upper Deck to be covered with Plate worked with Flush Joints, as shown on the Section, the Longitudinal Joints to be single riveted, Cross Joints double riveted; the thickness of the Plates to be 5/16 inch, excepting a Tie-plate 24 inches broad on each side of the hatchways, Diagonal Tie Plates 24 inches broad as shown on the plan of Upper Deck, and a Stringer Plate 3 feet 6 inches broad round the side, which are to be ⅛-inch thick worked on the top of the 5/16 inch Plates. The Butt Straps to be double and treble riveted; the whole to be worked in lengths of at least 15 feet, and secured to the beams as may be directed; the rivet holes to be countersunk on the upper side of the Plates, and all Joints to be caulked and made watertight. The Side Stringer to be attached to the sheer strake by Angle Irons 6 × 4 × ¾ inches for 20 feet before and abaft the Armour Plates. The remainder to be 5 × 3½ × ⅝ inches; and short Angle Irons 4 × 4 × 9/16 inches between the frames under the Stringer, as on the Main Deck.

The entire surface of the Main Deck is also to be covered with Plates ¼ inch thick; a Tie-plate 20 inches broad is to be fitted on each side the Hatchways, and a Stringer Plate 4 feet 6 inches broad all round the side, excepting at the termination of the recess, where it is to be as required; both Tie and Stringer Plates are to be ⅝ inch; the whole to be worked in lengths of at least 15 feet, and secured to the beams as may be directed. The joints of the Plates to be flush, and secured as on the Upper Deck; the holes are to be countersunk on the upper side, and the joints to be caulked and made water-tight as required by the Overseer. The Deck Plating is to be scored home to the side of the Ship, and united thereto by short Anglo Irons above and below 4 × 4 × 9/16, and to the Reverse Irons of the frame by an Angle Iron on the upper side 4 × 4 ×9/16 inch.

LOWER DECK to have a Stringer Plate round the side to the breadth of the Wing Passage, with all necessary Angle Irons, of the sizes given for those of the Main Deck, and Tie-plates at the side of Hatchways, as shown on the Drawings, all ½-inch thick.

Plates ½-inch thick are to be attacked to the Deck Beams in the wake of the Mast Holes, Bitts, &c. on all Decks, and wherever else the Overseer may direct.

PILLARS IN HOLD AND BETWEEN DECKS To be wrought Iron Tubes, with heads and heels welded in solid, and firmly accured to the Beams, &c. Every Beam to be pillared, trussed, or otherwise supported, as shall be directed. The diameter and thickness of the Pillars to be as follows:-

Pillars in Hold   7 inch Diameter ½ inch thick
Pillars on Lower Deck 5 inch Diameter 3/16 inch thick
Pillars on Main Deck   4½ inch Diameter 5/16 inch thick

Solid Pillars are to be fitted wherever required in the Engine and Boiler rooms.

WATERTIGHT BULKHEADS TRANSVERSE To be arranged as shown on the Plans, or as may hereafter be directed; to be well secured to the bottom Plates by double Angle Irons; the Plates of the Bulkheads are to be carefully fitted to each other, to the bottom of the Ship, and round all Keelsons and Stringers, to be supported by Angle Irons 4½ × 3½ × 5/16 in placed vertically 30 inches apart, the joints to be carefully caulked and made water-tight, to the satisfaction of the Overseer. The Bulkheads are to be double where required, so as to enclose a water-tight space between them, as shown in the Drawings. The thickness of the plates to be as follows:-

After Bulkhead to receive Stuffing Box

Plates below Lower Deck, ⅞ inch.
    Do.   above   - ⅝ inch.

Bulkheads receiving thick Armour Plates:-

⅝ inch thick to Lower Deck, and above Lower Deck ½ inch thick.

Remainder all ⅝ inch to about 14 feet water-line, thence to Lower Deck 9/16 above   Lower Deck 7/16 inch.

Screen Bulkheads, with Doors, &c., are to be fitted as required round all water-tight Doors. A sounding tube to be fitted in each compartment; and a sluice valve or cock, as may be directed, to be fitted on each side the Bulkheads, with Levers for opening or closing them; such Levers or the bars attached to them to pass through Stuffing Boxes as may be required. Sea-cocks are to be fitted through the side where directed, for the purpose of admitting sea water into any of the compartments; the cocks to be cased over and otherwise secured to the satisfaction of the Overseer; also pipes are to be led from the sea-cocks to the compartments, as may be required.

WING PASSAGE BULKHEADS To have a longitudinal water-tight Bulkhead on each side at about three feet within the inner edge of the frame Angle Irons, or as shown on the Plans, and extending up to Main Deck Plating, to which it is to be secured by Angle Irons; the Plating of the Bulkheads to be 9/16-inch at lower part and $7/16$ inch at Lower Deck, and 6/16 inch between Decks, to be supported by Angle Iron placed vertically 1 foot 10 inches apart, and to have sliding doors at the upper part as required.

To have transverse divisional Bulkheads of the same thickness of Plate as the Wing Passage Bulkheads, and as shown on the Plans, each compartment to be fitted with a flat below the Lower Deck of Iron as may be directed. Sluice Valves or Cocks to be fitted in the Bulkheads, Wood chocks may be attached to the Bulkheads between the beams, if necessary to make them watertight; or such other means adopted for this purpose as may be directed by the Overseer. Between the Stuffing-box Bulkheads and the Sternpost vertical Transverse Plates $\frac{1}{2}$ inch thick are to be fitted, and firmly secured to each frame. Horizontal flats of the same thickness are also to be fitted in this space, and secured to the vertical Transverse Plates. The hole for the Propeller Tube will be cut out of these Transverse Plates, and care is to be taken that it is not made unnecessarily large. The whole is to be arranged agreeably to a Sketch that will be furnished, and secured as may be directed by the Overseer.

SHAFT PASSAGE The Shaft Passage, and the Passage connecting the Engine and Boiler Rooms, to be formed as may be directed with Plates $\frac{1}{2}$ inch thick, and Angle Irons $3 \times 2\frac{1}{2} \times \frac{3}{8}$ inches placed 18 inches apart, made watertight. These bulkheads are to extend up to the Lower Deck, and to have suitable air tubes fitted at the after end.

EXTERNAL LONGITUDINAL STRINGERS To have Longitudinal Stringers as shown on the Midship Section, formed of a Plate $10 \times 9/16$ inches with Angle Irons $4\frac{1}{2} \times 3\frac{1}{2} \times 9/16$ inches on the inner edge.

BILGE KEELS To be fitted as shown on the Midship Section, two on each side, formed of Plate 13/16i inch thick and 15 inches deep, with half-round Irons on the edge, secured to the bottom Plates by two Angle Irons $5 \times 4\frac{1}{2} \times \frac{5}{8}$ inches. The upper Bilge Keel to be about 07 feet long; the lower one 153 feet long.

INTERNAL LONGITUDINAL STRINGERS Longitudinal Plates $\frac{3}{8}$ inch thick, and bent Angle Irons $3 \times 3 \times \frac{1}{2}$ inches are to be fitted for the support of the frames between the ports on the Main Deck, as

shown on the Midship Section.

CONNING HOUSES Are to be fitted as shown on the Plans, and as will be described by a Sketch.

IRON-PORT SILLS Iron-Plate Sills $\frac{1}{2}$ inch thick, with bent Angle Irons, are to be fitted for securing the heads of intermediate frames, and to receive the Wood Sills, &c. for framing the Ports.

COAL BUNKERS Coal Bunkers to be built of the required capacity, the thickness of Plates, size of Angle Irons, and general arrangement to be as may be directed. The Plates are to be carefully fitted, caulked, and made watertight; the Flats to be of wood or iron as directed.

CAULKING, &c. The precautions required in fitting and caulking the bottom Plates are also be to carefully attended to for the Plates of the several Bulkheads; and the overseer will have power to reject all work not fitted to his entire satisfaction. All iron Bulkheads to be lined with wood where required.

BREAST HOOKS AND MIDDLE LINE BULKHEAD FORWARD To be fitted as shown on the Profile and Plans; the general arrangement and thickness of Plates to be more particularly described by a Sketch.

BULKHEADS ENCLOSING THE WELL FOR THE SCREW To be formed of Plate $\frac{5}{8}$ inch thick, and in size and form as may be hereafter directed.

ENGINE BOILER AND SHAFT BEARERS to be fitted as directed, and continued forward and aft as required for Keelsons. $\frac{1}{2}$ inch Plates to be worked on the frames under the Engine Bearers wherever required by Engineer.

IRON FRAMINGS ROUND MAST HOLES On the various Decks to be formed and fitted as directed.

MAST STEPS To be fitted as shown on the plans, or as shall be directed.

STERN FRAME, QUARTER GALLERIES, &c. The Stern Frame to be formed of $\frac{1}{2}$ inch Plate, and Angle Irons $5 \times 4 \times \frac{5}{8}$ inches, with a Reverse Angle $3\frac{1}{2} \times 3 \times \frac{1}{2}$ inches.

The Plating to be 9/16 inch thick, or as may be directed.

Oak Timbers are to be placed where necessary for fitting Ports, Dead-lights, Sashes, &c.

The Stern above the Counter Rail to be berthed up inside with English Oak 2 inches thick. The Stern to have all usual and necessary Rails and Mouldings. The Quarter Galleries to be built and completed in all respects as usual in H.M. Service. The Stern Ports to be fitted with Sashes; Deadlights, either of iron or wood, as directed; Jalousie Blinds, &c., and in accordance with the Admiralty model description fo fitting Stern Sashes, &c. The whole to be completed in the very best style, with Brass Fittings as may be required, to the entire satisfaction of the Overseer. The Gallery Ports to be fitted with dead doors as usual.

TOPSIDE TIMBERS The Roughtree Timbers [bulwark stanchions] are to be of English Oak or Teak, sided 10 inches, moulded as shown on the Section, and spaced as will be directed. The Heels of the Timbers behind the Armour Plates are to be worked as shown on the Section; – before and abaft this, the Heels are to be secured as will be described by a sketch that will be furnished.

GUNWALE To be worked on the Upper Deck Waterways as shown on the Section; to be 6 inches thick and 25 inches broad, of Oak or Teak.

PLANKSHEER To be Teak or Mahogany, worked as shown on the Section.

TOPSIDE PLANKING To be of Teak or Mahogany, in thickness as shown on the Section; the edges to be caulked and made watertight.

KNIGHT-HEADS AND HAWSE TIMBERS Knight-heads to be of Oak of the size directed, to be well secured to the Cross Bulkhead, and to have Chocks for Bowsprit Hole, fitted as may be directed by the Overseer. The whole to be worked as shall be described by a Sketch showing the general arrangement of the Head.

SHIPS' HEAD The Head of the Ship to be formed and fitted as shall be directed, to be completed with all necessary Rails, Timbers, Cheeks, Bolsters, Carlings, Straps for Gammoning and Bobstays, Berthing, Seats of Ease, Urine Dales, Boomkins, Head Pump, and all other necessary and usual fittings, in accordance with the directions of the Overseer.

CATHEADS To be of English oak, 20 inches sided, and 18 inches deep, fitted with supporters, and completed with Shives, Slip-stoppers, Cleats, Bolts, &c, as directed. Cat's Whiskers to be fitted if required.

ARRANGEMENTS FOR FITTING ARMOUR PLATES, WOOD BACKING. &c. The Armour Plates and Wood Backing on the side of the Ship are to be worked in a recess formed as shown on the Midship Section, and described by a Sketch: the Backing is to be composed of two thicknesses of East India Turk, sound and free from all defects; to be worked on a Teak Shelf, which is to be first secured to the Plates of the Ship as shown on the Section. The inner thickness of Backing is to be 10 inches longitudinally; the outer thickness to be 8 inches, worked vertically; the whole to be secured to the Plating of the side; to be bolted and dowelled together as shall hereafter be directed. A layer of fearnought, saturated with red or white lead or other substance, as may be directed by the Overseer, is to be laid between the faying surfaces of the Iron Plates and Wood Shelf round the edges of the recess; all other faying surfaces are to be thickly coated with red lead or other approved material. The greatest care is to be taken that the Backing is well fitted to the Side plates of the Ship, and the two thicknesses to each other. The Butts and Joints are to be arranged so as to clear the fastenings of the Thick Plates, and the Butts of the inner thickness are to be properly shifted to the satisfaction of the Overseer, the general arrangement being submitted to him for approval before the work is commenced. The Joints of each thickness of Backing are to be carefully caulked, and made watertight to the satisfaction of the Overseer, the number of threads

oakum and spunyarn being as usual in Her Majesty's Service for similar thicknesses. As more than ordinary care will be required to prevent leakage between the Iron Shelf Plate and Wood Backing at the edges of the recess, the Overseer will have authority to introduce any additional means for effecting this object without additional charge. In working the Armour Plates care is to be taken that the edges and butts are planed and well fitted; they are to be formed so as to be tongued and grooved, billed or otherwise recessed into each other, and to be worked fair and even.

ARMOUR BULKHEADS The Transverse Bulkheads which receive the Armour Plates are to be fitted and supported as shown on the Plans; to have two thicknesses of 9 inches East India Teak under the Armour Plates; the whole to be fitted and secured as directed by the Overseer. The Armour Plates and Wood Backing to be bolted or otherwise secured to the side and Transverse Bulkheads as will be hereafter directed or described by a Sketch.

WATERWAYS The thick Waterways on the several Decks are to be of Teak or African, and worked as shown on the Midship Section; the several lengths to be secured at the Butts by a Plate at the Back; to be well bolted to the Stringer Plates and to the Angle Irons on them, and to the Ship's Frames, as shall be directed by the Overseer.

Dimensions to be-

		Inches
Upper Deck	Broad	12
	Deep	12
Main Deck	Broad	11
	Deep	11
Lower Deck	Broad	11
	Deep	6

Thin waterways are to be of Dantzic Oak or East India Teak as may be directed, to be worked as shown on the Midships Section, and well secured to the Stringer Plate, and bolted edgeways to the thick waterway.

DECK FLATS Upper Deck; 4-inch Dantzic Deals, except the Strakes next the side for 12 feet out, which are to be Oak or Teak, if so directed.

Main Deck; Dantzic Oak, 4½ inches thick, from the thin waterway to within three strakes from the sides of the hatchways, or as may be required for stopper bolts or within range of the cable; from thence to the middle line to be 6 inches thick.

Lower Deck; Dantzic Deals, 4 inches thick.

The underside of the Deck Deals to be trimmed straight and fair, and the edges to be planed before being laid, so as to leave a proper seam for caulking. The Decks are to be thoroughly caulked with the number of threads of oakum usual in Her Majesty's Service, and made perfectly watertight. The seams of the Upper Deck to be payed with Jeffery's Marine Glue, and those of the Main and Lower Decks, with main or pitch as may be directed.

All wood work of the Deck is to be kept at least 18 inches from the funnel.

The whole of the material is to be well seasoned, and free from all objectionable knots, and sapwood, and other defects.

CEILING OF HOLD The Ceiling of the Hold where required is to consist of Red Pine, 3 inches thick on the flat of the bilge, and 2½ inches thick from thence to the Lower Deck. This Wood Ceiling may be either wholly omitted, or substituted by wood battens, or half round bars of iron, at the discretion of the Overseer. The bars to be about ⅞ inch thick and 2½ inches broad. The Wood Ceiling or battens are to be secured to the reverse Angle Irons of the frame by galvanized screw bolts; the half round strips to be riveted thereto. The Wood Ceiling is to be caulked and made watertight where required. The battens or bars are to be spaced as directed.

GENERAL ARRANGEMENT OF HOLDS AND PLATFORMS The Flats of the Platforms below the Lower Deck are to be of iron, except where otherwise directed or shown on the Drawings. The Plates to be ⅞-inch thick, roughed on upper surface, worked with flush or lap joints as may be directed; to be single riveted longitudinally, with double riveted cross joints, and to be carefully caulked and made watertight; the Plates next the side being scored round the frames, and secured to the outside Plates. Wood chocks are to be fitted where required, to make the joints watertight. Man holes are to be fitted, to give access to these compartments.

AFTER PLATFORM The Store-rooms and Dispensary on Low Deck and After Platform to be as shown on the Plans, the Bulkheads of the latter to be of ³⁄₁₆-inch Plate, with suitable Angle Irons; the whole to be protected by battens, or cased with deal, as may be directed by the Overseer. Store-rooms to be fitted with bins and racks as may be required.

FORE AND AFTER MAGAZINES The iron Bulkheads forming the Magazines are to be lined with 2-inch Teak, rabbetted or tongued, and grooved, and well secured to them as may be directed by the Overseer. The remaining Bulkheads, include those of the light rooms, handing rooms, &c., also the Flat and Crown of the Magazines, are to be worked as is usual in Her Majesty's Service; the whole to be caulked and made watertight, and the Bulkheads scraped before the linings are worked; the outside and inside linings to be worked as usual in Her Majesty's Service, and as will be directed by the Overseer. The Magazines to be fitted complete with Racks, Dunnage Battens, Supply and Return Scuttles, with Flaps, Fearnought Bags, and all usual and necessary fittings. The flat of the Handing Room to be covered with lead as usual in Her Majesty's Service; the Light Rooms to be fitted with illuminators, and lined with copper. The whole to be fitted complete in accordance with the directions and to the entire satisfaction of the Overseer.

The Crown of the Magazine to be lined with lead

weighing 8lbs to the square foot, the joints being soldered and made perfectly watertight. Over the lead, Dunnage Battens are to be laid and secured (but not nailed through it), for the reception of the Tanks.

PROVISION ROOMS The Bulkheads of the Provision Rooms and the Shaft Passage within it, are to be battened, if required by the Overseer.

ATTENDANCE ON ENGINEERS Shipwrights and other workmen are to attend as usual on the Engineers, chock the boilers, lay all necessary flats in the Engine and Boiler Rooms, and complete all fittings required by the Overseer.

WATER COURSES AND LIMBER CHAINS IN HOLD Water Courses and Limber Chains are to be fitted throughout the Engine and Boiler Rooms, Coal Bunkers, and such other places as the Overseer may direct.

BULKHEADS OF CHAIN LOCKERS, &c. The Bulkheads of the Chain and Shot Lockers of the Shell and Spirit Rooms and of the Officers' Store Rooms are to be of ½-inch plate, properly stiffened with Angle Irons; to be well-fitted, and caulked and made watertight, if required; wood or iron Flats are to be laid as directed. The Bulkheads enclosing the Shell Rooms are to be lined with 2-inch Teak, grooved and tongued, the flat and crown to be 3-inch Teak; the whole to be caulked, and lined with one thickness of Deal, as is usual in Her Majesty's Service, and to be fitted complete, with Stanchions, as may be directed. A Light Room is also to be fitted to each Shell Room, complete with Illuminators, &c., as directed for those of the Magazines. The Bulkheads of the Chain Lockers, Shot Lockers, Spirit Room, and Officers' Store Rooms are to be battened, if required by the Overseer. Provision is to be made for securing the clench of the Cables, either by Forgings, Plates, or otherwise.

ENGINEERS' STORE ROOM The Engineers' Store Room to be built as shown on the Plans; to be fitted complete, with all usual and necessary fittings.

CABLE TIER Dunnage Battens are to be fitted in the Cable Tier, but not secured through the Iron Flat.

SHELL ROOM To be built as shown on the Plans; the Iron Bulkheads enclosing it is to be cased with Deal, and fitted with Dunnage Battens, as usual; the upper part of the Bulkhead to be fitted with Iron Bars; Sliding Doors, and Rollers, as may be directed.

BOLTS AND CRANKS IN LOWER DECK BEAMS Screw Bolts are to be placed in the Lower Deck Beams, as may be required, for the purpose of removing Casks, Packages, &c. in the Hold. Cranks are also to be fitted between the Beams; Hawser and Cordage Reels, Rollers to working Hatchways, and all similar fittings to be completed as directed by the Overseer.

WARRANT OFFICERS' STORE ROOMS To be fitted completed with all bins, racks, cordage-reels, &c. as usual in Her Majesty's Service.

DISTILLING APPARATUS The Distilling Apparatus to be supplied by the Government; to be fitted and enclosed by bulkheads by the Contractor. The whole of the work connected with Kingston's Valves and Cocks through the bottom to be performed by the Contractor, unless otherwise arranged by the Government.

CABIN BULKHEADS ON LOWER DECK The Bulkheads on the Lower Deck are to be framed as usual in Her Majesty's Service. The Bulkheads are to be of Fir, panelled, with shifting or fixed jalousie blinds of mahogany, and shutters thereto, as may be required. When the Bulkheads are Iron, they are to be covered on each side with panelled or plain framing as may be directed. The Doors to be of Mahogany or Fir, as usual in Her Majesty's Service, to be made to slide, or to be hung as may be required; the slides, hinges, locks, and other fittings to be of the same pattern and quality as is usual in Her Majesty's Service. Patterns of these will be furnished. The Gun Room to be fitted with the usual Side Boards, Glass Racks, Drawers, &c.

ENGINEERS' MESS ROOM AND MIDSHIP-MEN'S BERTH The Engineers' Mess Room and Midshipmen's Berth to be fitted with Lockers as may be directed.

STEWARD'S BERTHS The Steward's Berths are to be fitted with the usual Lockers and Drawers, Bins, Glass and Plate Racks, &c.

MARINE SLOP ROOM The Marine Slop Room is to be fitted complete with Racks as may be required.

BATH ROOMS Baths are to be fitted for Engineers and Stokers with all necessary appartenances.

DECK PIPES AND COMPRESSORS ON LOWER AND MAIN DECKS Cast Iron Pipes for the Passage of the Cable, are to be fitted in suitable chocks as shown on the Plans; the size and thickness of the Pipes to be as usual in Her Majesty's Service; to have Compressors of the size and form directed by the Overseers. Iron Covers are to be attached to the Deck Pipes, and Eye Bolts for Compressors to be fixed in the Deck Beams with all other usual and necessary fittings.

PUMPS To have two 12-inch, and four 9-inch, Downtown's Pumps, complete with all Copper Pipes, Mixed Metal Valves, cocks, and other Fittings; the whole to be supplied and fitted by the Contractor.

A Sketch will be furnished showing the position of Pumps, size and direction of Copper Pipes, &c. All Lead Pipes to Pumps for salt and fresh Water are to be supplied and fitted by the Contractor.

CAP SCUTTLES AND GRATINGS Gratings or Cap Scuttles, or both, where required, are to be fitted to all Hatchways, Ladderways, and Scuttles; Gratings to be either of Wood or Iron; the whole to be completed as directed by the Overseer.

MADE SCUTTLES To be fitted on Lower Deck, before and abaft the Armour Plates, as may be directed.

MIZZEN STEP A suitable step of Iron to be fitted on the Lower Deck, and properly supported from below.

SHOT RACKS Shot Racks (Wood or Iron) are to be fitted as shown on the Plans, and as shall be directed by the Overseer.

BAG RACKS Bag Racks formed either of Wood Quartering and Battens, or Iron Bars, are to be fitted as usual in Her Majesty's Service, or as may be directed.

COAL SCUTTLES ON LOWER AND MAIN DECKS Coaling Scuttles are to be fitted with suitable castings and covers in number and position as may be directed; those on the Main Deck are to be fitted with gratings in addition to solid covers; the whole to be as usual in Her Majesty's Service.

COAL SHOOTS BETWEEN DECKS To be of Plate Iron, and in number and size as may be directed by the Overseer.

MESS TABLES AND STOOLS To be in number and dimensions as may be required; made and fitted as usual in Her Majesty's Service. The Iron Cranks for the Tables, and Legs for the Stools, are to be made in accordance with the patterns to be supplied.

SEAMEN'S SHELVES AND PLATE RACK To be fitted along the side as may be required.

THERMOMETER TUBES To be fitted through the Lower Deck into the Coal Bunkers as shall be directed.

HAMMOCK HOOKS, &c. Hammock Hooks or such other fittings as may be required for berthing the crew, are to be fitted as directed, both in the Main and Upper Deck Beams.

CORDAGE REELS ON LOWER DECK To be fitted as may be directed by the Overseer.

GUARD RAILS ROUND HATCH AND LADDER-WAYS To be of Iron round the Hatchway on the Lower Deck; to be fitted as may be directed.

SPARE STEERING WHEELS, &c. To be fitted with Stantions and all other usual and necessary fittings complete for the reception of the Tillar Ropes, and in accordance with the directions of the Overseer.

CEILING BETWEEN MAIN AND LOWER DECKS If of Wood to be of Dantzic Fir or Red Pine 2 inches thick; the edges to be caulked; $\frac{1}{4}$ inch Plate to be substituted, if required. The Ceiling is to be wholly omitted behind the longitudinal Bulkhead shown on the Section.

RIDING BITTS To be of African or English Oak timber 23 inches square at the head, and to taper from about 6 inches below the beam to the heel, where they are to be 16 inches square; to be fitted with Iron Castings and cross pieces complete, as shown upon the drawings, or as is usual in Her Majesty's Service.

STANDARDS TO RIDING BITTS To be of English Oak sided 15 inches, worked as shown on the Drawings.

CABIN BULKHEADS ON MAIN DECK To be built as shown on the Plans; the cants to be secured with Metal Screws, and fitted to shift if required. The Bulkheads are to be pannelled; to be fitted with Jalousie Frames and Shutters, or with Ground Plate Glass Panels, if so directed. The transverse Bulkheads to be fitted to slide into midships, and the longitudinal

Bulkheads to be fitted with loose pin hinges so as to turn up or unship as may be required; to have all necessary door handles, with metal locks and hinges of approved construction, and to be completed with all other usual and necessary fittings, except portable cabin furniture. The steward's berth to be fitted with side boards, drawers, plate and glass racks, hooks, &c. The whole to be completed to the satisfaction of the Overseer.

QUARTER GALLERY FITTINGS Quarter Galleries to be fitted complete, with waterclosets, bath &c., as usual in Her Majesty's Service.

WATERCLOSETS FORWARD ON MAIN DECK To be built as shown on the Plans, and completed with all necsary fittings.

CARLINGS (WOOD OR IRON) BETWEEN DECK BEAMS To be fitted wherever required, and of such material as the Overseer shall direct.

COAMINGS AND HEAD LEDGES ON THE SEVERAL DECKS To be of Cuba Mahogany or African Timber, as may be directed, and of the dimensions required by the Overseer; to be well secured to the framework of the Deck; the edges to be protected by Plates where directed. Hatch bars with locks thereto, to be fitted as may be directed.

CAPSTANS AND FITTINGS To be in number and position as shown on the Plans, fitted complete with sprocket-wheels or flanges, as may be required, with all necessary bars. A descriptive Sketch will be prepared, from which no deviation will be allowed without the permission of the Overseer. Rollers or fair leads, and all other fittings for the Messenger, to be completed as may be directed.

All the fittings, including Messenger, to be supplied by the Contractor.

CONTROLLERS To be supplied, and fitted, if required.

MAST PARTNERS AND CAPSTAN PARTNERS THROUGHOUT THE SHIP To be of English Oak or African Timber; to be fitted complete to the satisfaction of the Overseer.

FRAMING TO PORTS AND CHOCKS TO RING AND EYEBOLTS Port Sills and Timbers, with all necessary Chocks, to be of East India Teak, fitted as shall be directed, and as will be described by a Sketch.

SPIRKETTING UNDER MAIN DECK PORTS To be of East India Teak, 6 inches thick, or of Iron Plate as may be directed.

LINING AT SHIP'S SIDE BETWEEN MAIN AND UPPER DECKS To be of East India Teak, 2 inches thick, or of Iron Plate as may be directed.

RING AND EYEBOLTS TO PORTS To be fitted as will be shown by a Sketch; also Breeching, Muzzle Lashing, and Intermediate Eye Bolts and Train Tackle Bolts, with all necessary Breeching Plates and Chocks, as may be directed.

STOPPER BOLTS To be fitted as usual.

OTHER IRON WORK As usual, or as may be required.

BOWSPRIT PARTNERS To be fitted as shown on the Plans.

BITTS ROUND MAIN MAST ON MAIN DECK To be fitted complete, with all Iron work and other fittings, as may be directed by the Overseer.

MANGER To be fitted complete with Ballers for Messenger, and all other fittings, as usual in Her Majesty's Service.

HAWSE PIPES AND STERN MOORING PIPES To be fitted as usual in Her Majesty's Service; to be in size and form as may be directed; to be fitted complete, with all necessary Plugs, Bucklers, Buckler Bars, &c., as may be directed by the Overseer.

GALLEY CANTS, &c Cants are to be fitted, if required, enclosing the space allotted to the Ship's Galley, and the Cants, and Deck Flat within them, are to be covered with lead and copper of the thickness required, the Flat being first well caulked and coated with tar or paint. The Wood Coamings over the Galley are to be covered with lead and tin as may be directed. The whole, with the Ringbolts for securing the Galley, to be completed as usual in Her Majesty's Service, and to the satisfaction of the Overseer.

SHOT RACKS (Of Wood or Iron) to be fitted between the Ports and round the Hatchways of all the Decks, or wherever may be directed.

VENTILATING TUBES To be fitted, if required; to be completed with all necessary Castings, Cowls, &c. as may be directed.

MEAT SAFES AND SCREENS Meat Safes and Screens round the Galley and in other places, to be fitted as usual in Her Majesty's Service.

SCUPPERS ON THE SEVERAL DECKS Iron and Lead Scuppers are to be fitted, in accordance with the directions of the Overseer.

Those in the wake of the Armour Plates are to be led into a Wrought-Iron Tube or Pipe, 11 inches diameter in the clear, fitted under the Main Deck Beams, and emptying itself through the side before and abaft the Armour Plates.

The Scuppers and Tubes are to be fitted as directed; the whole to be completed to the satisfaction of the Overseer.

HATCHES OVER PROPELLER WELL To be fitted complete, with all necessary Carlings, Gratings, &c., as usual in Her Majesty's Service.

STEERING WHEELS AND STANCHIONS To be fitted complete in accordance with the Sketch that will be supplied, and as is usual in Her Majesty's Service. Slide Boxes for Tiller Ropes, and all other usual and necessary fittings to be completed by the Contractor.

IRON WORK Bolts round Masts, Train Tackle bolts, and all Ring and Eye bolts, and Outriggers connected with the Rigging, to be fitted as may be directed by the Observer.

BOATS CRUTCHES AND CRUTCHES FOR BOOMS, &c To be fitted complete, of the size and form directed by the Overseer, and fixed in the positions required for the Stowage of the Boats, &c. To have all necessary Bolts for Boats' Gripes, &c., as may be directed.

SKYLIGHTS, COMPANIONS, AND GRATINGS ON UPPER DECK To be fitted complete, as may be directed. The Hatch and Ladderways, Skylights, &c. on the Upper Deck, to be protected by Strong Bars of Iron, fitted as will be hereafter directed.

BLOCKS, FAIRLEADS, &c To fit all fixed Blocks, Fair Leads, Kevels, Belaying Cleats, Pin Racks, and Relaying Pins. The Blocks and Pin Racks to be completed, with all necessary Shives; the whole of the Shives to be of Brass, or Brass-bushed, as shall be directed.

SECURITY FOR MAIN STAYS To have all necessary Provision for securing the Main Stays.

HAMMOCK STANCHIONS AND BERTHING To be fitted complete, with Rails, &c. all round the side, as shown on the Midship Section. To have Mahogany End Boards at Gangways and wherever directed, completed with Brass Bindings.

To fit all necessary and usual Brass work for the reception of the Man-ropes, &c., at the Gangways, with Shutters complete.

OUTBOARD WORKS

PORT LIDS Port Lids, or Bucklers and Half-ports, to be fitted and cased with Iron, as may be directed; to be fitted complete with Iron Hinges, Ring Bolts, and Pendants, and all necessary and usual fittings, including Scuttles, Port-Riggles, and Nozzles and Hoses for Pendants. Sashes are to be fitted in the Side Ports, if required. The whole to be completed to the satisfaction of the Overseer.

CHANNELS To be fitted in accordance with the Drawings and as directed by the Overseer; to be completed with all necessary Dead-Eyes for Shrouds and Backstays, with all Chain Plates, Proventer and Tee Plates, Shackles, Eye Bolts, Preventer Bolts for Shrouds, Eye Plates and Goose Necks for Booms, and all other usual and necessary fittings.

ACCOMMODATION LADDERS AND STEPS TO THE SIDE To be fitted with Steps to the Side and Accommodation Ladders, with all necessary Stools, Rails, and Stanchions (Wood or Iron), and Gratings; the whole to be completed as usual in Her Majesty's Service, and to the satisfaction of the Overseer.

FITTINGS FOR ANCHORS To have all necessary Timber Heads, Eye Bolts, Lashing Bolts, Slip-Stoppers, Bill-Boards, Tumblers to Sheet Anchors, and Fish Davits, fitted complete, as usual in Her Majesty's Service.

RUDDER AND STEERING APPARATUS Rudder Frame to be of the best best Hammered Scrap Iron; the head to be 10 inches diameter, and to be tapered towards the heel as required. To be plated with $\frac{7}{16}$ inch plates, and fitted so as to unship afloat. To have Tiller, Spare Tiller (or Yokes), Blocks, Chains, Rudder Pendants, and suitable means for locking the Rudder, with such other Fittings as are required to complete the steering apparatus to the entire satisfaciton of the Overseer, and as is usual in Her Majesty's Service. To fit eyebolts for rudder pendants as may be directed.

BOATS' DAVITS, &c. To be fitted as may be required, complete with Blocks, Chain Guys, and other Fittings, as may be directed by the Overseer.

AWNING STANCHIONS To be fitted as may be directed.

FIGURE HEAD AND STERN ORNAMENTS To be fitted complete in accordance with a design to be furnished or approved by the Controller of the Navy.

GENERAL FASTENINGS AND QUALITY OF MATERIALS All Rivets are to be Low Moor or Bowling Iron. The joints of the outside Plates, butts of Deck Covering Plates, to be double rivetted; all the remaining joints, where not otherwise specified, are to be single rivetted. The breadth of the laps, size and distance of rivets, to be as may be directed by the Overseer. The rivetting is to be executed in a careful and workmanlike manner, the rivets thoroughly fitting the holes, and the greatest care is to be taken in punching to prevent unfair holes; all such are to be rimed-out before rivetting: the countersinking is also to be carefully done. The Overseer may require any holes to be drilled, and Bolts turned for them, or he may substitute Bolts for Rivets, or make other changes of this kind wherever he may think it desirable, without additional charge.

The whole of the remaining Bolt and Screw Fastenings throughout the Ship are to be of the very best material and workmanship; to have Copper or Mixed Metal Fastenings where usual in the internal and other fittings in Her Majesty'S Service; the whole to be to the entire satisfaction of the Overseer.

The Upper and Lower Keel Strakes, the After Plates in the vicinity of the Screw Shaft, the Sheer Strake, and Angle Iron round the recess for the Armour Plates and backing, to be of Low Moor or Bowling Iron, or other Iron approved by the Controller of the Navy.

The Frame of the Ship (excepting the Angle Irons, set to a great bevelling,) all Bulkheads above the Lower Deck, the Bulkheads of Shell Rooms and Chain Lockers, and all Bulkhead Angle Irons, (excepting those round the edge of the Bulkheads at the sides of the Ship,) the Plating on the floors, (excepting the Flat Keelson Plate,) and the Plate of Bilge Keels, are to be of best Boiler Plate. The remaining portion of the Iron is to be of *best best* Boiler Plate, unless otherwise specified. The name of the makers of whom it is proposed to purchase to be submitted to the Controller of the Navy for his approval, and the whole to be attested by the certificates or invoices of the firms supplying the same, if required, and to have the maker's name stamped in a legible manner on each Bar or Plate.

The strength must be such as to bear a tensile force of 22 tons to the square inch; and Overseer will have power to test the strength, dactility, and other qualities of the by any suitable means.

Samples will be selected by him, to be torn asunder and otherwise tested in his presence should they break with less than 22 tons to the square inch, or prove otherwise damaged or of inferior quality, the lot from which the sample has been selected, may be rejected.

The apparatus required for pulling asunder the samples, and otherwise testing the material, as well as the samples themselves, shall be provided by the Contracts own cost and charge; and he shall find all necessary for the process of for any other experiment the Overseer may desire to try upon the work.

WEIGHT OF HULL The greatest care must be observed to keep the Weight of the Hull within the estimate; and with a view of accomplishing this object, the Overseer is authorized to insist, that the extreme latitude allowed in Rolling Iron shall not exceed the scantling specified.

ARMOUR PLATE Armour Plates are to be made of such quality of Iron, and in such a manner, and Iron and Plate are to be manufactured by such parties, as the Controller of the Navy shall approve. To be called if required. Iron Work is to be carefully scraped and cleaned before being painted; and each portion of it, as it is turned out of hand, is to have a coat of thin rod-lead paint or other substance, as may be directed, as soon as it is sufficiently completed to receive it, in order to prevent as far as possible, the Iron Work from becoming in any degree oxidized. In addition to this, the whole of the Ship, both inside and out, as well as the Plating behind the Wood backing, and all Iron surfaces covered with Wood, is to have three coats of the best oil paint; the Controller of the Navy, however, having the power to direct that the third coat of paint on the outside of the Bottom Plating shall be substituted by an species of composition or coating; and also that the third coat of paint on the inside of the bottom may be substituted by any species of composition or cement. All Woodwook is to be painted in the best manner with three coats of good oil paint, of such colour, and with such portions grained, as the Overseer may direct. Should any slight deviations from the Drawings or Specification be considered desirable during the progress of the work, the overseer shall have the power to order the same to be performed, without additional charge, except in cases when the contrary shall have been previously agreed to

in writing; and the Contractor shall attend to, and forthwith execute, all such directions as may from time to time be given him by the Overseer.

This Contract is intended to include the entire completion of the Hull of the Ship for sea, as usual in Her Majesty's Service, with the exception of portable cabin furniture. It is therefore to be expressly understood that all minor fittings which may not be shown on the Drawings, or mentioned in the Specification, but which may be considered by the Overseer as requisite for the proper completion of the work, are to be provided by the Contractor, without extra charge.

The ship is to be launched by the Contractors at their own risk and cost, and delivered up afloat on the date stipulated by the Controller of the Navy. Throughout they must act to the satisfaction of the Controller of the Navy who may select certain officers to inspect the manufacturing of the iron to make such directions as they may think proper, and to inspect the workmanship during progress of the building and fitting of the Ship. These persons shall have the power to reject all such portions as, in their opinon, are inferior in strength, quality of materials or workmanship; and the decision of the Controller of the Navy on such matters shall be final and binding upon the Contractors.

With the full understanding that if any omission be discovered in the Specification of Drawings, such omission is to be supplied by the Controller of the Navy; and the Contractors are bound to comply with the part thus supplied, without any extra charge, in the same manner as if it had formed part of the original Specification or Drawings. And further, that if any doubt arise respecting the meaning of any part of the Specification or Drawings, or any appeal be made respecting matters of any kind relating to the carrying out of this contract, about which there may be any dispute or difference of opinion between their Lordships Officers and the Contractors, the Controller of the Navy is to decide, and his decision is to be final.

The Contractors are to provide security in a bond [for] the due performances of the Contract in the manner and in the time specified therein.

The builders must state the time within which the vessel will be delivered [   ] on the River Thames in a fit state to receive the engines.

Bibliography

Further reading on the subject of *Warrior* is difficult to recommend. Walter Brownlee's *HMS Warrior* provides an excellent introduction to the ship, while John Well's forthcoming book should add some more details of her career. Elsewhere the list becomes more general. The best survey of the ironclads, both of Britain and her rivals comes in *Conway's All the World's Fighting Ships 1860–1905*. This encyclopaedic work is well illustrated and authoritative. Elsewhere J P Baxter's *The Introduction of the Ironclad Warship* provides a seminal text on the naval policy of the ironclad era, in Britain, France and the USA. Later work has supplemented his study, and his conclusions on technical matters are not entirely reliable. I have pointed out some of these errors in my *Battleships in Transition: The creation of the steam battlefleet 1815–1860* which covers the wooden period up to the design of *Warrior*. Other erstwhile authorities on *Warrior* have been shown up as inadequate or unreliable by work carried out during the reconstruction; Oscar Parkes' book relied heavily on Admiral Ballard and Baxter. As a result he repeats several errors of fact, such as the idea that *Black Prince* had a fixed propeller.

Official documents remain the only unimpeachable source, and cannot be avoided in any serious study. The secondary sources cited all have something to offer, but in total they can only provide a partial and unsatisfactory picture of the Navy in the 1860s and 1870s. They are long overdue for replacement by some coherent work.

UNPUBLISHED PAPERS

Public papers held at the Public Record office
Admiralty Papers, particularly:
ADM 1. Secretary's In Letters
ADM 2. Secretary's Out Letters
ADM 3. Special Minutes
ADM 12. Digest
ADM 50. Admiral's Journals
ADM 84. Steam Department
ADM 87. Surveyor's Department
ADM 91. Materiel, Departments: Out Letters
ADM 92. Surveyor's Submission Book
ADM 180. Progress Book

Public Papers held at the National Maritime Museum
Admiralty Papers
Ship's Draughts

Private Papers
CODRINGTON MSS, National Maritime Museum
GLADSTONE MSS, British Library Add Mss
HALIFAX MSS, British Library Add Mss; and Borthwick Institute, York
MARTIN MSS: ADMIRAL SIR WILLIAM FANSHAWE; British Library Add Mss
MILNE MSS, National Maritime Museum
NAPIER MSS, British Library Add Mss, Public Record Office, and National Maritime Museum
PALMERSTON MSS, Broadlands Mss at the National Register of Archives, and British Library Add Mss
WALKER MSS, National Maritime Museum (now only available on microfilm)

PUBLISHED DOCUMENTS
Great Britain: Parliament
Parliamentary Papers, particularly:
1847–8 vol xxi
1852–3 vol ix
1856 vol xi
1859 vols xiv & xv
Hansard's Parliamentary Debates 1845–1863

Journals and letters
STANLEY, LORD *The Political Journals of Lord Stanley*, edited by John Vincent, London 1979
VICTORIA, QUEEN *The Letters of Queen Victoria: A Selection from Her Majesty's correspondence between the years 1837 and 1861*

SECONDARY SOURCES

Articles
BROWN, D K 'The First Steam Battleships', *The Mariner's Mirror*, 63, 1977
BROWN, D K 'Shells at Sebastopol', *Warship*, 10, April 1979
BROWN, D K 'The Structural Improvements to Wooden Warships instigated by Sir Robert Seppings', *The Naval Architect*, May 1979
BROWN, D K 'Thomas Lloyd CB' *Warship*, 20, October 1981
BROWN, D K 'Developing the armour for HMS *Warrior*' *Warship* 40, October 1986
BROWN, D K 'The First Iron Warship' *Warship*, 8 October 1977
BROWN, D K & WELLS, CAPTAIN J 'HMS *Warrior*' *Transactions of the Royal Institution of Naval Architects* 1986
LAING, E A M 'The Introduction of the Paddle Frigate into the Royal Navy' *The Mariner's Mirror*, 66, 1980
MABER, J 'Greenock' *Warship* 23 & 24, August, October 1981
OSBON, G A 'The First of the Ironclads', *The Mariner's Mirror*, 50, 1964
OSBON, G A 'Paddlewheel Fighting Ships of the Royal Navy', *The Mariner's Mirror*, 68, 1982
PACKARD, J J 'Sir Robert Seppings and the Timber Problem', *The Mariner's Mirror*, 64, 1978
RODGER, N A M 'The Design of the *Inconstant*' *The Mariner's Mirror*, 61, 1975
SLAYMAKER, E 'The Guns of HMS *Warrior*' *Warship* 37, 38, 39, January, July, August 1986

Unpublished Dissertations
BAXTER, C F 'Admiralty Problems during the Second Palmerston Administration', University of Georgia 1965
ROPP, T 'The Development of a Modern Navy', Harvard 1937
WALLIN, FRANKLIN 'The French Navy during the Second Empire', University of California 1953

Index

Abbreviations: (F) French, (M) merchant ship, (US) American

Aaron Manby (M) 63
Achilles 14, *19*, 21, 22, 26, *28*, 29, 32, 33, 35, 41, 48, *63*, *64*, *65*, 73, 82, 107, 113, 116, 118, 125, *126*, 128, 133, 135, 150, 172, 173
Admiralty, Board of 11, 12, 13, 15, 16, 18, 28, 168
Aetna 21
Agamemnon 10, *11*, 12, 24, 106
Agincourt 33, 38, 125, 135, *173*
Airey, Sir George 63
American Civil War 1861-5 37, 38, 73, 102
Anchors 162-5, *162*, *165*, 170
Anglo-French Naval Rivalry 7, 10, 14, 15, 37, 39, 171-3
Archimedes (M) 103
Armour, trials 11, 12, 13, 16, 29, 30, 65-72
Armstrong gun 16, *83-102*, 145, 149, 150
Audenet 12, 29

Barnaby, Nathaniel 30, 66, 133
Bartram, Jean 47
Barnett, Richard 155, 159
Bellerophon 31, 35, 66, 113, 116, 128, 157, 171, 172
Bermuda, dockyard and floating dock *34*, 38, *73*
Birkenhead 11, 64
Black Prince 20, 21, *23*, 28, *33*, 34, 35, 36, *37*, 38, 82, 106, 107, 110, 113, 118, 125, 127, 135, 150 *154*, 157, 170
Boats 158-162
Broadside ironclads 12, 171
Brown, D K 22, 69
Brownlee, Walter 51, 53
Brunel, I K 9, 10, 14, 15, 18, 66
Bulwark 11, 16, 17, 72

Caledonia 65, 75, 82
Capital ships, changing value of 171
Captain 31, 135
Centre battery ironclad 171
Channel, & Fleet 14, 28, 30, 33, 35, 36, 38, 39, 65, 103, 108, 124, 128, 129
Cleveland Combined Council of Churches 58, 60
Clyde 36
Coal consumption 123
Coast Guard 36, 39
Cochrane, Captain A A P *34*, 36, 37, 51,

101, 149, 158, 163
Compass deviation 63-4
Conning tower 149-150, *166-7*
Corry, H T L 17, 20
Corvette 8, 20
Cowper Coles, Captain C 31, 135, 172
Couronne (F) 12, *29*, 33, 34

Dacres, Rear Admiral Sir S 36-7
Defence 26, 27, *28*, 29, 30, 35, 36, 82, 107, 124, 128, 150
Deptford 19, 21
Derby Committee 15-17
Derby, Lord 15-17, 20, 28
Devastation 32, 35, 133, 157, 171-3
Devastation (F) 11
Devonport 19, 21, 44, 158, 163
Disraeli, Benjamin 16-17
Dockyards, Royal 20-1
Donegal 36, 37
Dreadnought 1906, 171-2
Drying room *163*, 168
Duncan 11, 13, 22, *24*
Duke of Edinburgh, HRH Admiral 40, 45
Duke of Wellington, engines from 12
Dulake, Tom 46, 47, 49
Dupuy de Lôme 10, 12, 14, 39, 117

Edgar 36, 129
Enterprise 82
Erebus 17, 65, 67
Excellent, gunnery training ship 16, 18, 91, 102

Figurehead 153-5, *150-7*
Fisher, Lord 84, 161, 173
Floating battery 8, 11, *12*, 13, 73, 149
Friends of the *Warrior* 60

Gibraltar 11
Gladstone, William 30, 33
Gloire (F) 7, 12, 13, 15, 18, 22, 23, *24*, 26, 27, 28, 34, 35, 37, 39, *42*, *53*, 67, *68*, *70*, 71, 72, *76*, 84, 85, 108, 109, 110, 115, 123, *127*, 129, 149, 150, 171-3
Great Britain (M) 9, *10*, 45, 54, 61, 64
Great Eastern (M) *13*, 14, 15, 18, 66, 67
Great Western (M) 9
Greenock 64
Guns 81-99, *81-103*
Guns, replication 99-102

Hartlepool 6, *46*, 47, 48, 49, 54, 55, 56, 57, 58, 60, 65, 78, 117, 135, 144, 157, 173
Heads 157-8
Hector 28, *29*, 30, 82, 124
Hercules 41, 171-2
Himalaya (M) P & O liner 27, 64
Hockey, Ray 49
Hood (1919) 150
Howe 106

Indicated Horse Power 8
Inflexible 62
Invincible, see *Black Prince*
Irish Sea 40, 41
Iron armour, significance of 11
Ironclads, originally intended only for channel service 33
Iron Duke 40
Iron shipbuilding 63-72
Iron warship, pre-1854 10, 11, 20

Johnson, Keith 47, 100

Kagoshima, bombardment of 83-4
Kinburn, Battle of 1855 11, 12, 13, 149
Kronstadt 40, 41

Laird Bros shipbuilders 19, 21, 64
Lave (F) 11
Louis Napoleon, Napoleon III 7, 11, 22, 37, 67, 108
Lisbon 35, 37
Lissa, Battle of, (1866) 85
Liverpool 32, 36
Lloyd, Thomas 11, 67
Lord Clyde 113, 128
Lord Warden 113, 128

Machinery, steam *103-123*
MacArthur, Antonio 52
Magazine 96-8
Manifold Trust 45, 48, 49, 50
Manpower Services Commission (MSC) 54, 55, 56, 57, 122
Mare C & J, Shipbuilders 19, 20, 21
Maritime Trust 45, 46, 47, 49
Marlborough 36, 37, 43, 163
Mary Rose 54, 62, 100
Maudslay, Son & Field engine builders 103, 111, 113
Mediterranean, & Fleet 75, 108, 124
Merrimac (US) wooden screw frigate, influence on British designs 14, 22, 23, 83, 93
Mersey 13, 20, 21, 22, 24, *53*, 73, 82, 92, 93, 125, 130, 150, 173
Meteor 17, 27, 67
Milford Haven Pembroke
Milne, Admiral Sir A 36, 37, 73

Minotaur 15, 24, 26, 35, 39, 74, 84, 107, 113, 115, 118, 125, *126,* 128, 130, 135, 172, 173
Molten Iron Shell 7, 87
Monarch 31, 35, 171
Moore, John 51
Morrell, Stan 47, 49, 54, 72, 137
Murray Plan 146

Napoleon (F) *see* Louis Napoleon 7, *10,* 11, 22, 37, 67, 108
Napier, Admiral Sir C 63, 103
Napier, R. shipbuilding 19, 20, 21
Narcissus 145–153
Naysmyth, James 68
Nemesis 64, 71
Nominal Horse Power 6
Northumberland 15, 33, 38, 104, 113, 118, 120–1, 150

Ocean 124, 127
Orlando, 13, 22, 23, 44, 73, 81, 82, 106, 119

Paddle wheel frigate 7, 8, *10,* 103
Paget, Captain Lord 30
Paixhans, Henri 9, 125
Pakington, Sir John 15, 16, 20, 28, 34, 35
Pallas 82, 113
Palmer, shipbuilder 19, 21, 68
Palmerston, Lord 15, 28, 29, 33
Pembroke Dockyard/Milford Haven 15, 19, 44, 61, 72, 80
Plymouth 27, 33
Prince (M) 64
Prince Consort, HRH the 15
Prince Consort 82, 113, 128
Prison, aboard *Warrior* 169

Queen Victoria 15

Ram 85
Reed, Sir Edward 21, 31, 33, 66, 171–3
Repulse 124
Resistance 26, 36, 82, 85, 107, 124, 150
Revenge 36, 128
Revolvers, Colt 98–9, 102
Rig 19, 123–144
Robinson, Captain R S 33, 172
Rodney (1888) *157*
Royal Charter (M) 64
Royal Naval Museum, Portsmouth 62, 145
Royal Oak 17, 72, 73, 75, 82, 85, 128, 129, 150
Rudder 116, 129
Russian War 1854–6 7, 9, 27, 32, 64, 99, 103, 161, 171

Russian war scare 1878–9 40, 41, 82

Samuda Bros, shipbuilders 19, 21
Sans Pareil 1892 *172*
Scott-Russell, John 15, 17, 19, 20, 21, 34, 66, 67
Screw propulsion, vital for warships 9
Seppings, Sir Robert 9, 22
Shannon 41
Sheerness 19, 21
Ships Preservation Trust 46–50 *Sidon* 103
Simoom 12, 26, 65, 71
Sinope, Battle of (1853) 11
Small arms 98–9, 102
Smith, John 45
Solferino (F) *39,* 117, 173
Somerset, Duke of 28, 29, 30, 34
Southampton 32, 37
Spithead Reviews at 37, 41
Steam engines *see* machinery
Stern galleries *158*–9
Stevenson, Bill 47, 49, 51, 56, 100
Stove, drying room *160*
Symonds, Sir William 130
Swiftsure 108

Tactical diameter 116
Terrible 10, 37
Terror 73
Thames ironworks 27, 28, 56, 68
Thames shipbuilders 19, 21
Thunder 27
Thunderer (1855) 35
Thunderer (1874) 106–7
Thunderbolt 65
Tomlin, Richard 51
Tonnant (F) 11
Trident 64
Triumph 108
Trusty 82
Tryon, Admiral Sir George 36
Turret 82 see also under *Captain, Devastation, Monarch, Trusty* & Cowper-Coles

Unicorn Project 52

Valiant 30, 124
Vanguard 40, 41, 85
Ventilation 170
Vernon Torpedo Schoolship 36, 37, 40, 43, 44, 61, 117
Victory 9, 24
Victoria (1860) *16,* 22, *24, 52,*
Victoria (1890) 85, 172–3

Walker, Admiral Sir Baldwin 12–22, 27, 28–35 83, 103, 172–3

Warrior, aesthetics 26
  Association 60, 144
  a frigate, not a battleship 18, 22, 61, 103–4, 171–4
  Project 44–63, 72–80, 99–102, 117–122, 132–144, 174
  Illustrations *2–3, 19, 24, 27, 35, 36, 40, 41, 46, 48, 49, 51, 52, 54, 56, 57, 59, 60, 61, 67, 68, 76, 77, 78, 79, 80, 123, 126, 159, 168*
  Unique to the Royal Navy, 171
(1745) 28
(1906) *39*
(1946) *39*
Fleet Headquarters at Northwood 44, 154
Watts, Isaac 10, 20, 21, 22, 31, 66, 85, 172–3
Wells, Captain John 51
Westwood & Baillie, shipbuilders 19, 21
Whitworth gun 17, 82
Wilson, Jim 118, 120
Wood, Sir Charles 13
Wooden steam battleship 8, 10, 11
Woolwich 13, 19

Zealous 124